JUSTICE LEAGUE OF AMERICA
THE INJUSTICE LEAGUE

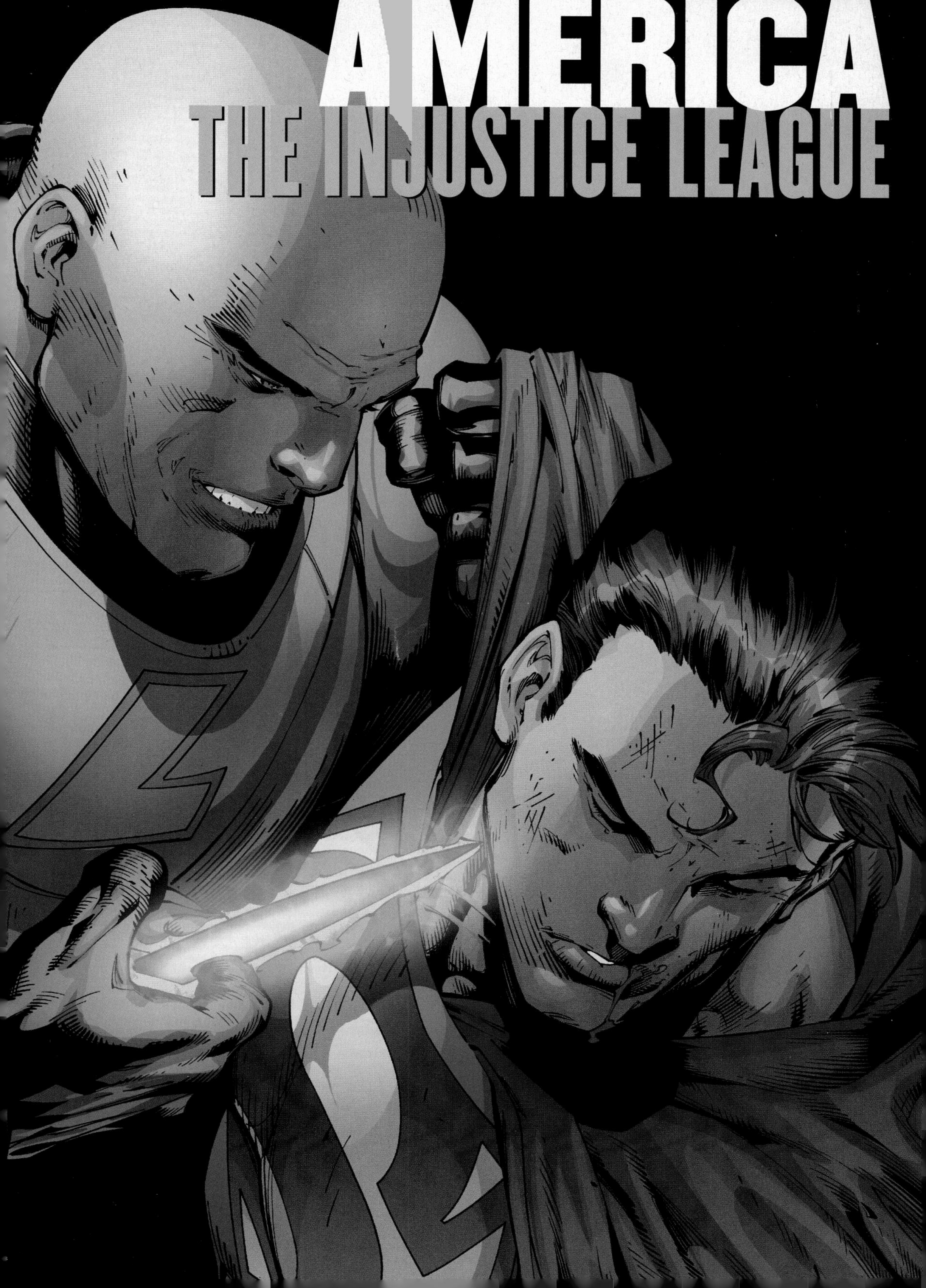

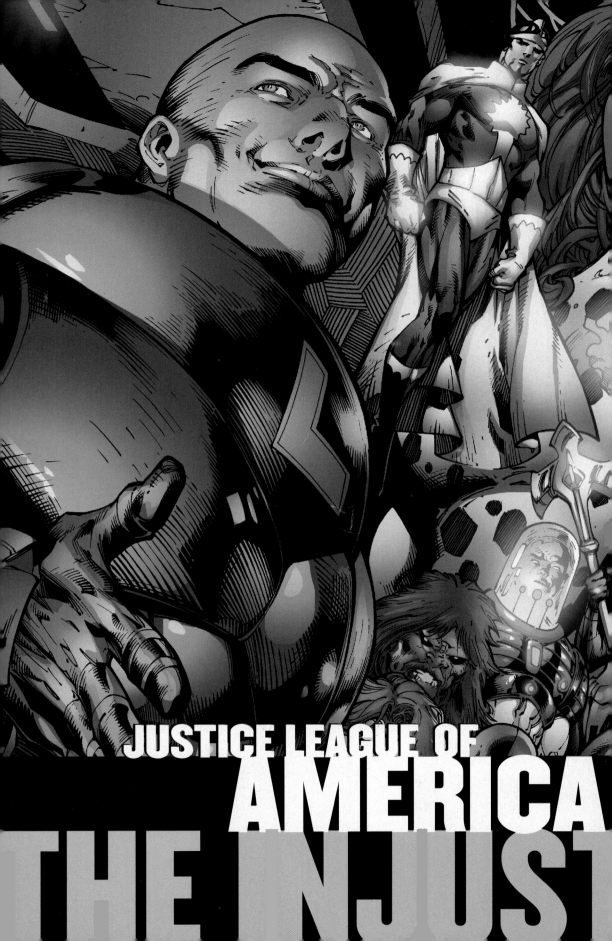

JUSTICE LEAGUE OF
AMERICA
THE INJUST

Dwayne McDuffie Writer

The Injustice League

Chapter 1
Mike McKone Penciller
Andy Lanning Inker

Chapter 2
Joe Benitez Penciller
Victor Llamas Inker

Chapters 3 + 4
Ed Benes Penciller
Sandra Hope Inker

A Brief Tangent

Joe Benitez Penciller
Victor Llamas Inker

Soup Kitchen

Alan Burnett Writer
Allan Jefferson Artist

Pete Pantazis
Alex Sinclair Colorists

Rob Leigh Letterer

ICE LEAGUE

Dan DiDio Senior VP-Executive Editor
Eddie Berganza Editor-original series
Adam Schlagman Assistant Editor-original series
Anton Kawasaki Editor-collected edition
Sean Mackiewicz Assistant Editor-collected edition
Robbin Brosterman Senior Art Director
Paul Levitz President & Publisher
Georg Brewer VP-Design & DC Direct Creative
Richard Bruning Senior VP-Creative Director
Patrick Caldon Executive VP-Finance & Operations
Chris Caramalis VP-Finance
John Cunningham VP-Marketing
Terri Cunningham VP-Managing Editor
Alison Gill VP-Manufacturing
David Hyde VP-Publicity
Hank Kanalz VP-General Manager, WildStorm
Jim Lee Editorial Director-WildStorm
Paula Lowitt Senior VP-Business & Legal Affairs
MaryEllen McLaughlin VP-Advertising & Custom Publishing
John Nee Senior VP-Business Development
Gregory Noveck Senior VP-Creative Affairs
Sue Pohja VP-Book Trade Sales
Steve Rotterdam Senior VP-Sales & Marketing
Cheryl Rubin Senior VP-Brand Management
Jeff Trojan VP-Business Development, DC Direct
Bob Wayne VP-Sales

Cover by **Ian Churchill & Norm Rapmund**
with **Alex Sinclair**
Logo designed by **Ken Lopez**

Justice League of America: The Injustice League

Published by DC Comics. Cover and compilation
Copyright © 2008 DC Comics. All Rights Reserved.

Originally published in single magazine form in
JUSTICE LEAGUE OF AMERICA WEDDING SPECIAL 1,
JUSTICE LEAGUE OF AMERICA 13–16.
Copyright © 2007, 2008 DC Comics. All Rights Reserved.
All characters, their distinctive likenesses and related elements
featured in this publication are trademarks of DC Comics.
The stories, characters and incidents featured in this
publication are entirely fictional. DC Comics does not read
or accept unsolicited submissions of ideas, stories or artwork.

DC Comics, 1700 Broadway, New York, NY 10019
A Warner Bros. Entertainment Company
Printed in Canada. First Printing.

HC ISBN: 978-1-4012-1802-7
SC ISBN: 978-1-4012-2050-1

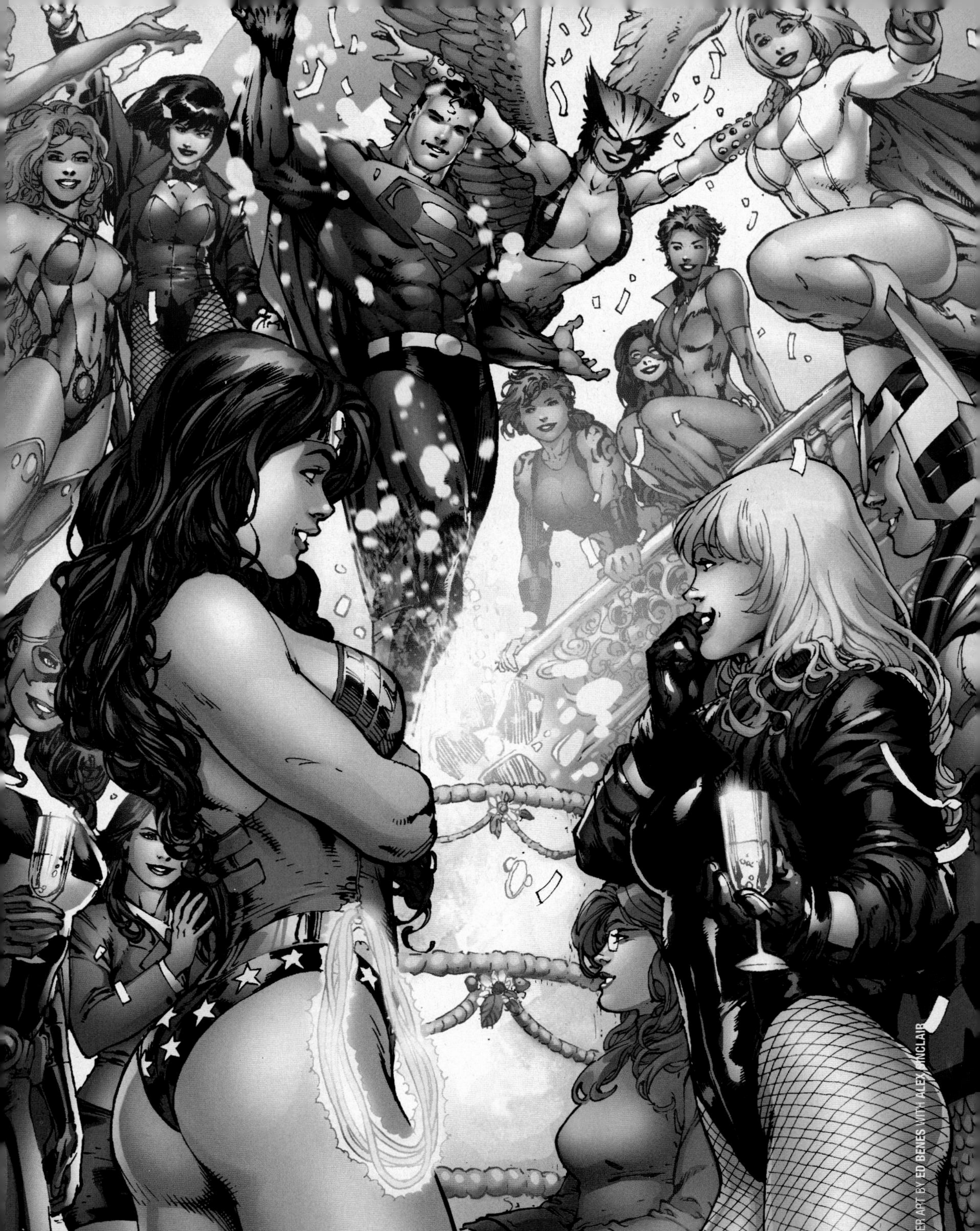
COVER ART BY ED BENES WITH ALEX SINCLAIR

JUSTICE LEAGUE OF AMERICA

CHAPTER ONE

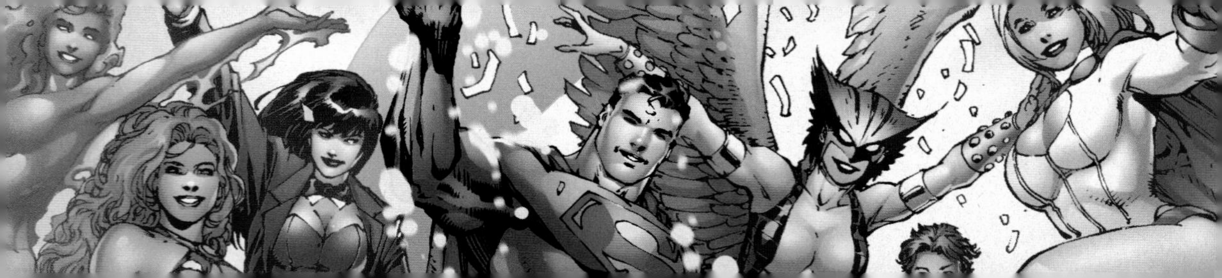

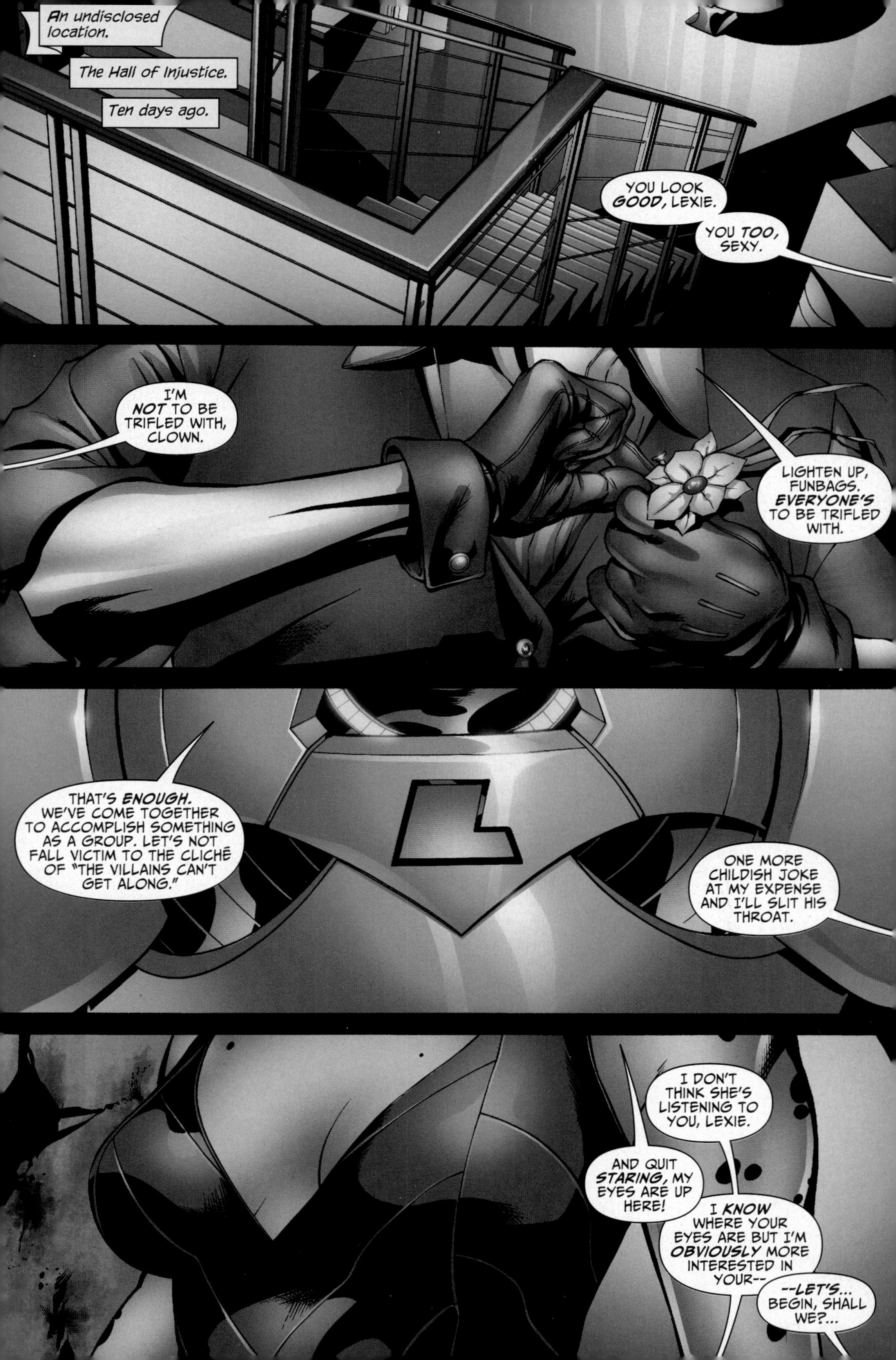
An undisclosed location.
The Hall of Injustice.
Ten days ago.
YOU LOOK GOOD, LEXIE.
YOU TOO, SEXY.
I'M NOT TO BE TRIFLED WITH, CLOWN.
LIGHTEN UP, FUNBAGS. EVERYONE'S TO BE TRIFLED WITH.
THAT'S ENOUGH. WE'VE COME TOGETHER TO ACCOMPLISH SOMETHING AS A GROUP. LET'S NOT FALL VICTIM TO THE CLICHÉ OF "THE VILLAINS CAN'T GET ALONG."
ONE MORE CHILDISH JOKE AT MY EXPENSE AND I'LL SLIT HIS THROAT.
I DON'T THINK SHE'S LISTENING TO YOU, LEXIE.
AND QUIT STARING, MY EYES ARE UP HERE!
I KNOW WHERE YOUR EYES ARE BUT I'M OBVIOUSLY MORE INTERESTED IN YOUR--
--LET'S... BEGIN, SHALL WE?...

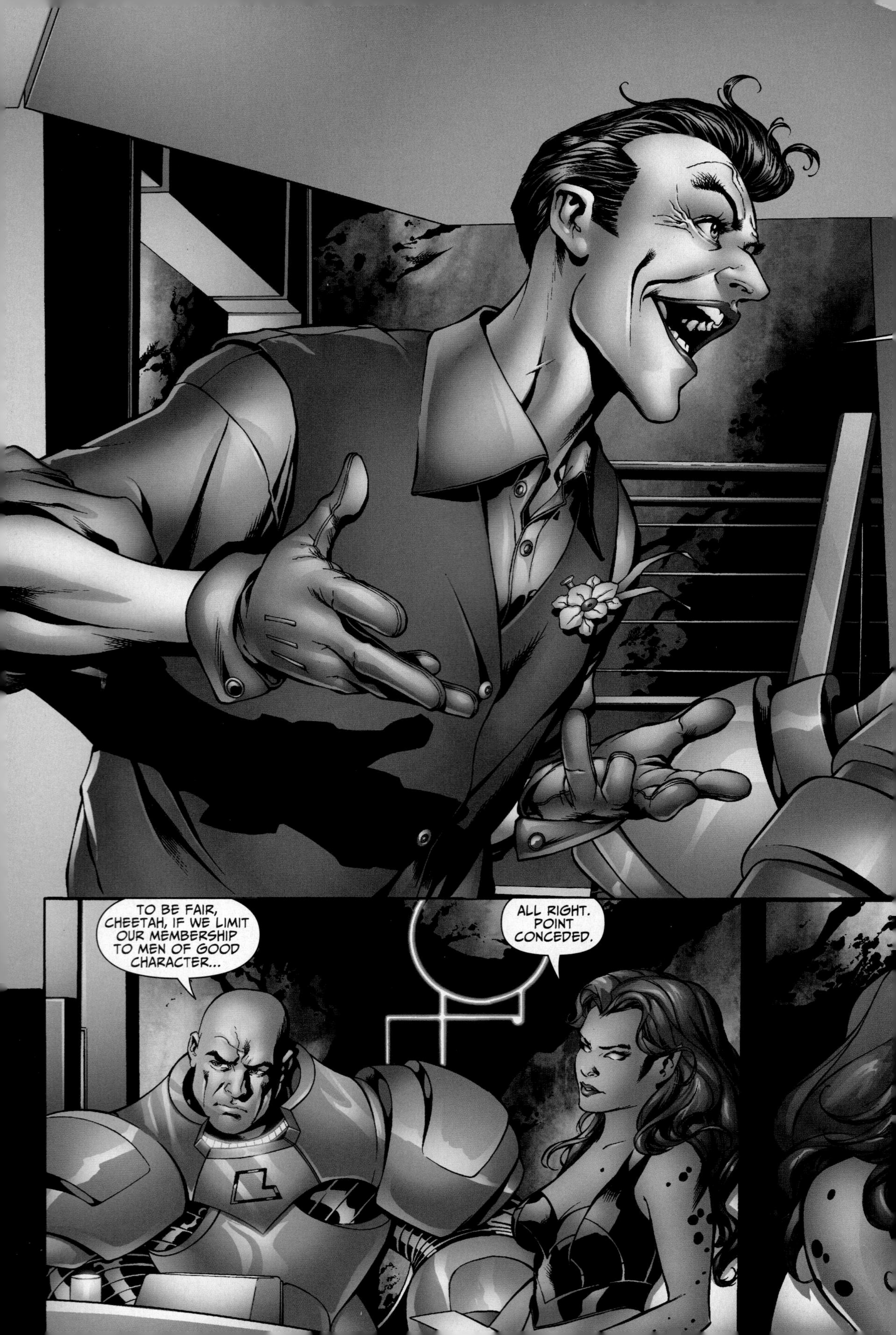
TO BE FAIR, CHEETAH, IF WE LIMIT OUR MEMBERSHIP TO MEN OF GOOD CHARACTER...
ALL RIGHT. POINT CONCEDED.

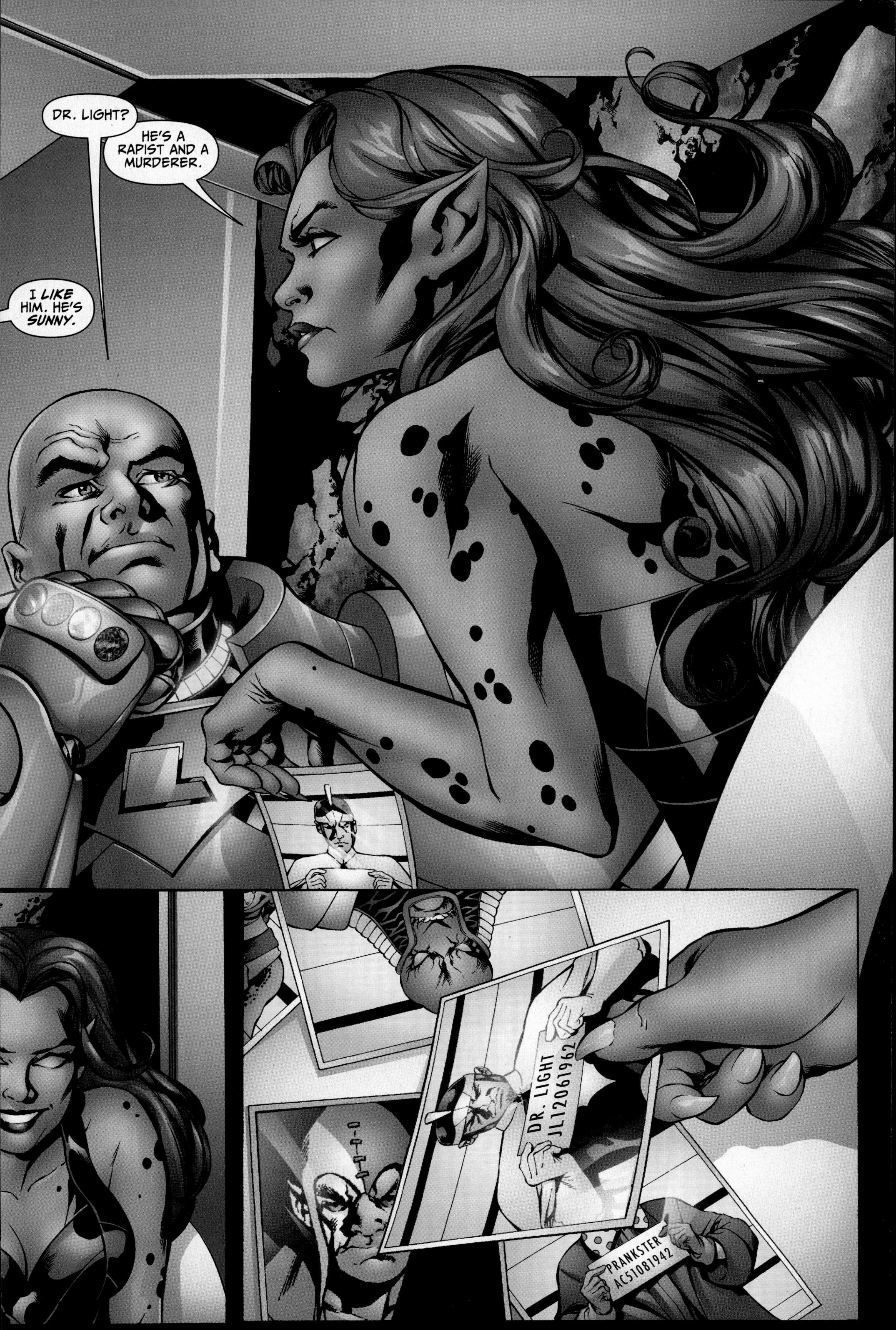
DR. LIGHT?
HE'S A RAPIST AND A MURDERER.
I LIKE HIM. HE'S SUNNY.
DR. LIGHT JL12061962
PRANKSTER AC51081942

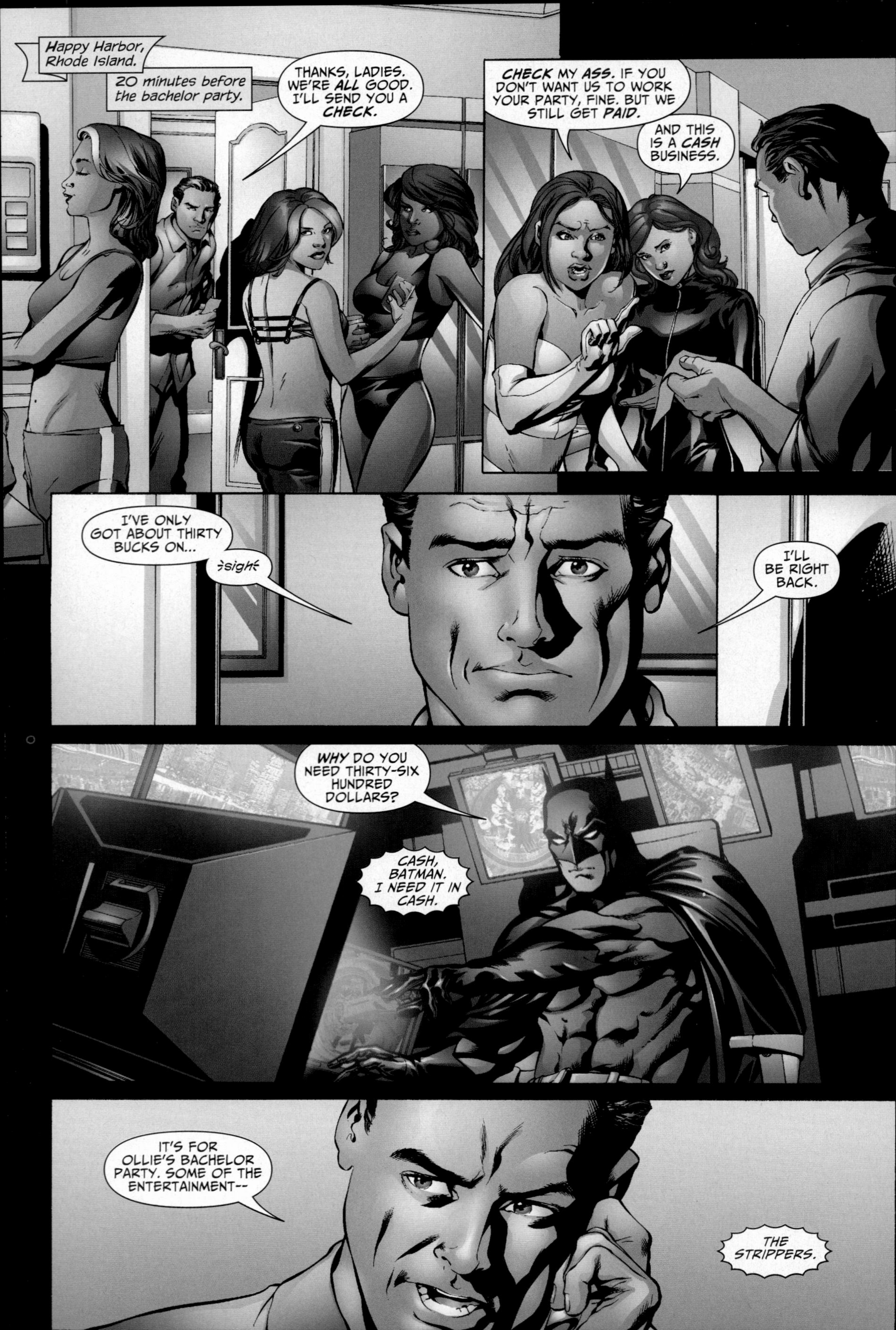
Happy Harbor, Rhode Island.
20 minutes before the bachelor party.
THANKS, LADIES. WE'RE ALL GOOD. I'LL SEND YOU A CHECK.
CHECK MY ASS. IF YOU DON'T WANT US TO WORK YOUR PARTY, FINE. BUT WE STILL GET PAID.
AND THIS IS A CASH BUSINESS.
I'VE ONLY GOT ABOUT THIRTY BUCKS ON...
sigh
I'LL BE RIGHT BACK.
WHY DO YOU NEED THIRTY-SIX HUNDRED DOLLARS?
CASH, BATMAN. I NEED IT IN CASH.
IT'S FOR OLLIE'S BACHELOR PARTY. SOME OF THE ENTERTAINMENT--
THE STRIPPERS.

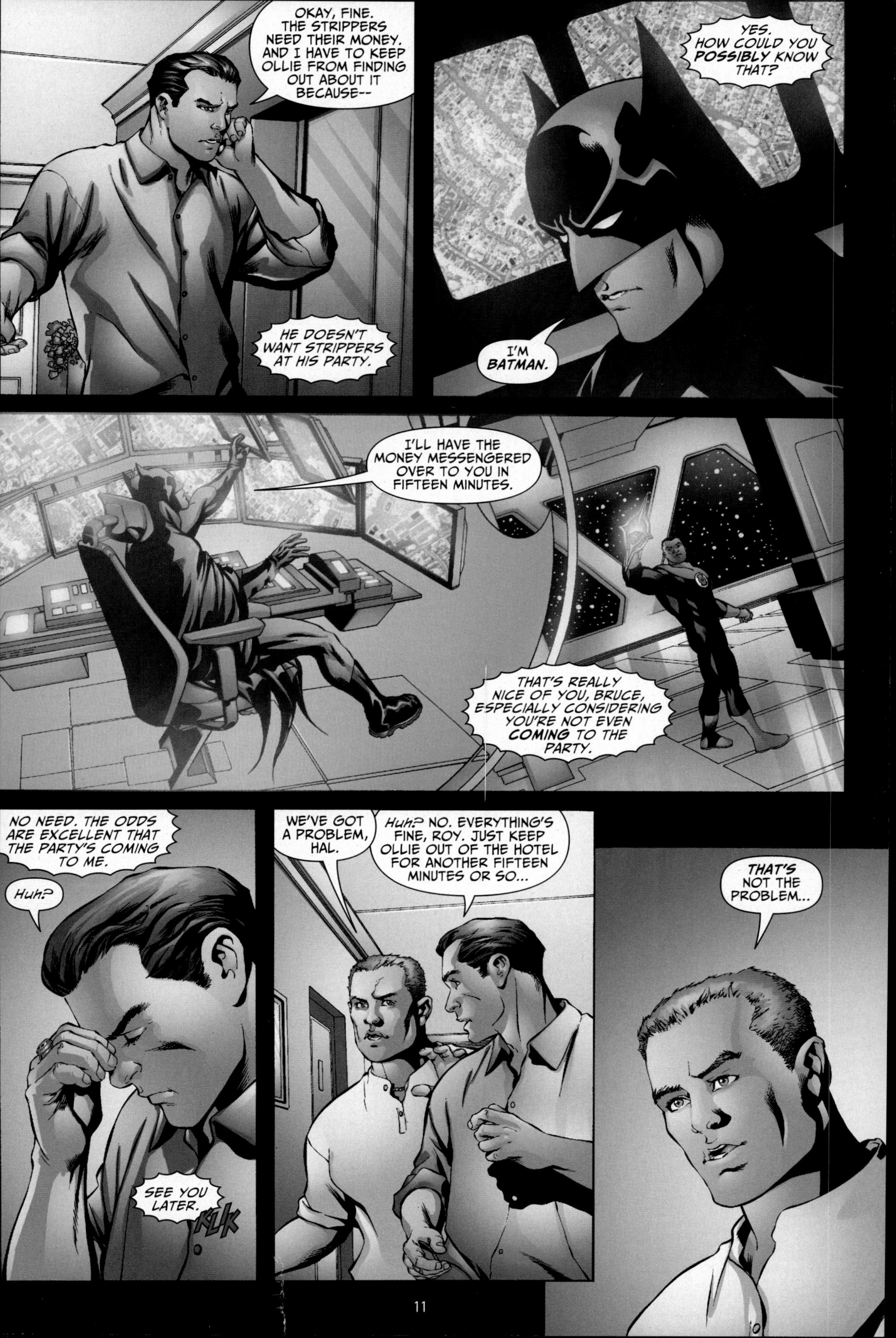
OKAY, FINE. THE STRIPPERS NEED THEIR MONEY. AND I HAVE TO KEEP OLLIE FROM FINDING OUT ABOUT IT BECAUSE--
HE DOESN'T WANT STRIPPERS AT HIS PARTY.
YES. HOW COULD YOU POSSIBLY KNOW THAT?
I'M BATMAN.
I'LL HAVE THE MONEY MESSENGERED OVER TO YOU IN FIFTEEN MINUTES.
THAT'S REALLY NICE OF YOU, BRUCE, ESPECIALLY CONSIDERING YOU'RE NOT EVEN COMING TO THE PARTY.
NO NEED. THE ODDS ARE EXCELLENT THAT THE PARTY'S COMING TO ME.
Huh?
SEE YOU LATER.
KLIK
WE'VE GOT A PROBLEM, HAL.
Huh? NO. EVERYTHING'S FINE, ROY. JUST KEEP OLLIE OUT OF THE HOTEL FOR ANOTHER FIFTEEN MINUTES OR SO...
THAT'S NOT THE PROBLEM...

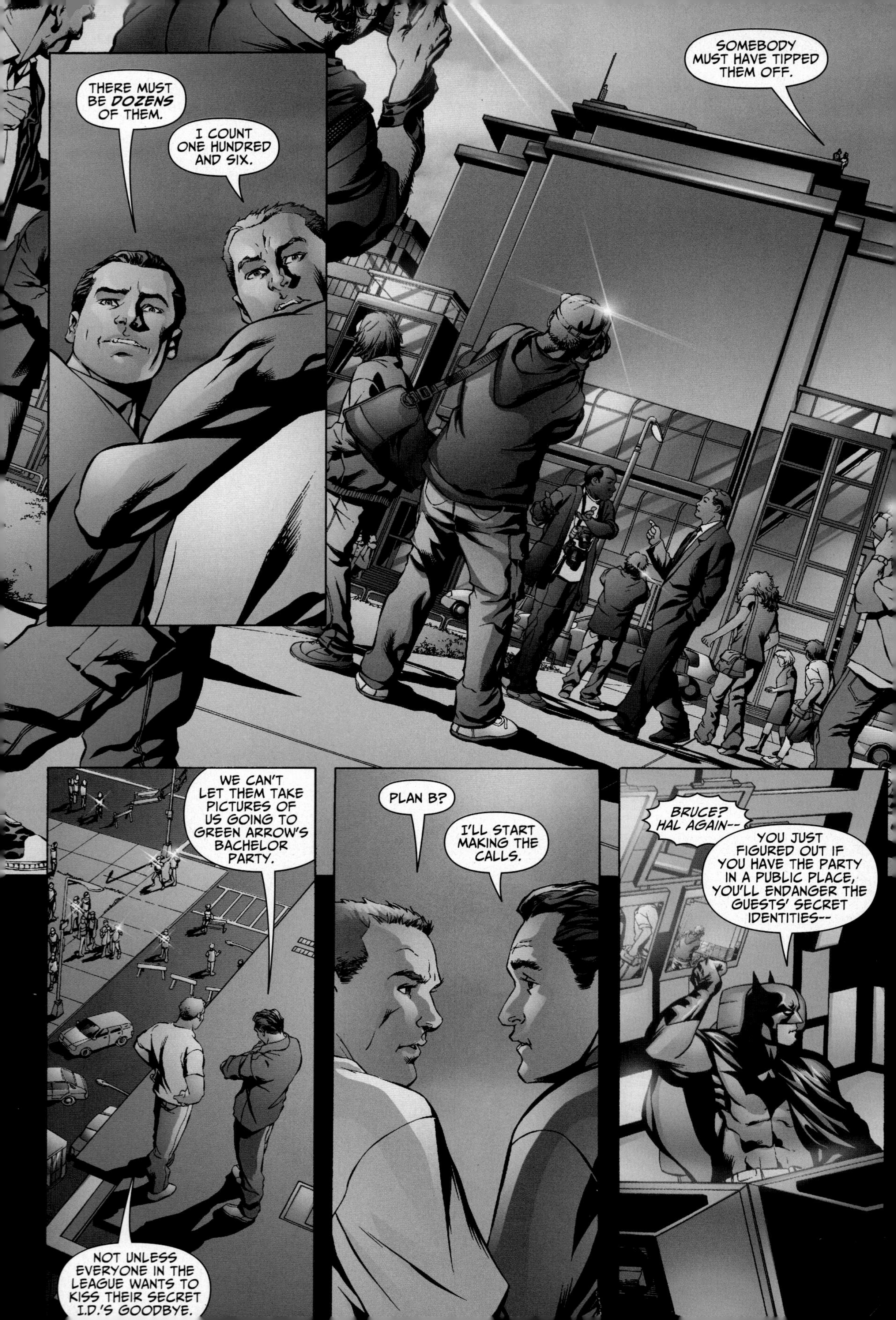
THERE MUST BE *DOZENS* OF THEM.
I COUNT ONE HUNDRED AND SIX.
SOMEBODY MUST HAVE TIPPED THEM OFF.
WE CAN'T LET THEM TAKE PICTURES OF US GOING TO GREEN ARROW'S BACHELOR PARTY.
NOT UNLESS EVERYONE IN THE LEAGUE WANTS TO KISS THEIR SECRET I.D.'S GOODBYE.
PLAN B?
I'LL START MAKING THE CALLS.
BRUCE? HAL AGAIN--
YOU JUST FIGURED OUT IF YOU HAVE THE PARTY IN A PUBLIC PLACE, YOU'LL ENDANGER THE GUESTS' SECRET IDENTITIES--

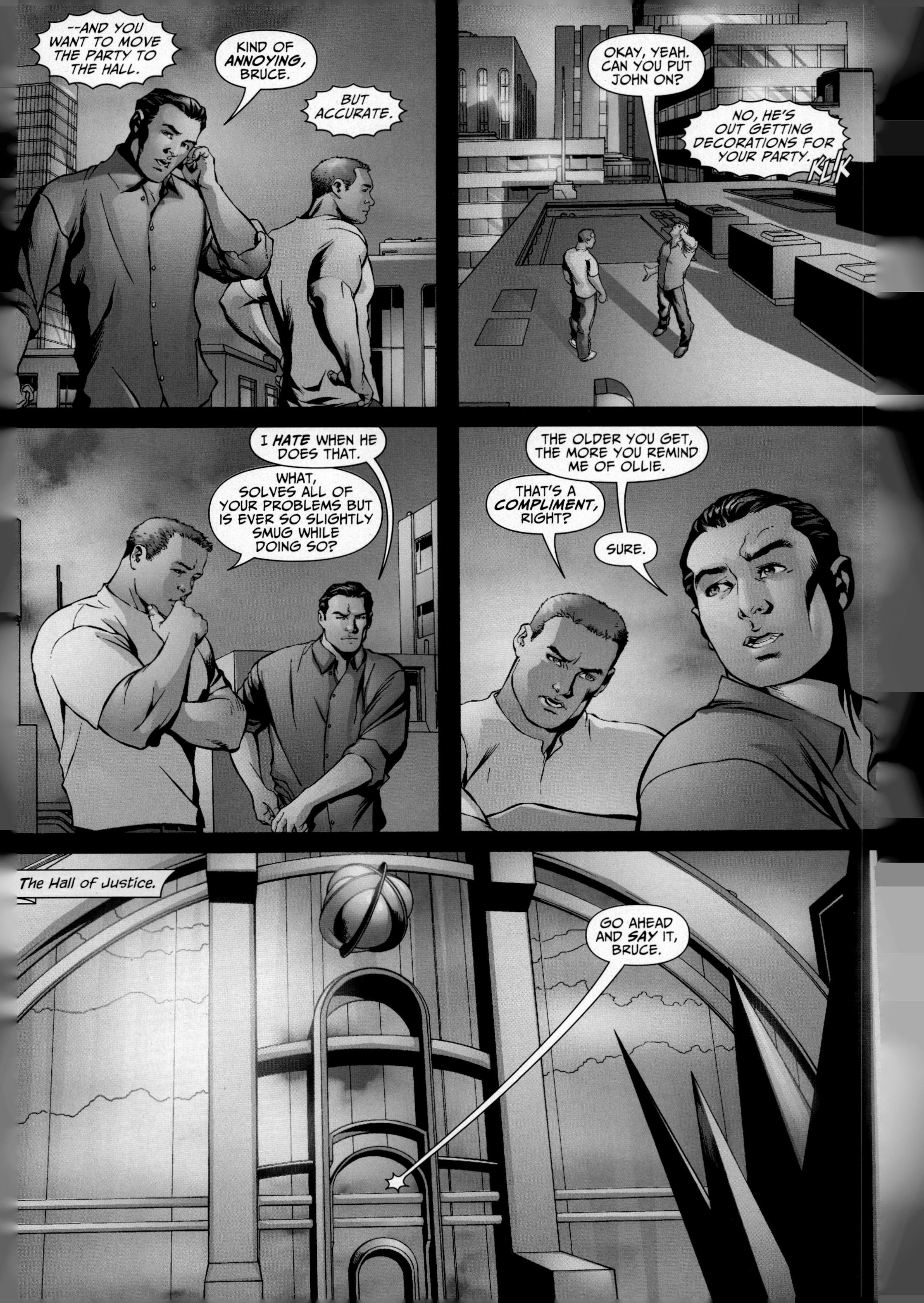

--AND YOU WANT TO MOVE THE PARTY TO THE HALL.
KIND OF ANNOYING, BRUCE.
BUT ACCURATE.
OKAY, YEAH. CAN YOU PUT JOHN ON?
NO, HE'S OUT GETTING DECORATIONS FOR YOUR PARTY.
KLIK
I HATE WHEN HE DOES THAT.
WHAT, SOLVES ALL OF YOUR PROBLEMS BUT IS EVER SO SLIGHTLY SMUG WHILE DOING SO?
THE OLDER YOU GET, THE MORE YOU REMIND ME OF OLLIE.
THAT'S A COMPLIMENT, RIGHT?
SURE.
The Hall of Justice.
GO AHEAD AND SAY IT, BRUCE.

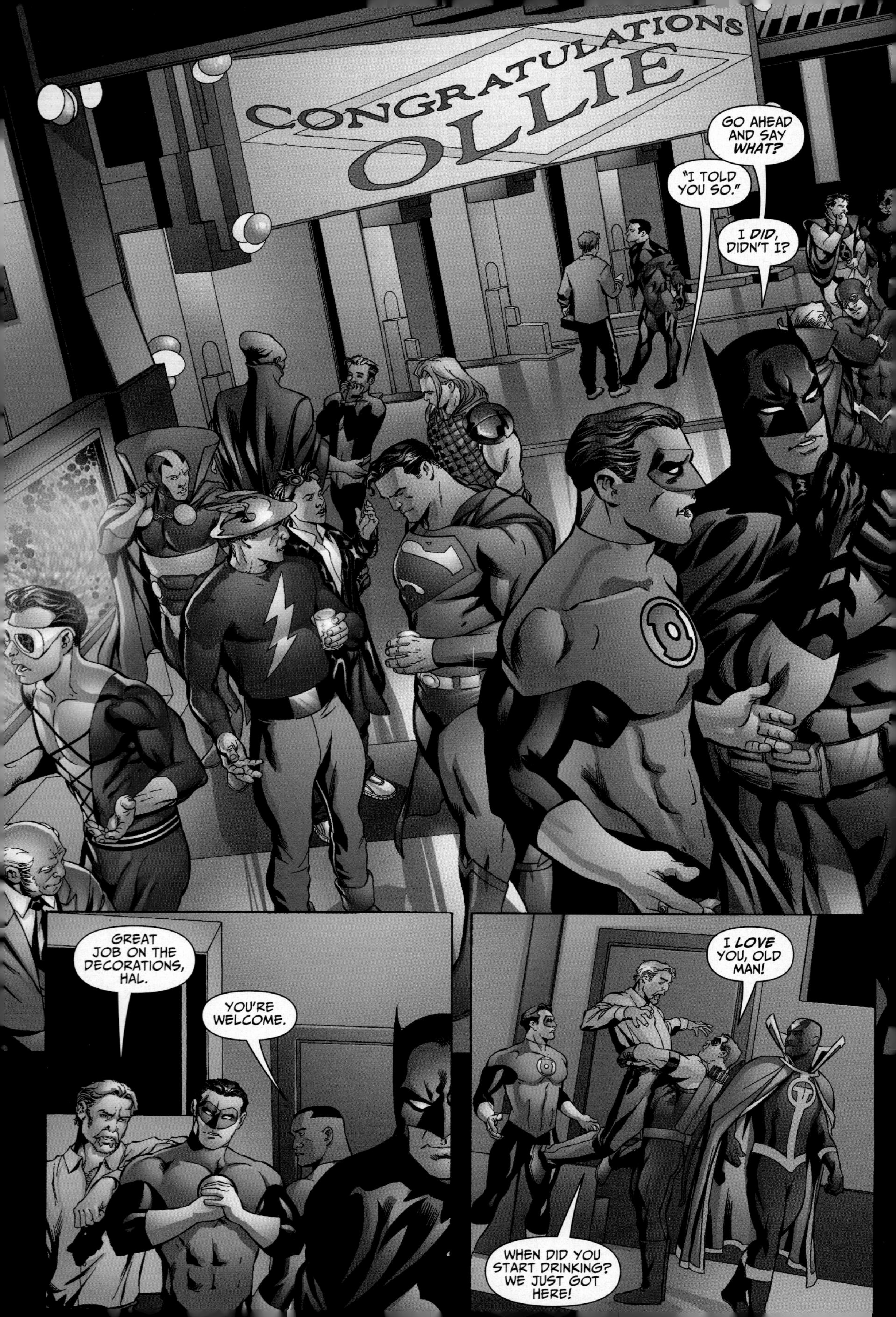
CONGRATULATIONS
OLLIE
GO AHEAD AND SAY *WHAT?*
"I TOLD YOU SO."
I *DID*, DIDN'T I?
GREAT JOB ON THE DECORATIONS, HAL.
YOU'RE WELCOME.
I *LOVE* YOU, OLD MAN!
WHEN DID YOU START DRINKING? WE JUST GOT HERE!

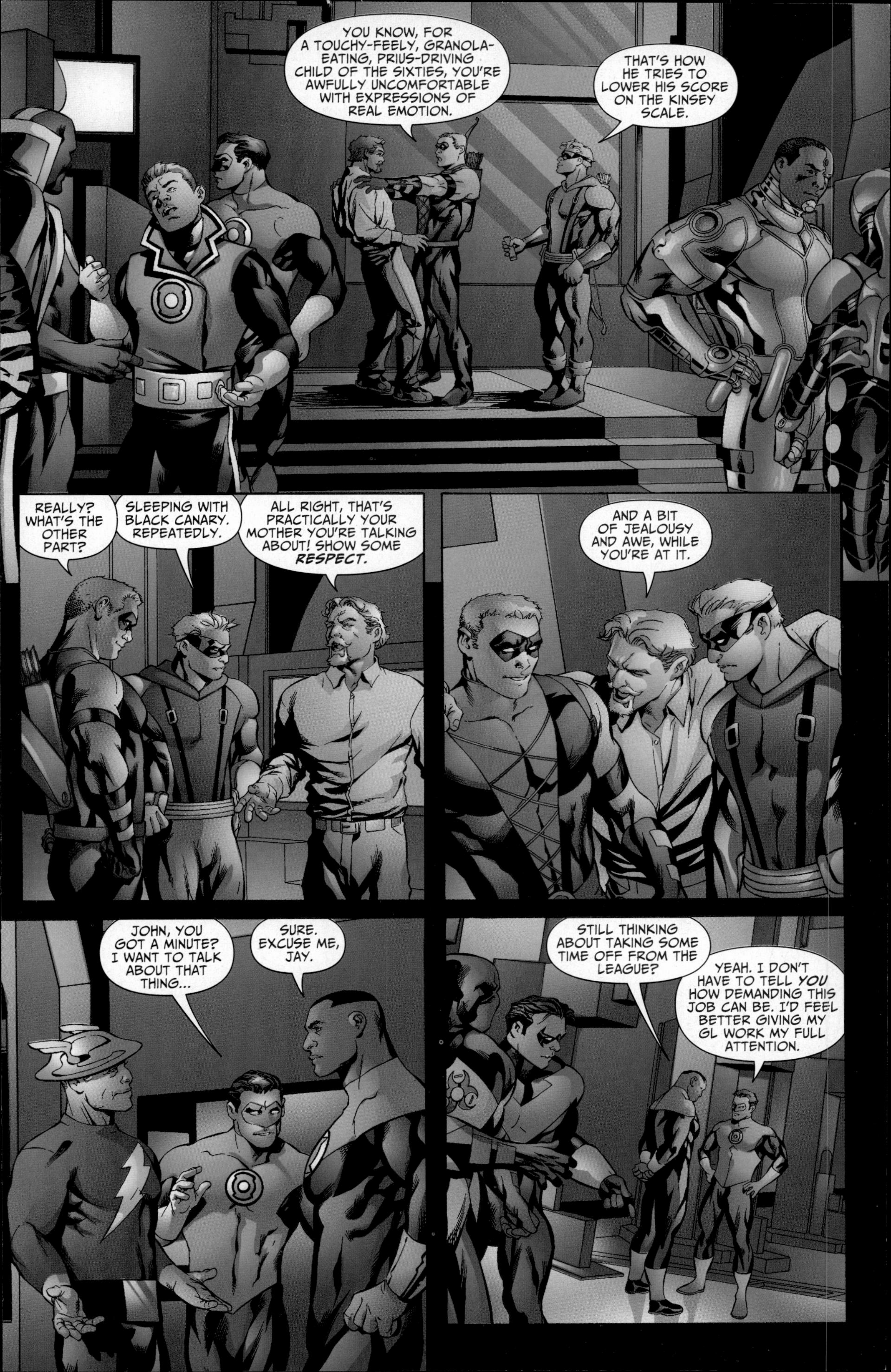
YOU KNOW, FOR A TOUCHY-FEELY, GRANOLA-EATING, PRIUS-DRIVING CHILD OF THE SIXTIES, YOU'RE AWFULLY UNCOMFORTABLE WITH EXPRESSIONS OF REAL EMOTION.
THAT'S HOW HE TRIES TO LOWER HIS SCORE ON THE KINSEY SCALE.
REALLY? WHAT'S THE OTHER PART?
SLEEPING WITH BLACK CANARY. REPEATEDLY.
ALL RIGHT, THAT'S PRACTICALLY YOUR MOTHER YOU'RE TALKING ABOUT! SHOW SOME *RESPECT.*
AND A BIT OF JEALOUSY AND AWE, WHILE YOU'RE AT IT.
JOHN, YOU GOT A MINUTE? I WANT TO TALK ABOUT THAT THING...
SURE. EXCUSE ME, JAY.
STILL THINKING ABOUT TAKING SOME TIME OFF FROM THE LEAGUE?
YEAH. I DON'T HAVE TO TELL *YOU* HOW DEMANDING THIS JOB CAN BE. I'D FEEL BETTER GIVING MY GL WORK MY FULL ATTENTION.

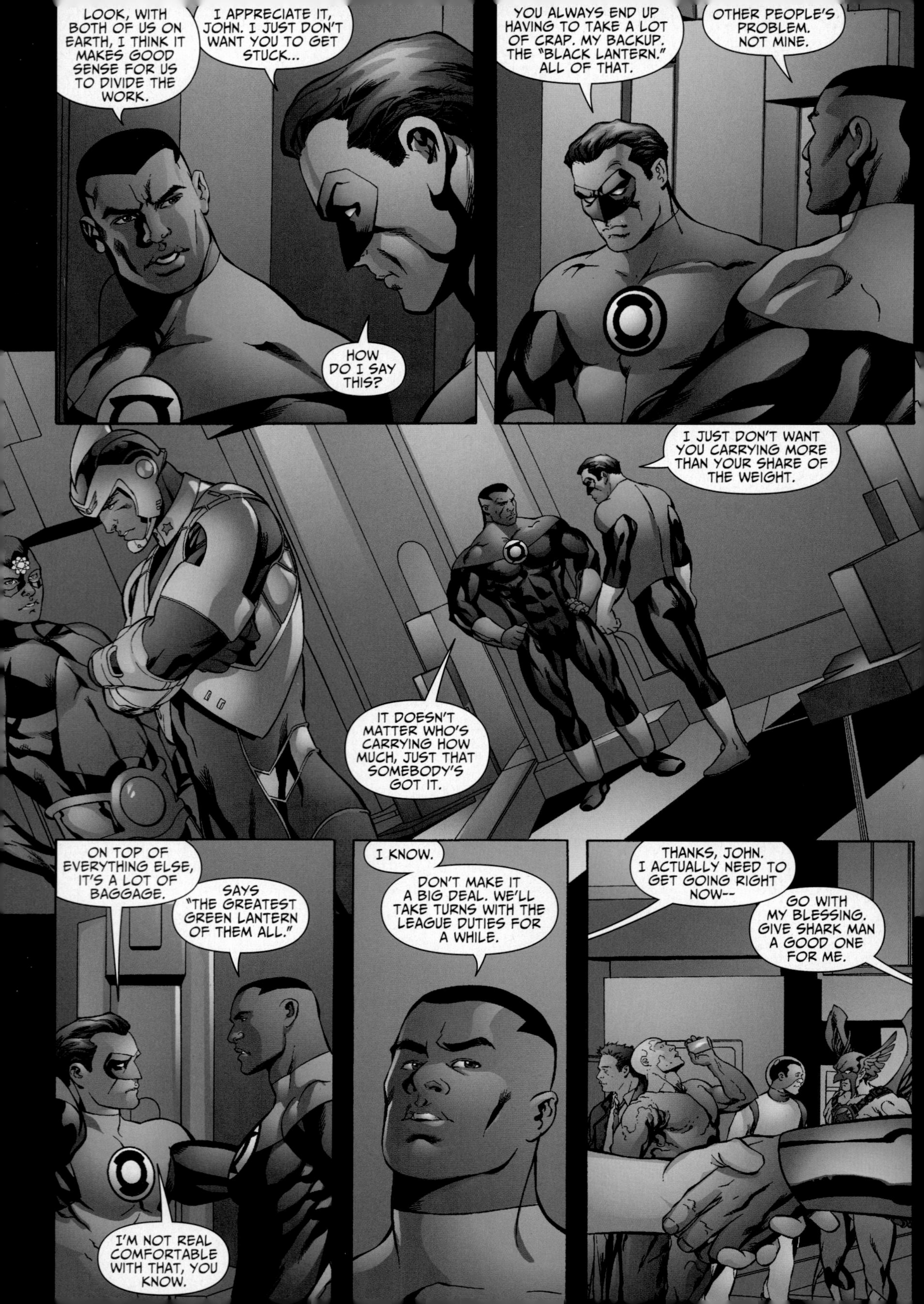
LOOK, WITH BOTH OF US ON EARTH, I THINK IT MAKES GOOD SENSE FOR US TO DIVIDE THE WORK.
I APPRECIATE IT, JOHN. I JUST DON'T WANT YOU TO GET STUCK...
HOW DO I SAY THIS?
YOU ALWAYS END UP HAVING TO TAKE A LOT OF CRAP. MY BACKUP. THE "BLACK LANTERN." ALL OF THAT.
OTHER PEOPLE'S PROBLEM. NOT MINE.
I JUST DON'T WANT YOU CARRYING MORE THAN YOUR SHARE OF THE WEIGHT.
IT DOESN'T MATTER WHO'S CARRYING HOW MUCH, JUST THAT SOMEBODY'S GOT IT.
ON TOP OF EVERYTHING ELSE, IT'S A LOT OF BAGGAGE.
SAYS "THE GREATEST GREEN LANTERN OF THEM ALL."
I'M NOT REAL COMFORTABLE WITH THAT, YOU KNOW.
I KNOW.
DON'T MAKE IT A BIG DEAL. WE'LL TAKE TURNS WITH THE LEAGUE DUTIES FOR A WHILE.
THANKS, JOHN. I ACTUALLY NEED TO GET GOING RIGHT NOW--
GO WITH MY BLESSING. GIVE SHARK MAN A GOOD ONE FOR ME.

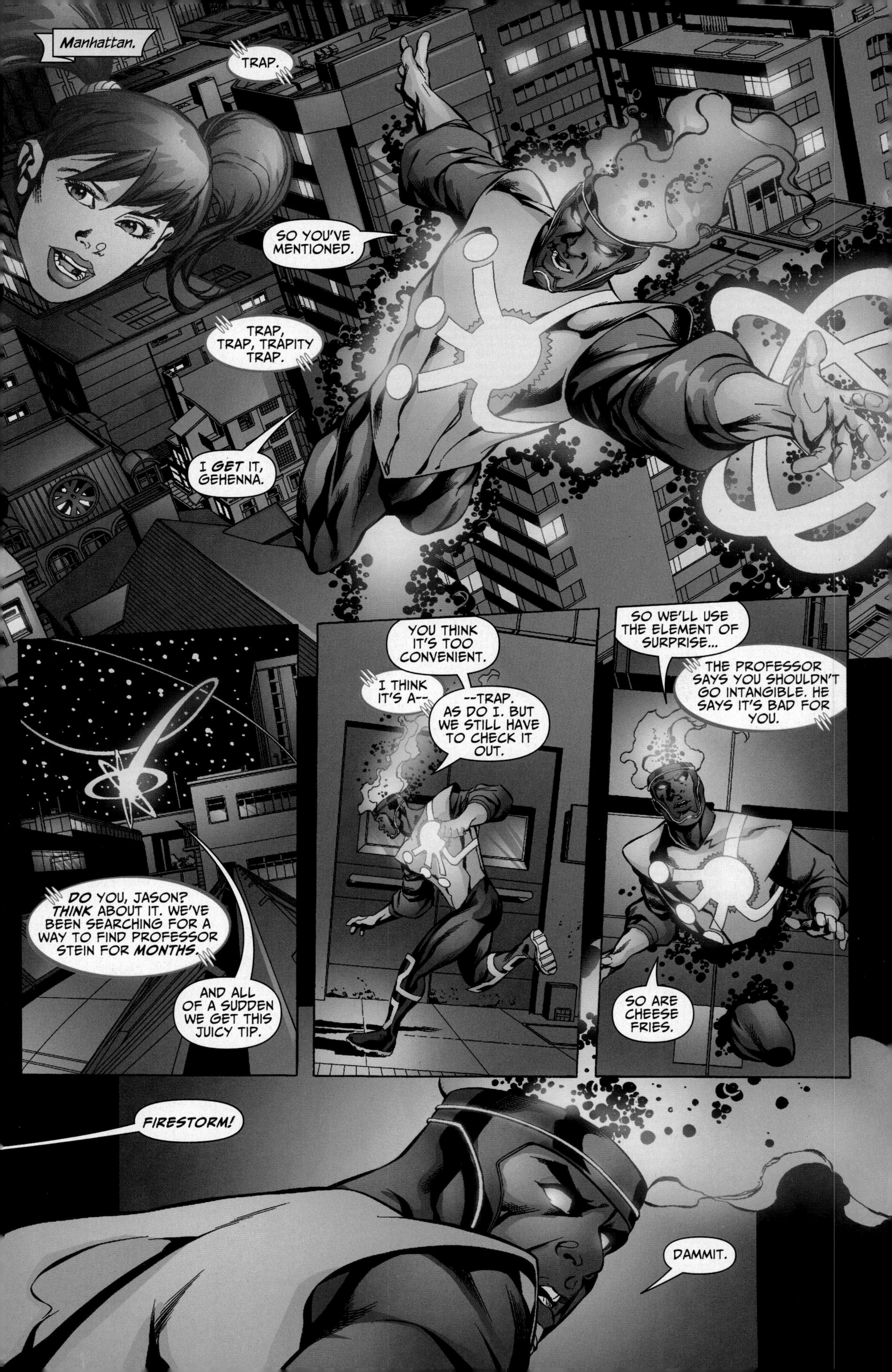
Manhattan.
TRAP.
SO YOU'VE MENTIONED.
TRAP, TRAP, TRAPITY TRAP.
I GET IT, GEHENNA.
DO YOU, JASON? THINK ABOUT IT. WE'VE BEEN SEARCHING FOR A WAY TO FIND PROFESSOR STEIN FOR MONTHS.
AND ALL OF A SUDDEN WE GET THIS JUICY TIP.
YOU THINK IT'S TOO CONVENIENT.
I THINK IT'S A--
--TRAP. AS DO I. BUT WE STILL HAVE TO CHECK IT OUT.
SO WE'LL USE THE ELEMENT OF SURPRISE...
THE PROFESSOR SAYS YOU SHOULDN'T GO INTANGIBLE. HE SAYS IT'S BAD FOR YOU.
SO ARE CHEESE FRIES.
FIRESTORM!
DAMMIT.

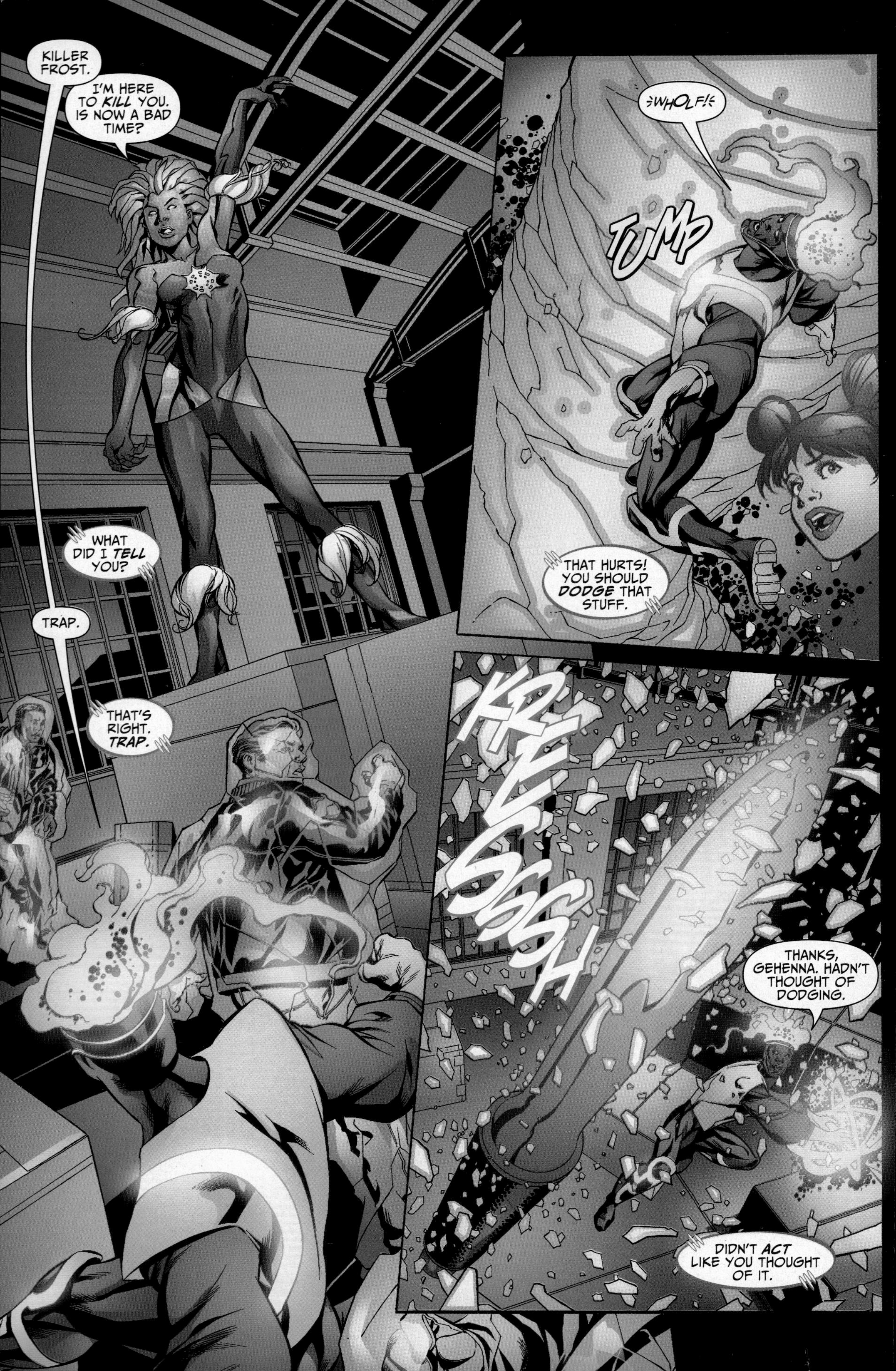
KILLER FROST.
I'M HERE TO KILL YOU. IS NOW A BAD TIME?
WHAT DID I TELL YOU?
TRAP.
THAT'S RIGHT. TRAP.
WHOLF!
TUMP
THAT HURTS! YOU SHOULD DODGE THAT STUFF.
KRRSSSSH
THANKS, GEHENNA. HADN'T THOUGHT OF DODGING.
DIDN'T ACT LIKE YOU THOUGHT OF IT.

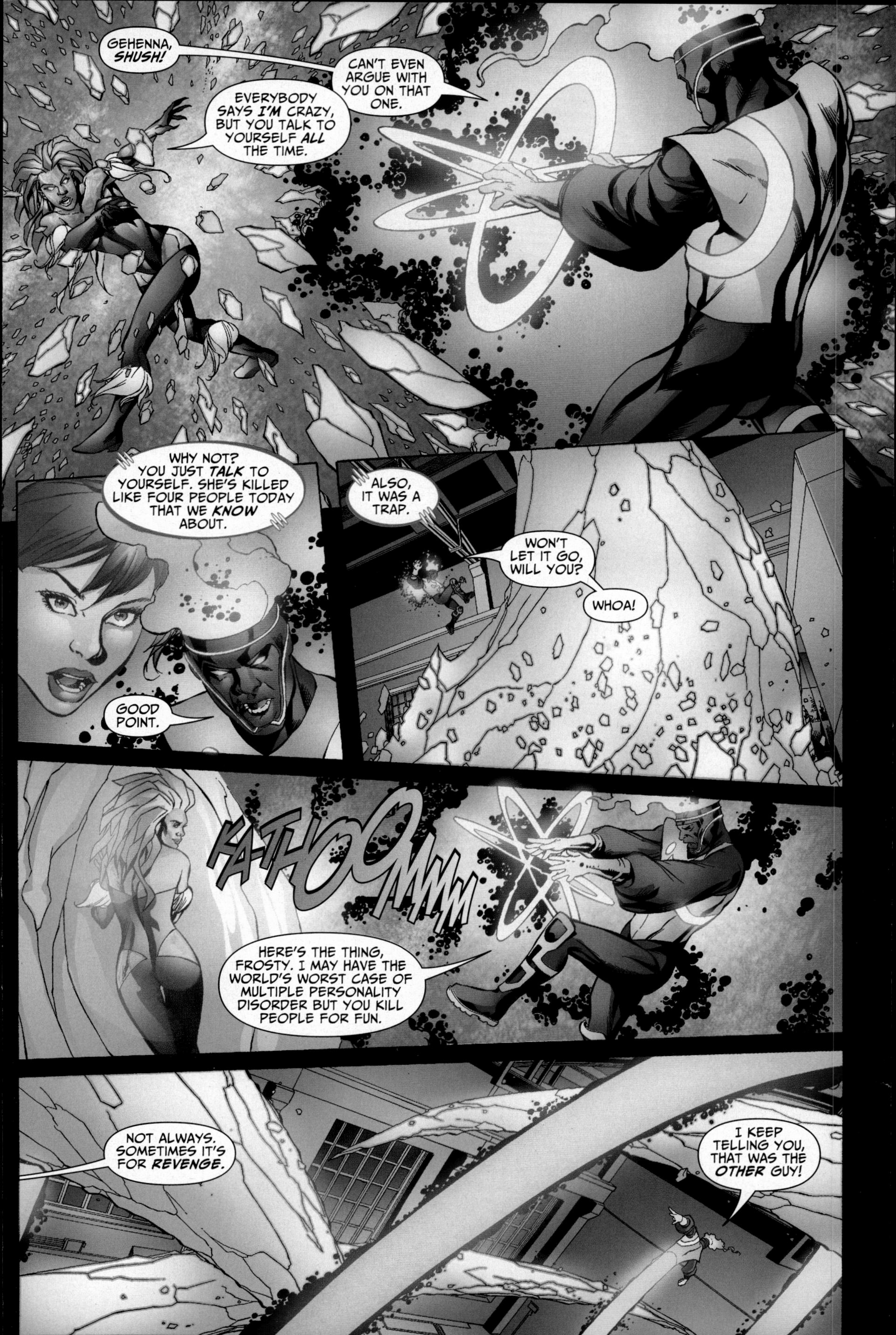
GEHENNA, SHUSH!
EVERYBODY SAYS I'M CRAZY, BUT YOU TALK TO YOURSELF ALL THE TIME.
CAN'T EVEN ARGUE WITH YOU ON THAT ONE.
WHY NOT? YOU JUST TALK TO YOURSELF. SHE'S KILLED LIKE FOUR PEOPLE TODAY THAT WE KNOW ABOUT.
GOOD POINT.
ALSO, IT WAS A TRAP.
WON'T LET IT GO, WILL YOU?
WHOA!
KA-FHOOMMMM
HERE'S THE THING, FROSTY. I MAY HAVE THE WORLD'S WORST CASE OF MULTIPLE PERSONALITY DISORDER BUT YOU KILL PEOPLE FOR FUN.
NOT ALWAYS. SOMETIMES IT'S FOR REVENGE.
I KEEP TELLING YOU, THAT WAS THE OTHER GUY!

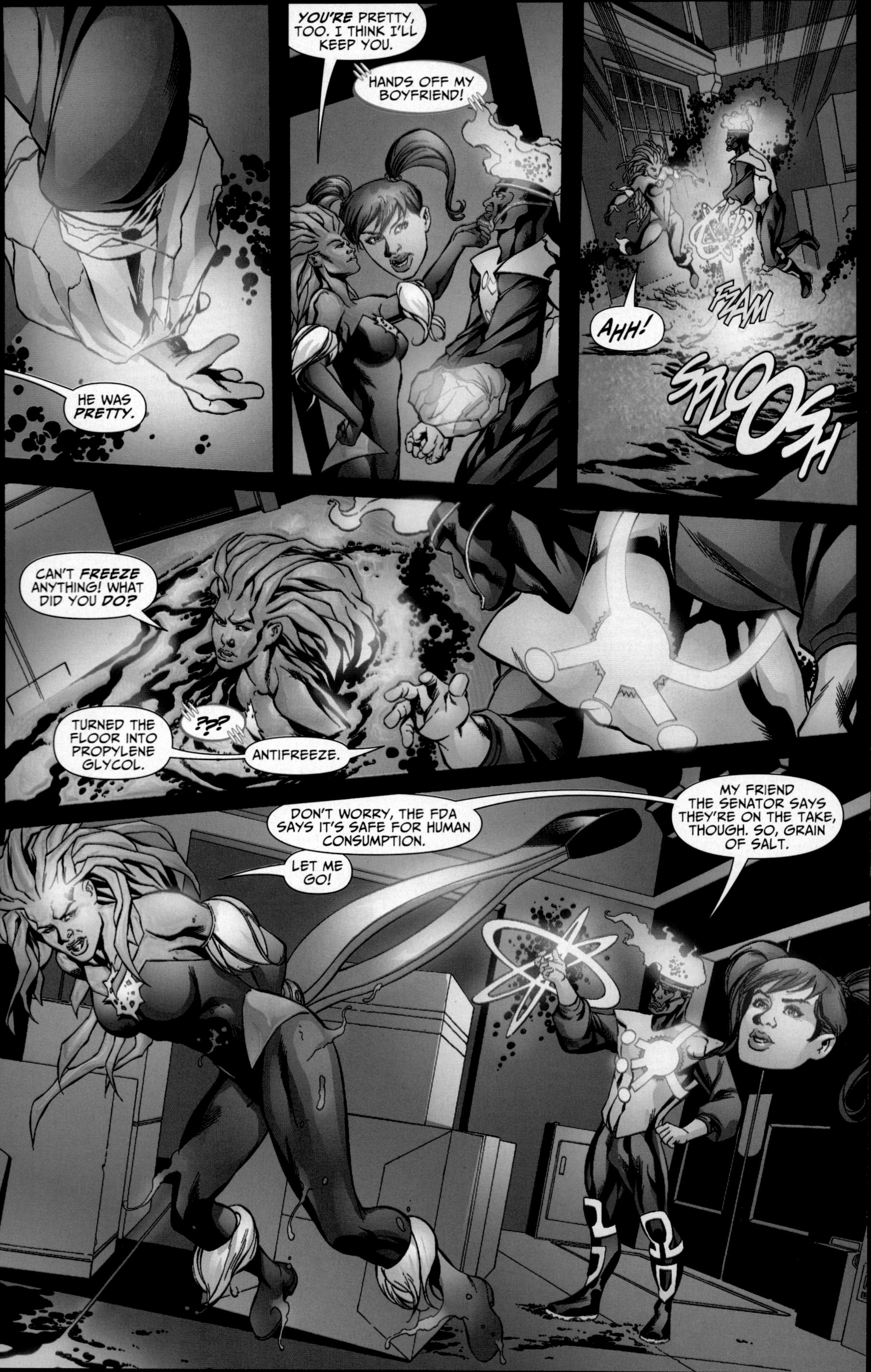
HE WAS PRETTY.
YOU'RE PRETTY, TOO. I THINK I'LL KEEP YOU.
HANDS OFF MY BOYFRIEND!
AHH!
FZAM
SPLOOOSH
CAN'T FREEZE ANYTHING! WHAT DID YOU DO?
TURNED THE FLOOR INTO PROPYLENE GLYCOL.
???
ANTIFREEZE.
DON'T WORRY, THE FDA SAYS IT'S SAFE FOR HUMAN CONSUMPTION.
LET ME GO!
MY FRIEND THE SENATOR SAYS THEY'RE ON THE TAKE, THOUGH. SO, GRAIN OF SALT.

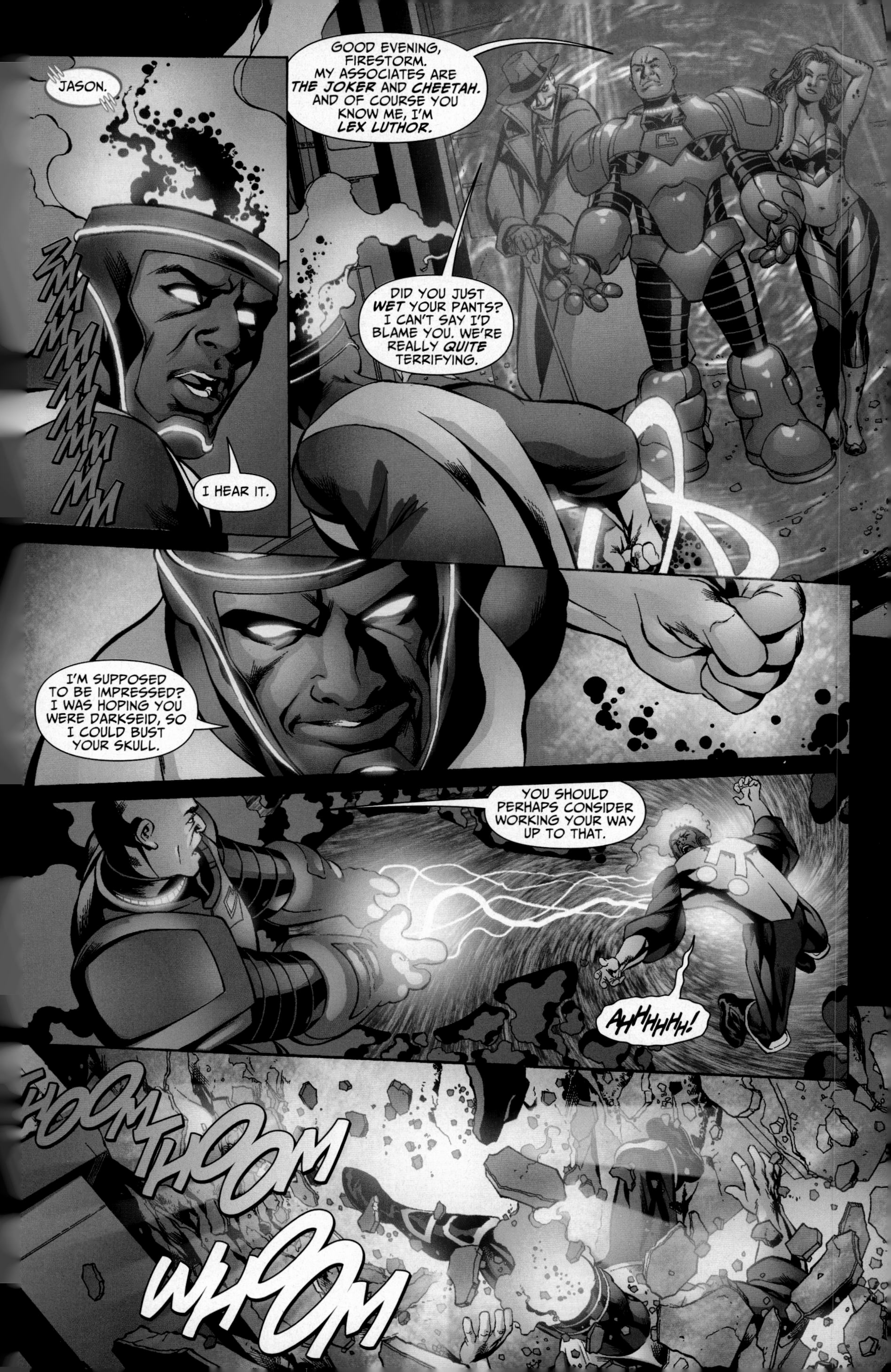
JASON.
GOOD EVENING, FIRESTORM. MY ASSOCIATES ARE THE JOKER AND CHEETAH. AND OF COURSE YOU KNOW ME, I'M LEX LUTHOR.
DID YOU JUST WET YOUR PANTS? I CAN'T SAY I'D BLAME YOU. WE'RE REALLY QUITE TERRIFYING.
ZMMMMMMMMMM
I HEAR IT.
I'M SUPPOSED TO BE IMPRESSED? I WAS HOPING YOU WERE DARKSEID, SO I COULD BUST YOUR SKULL.
YOU SHOULD PERHAPS CONSIDER WORKING YOUR WAY UP TO THAT.
AHHHHHH!
THOOM THOOM
WHOOM

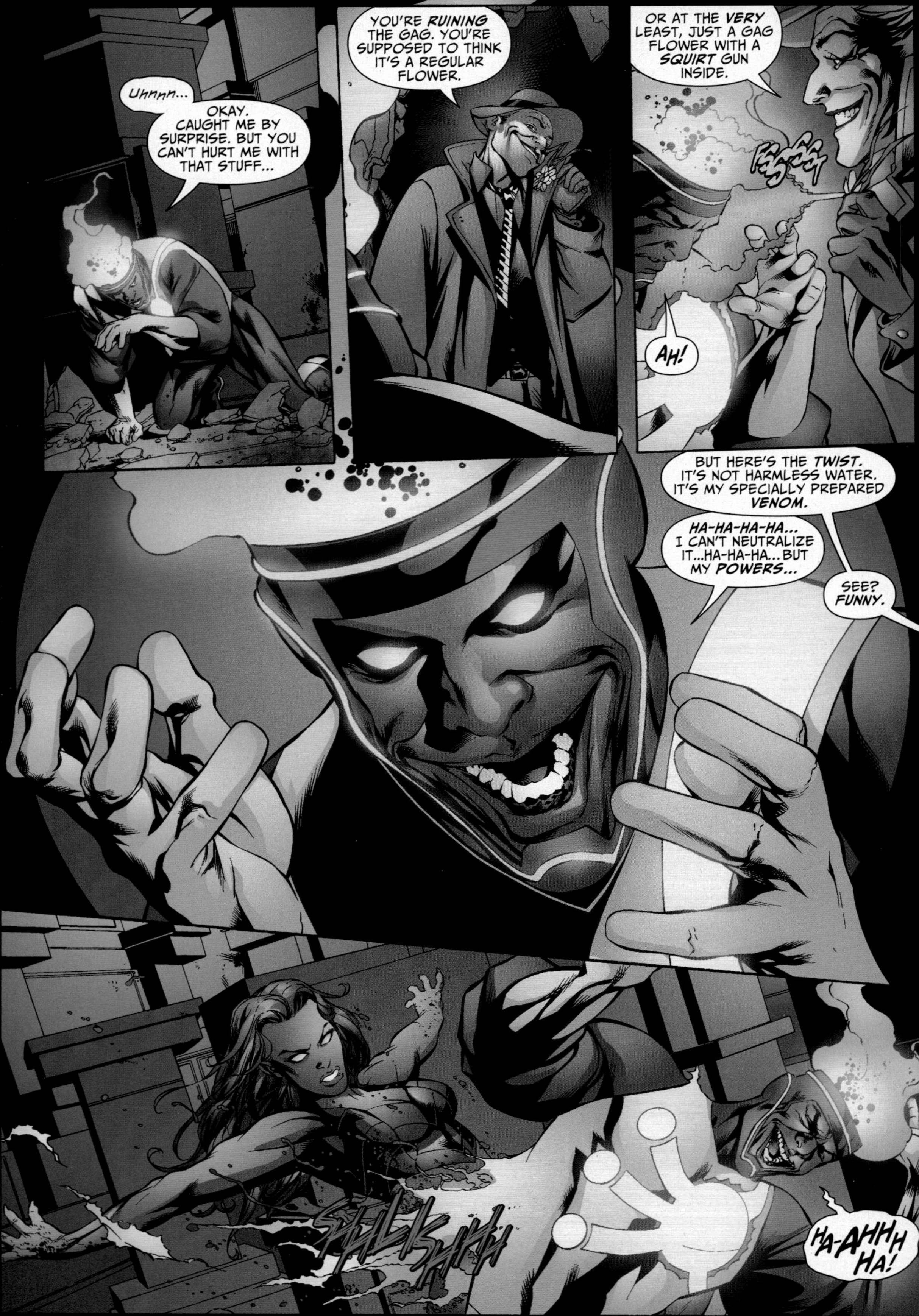
Uhnnn...
OKAY. CAUGHT ME BY SURPRISE. BUT YOU CAN'T HURT ME WITH THAT STUFF...
YOU'RE RUINING THE GAG. YOU'RE SUPPOSED TO THINK IT'S A REGULAR FLOWER.
OR AT THE VERY LEAST, JUST A GAG FLOWER WITH A SQUIRT GUN INSIDE.
FSSSSS
AH!
BUT HERE'S THE TWIST. IT'S NOT HARMLESS WATER. IT'S MY SPECIALLY PREPARED VENOM.
HA-HA-HA-HA... I CAN'T NEUTRALIZE IT...HA-HA-HA...BUT MY POWERS...
SEE? FUNNY.
SHLISHHH
HA-AHHH HA!

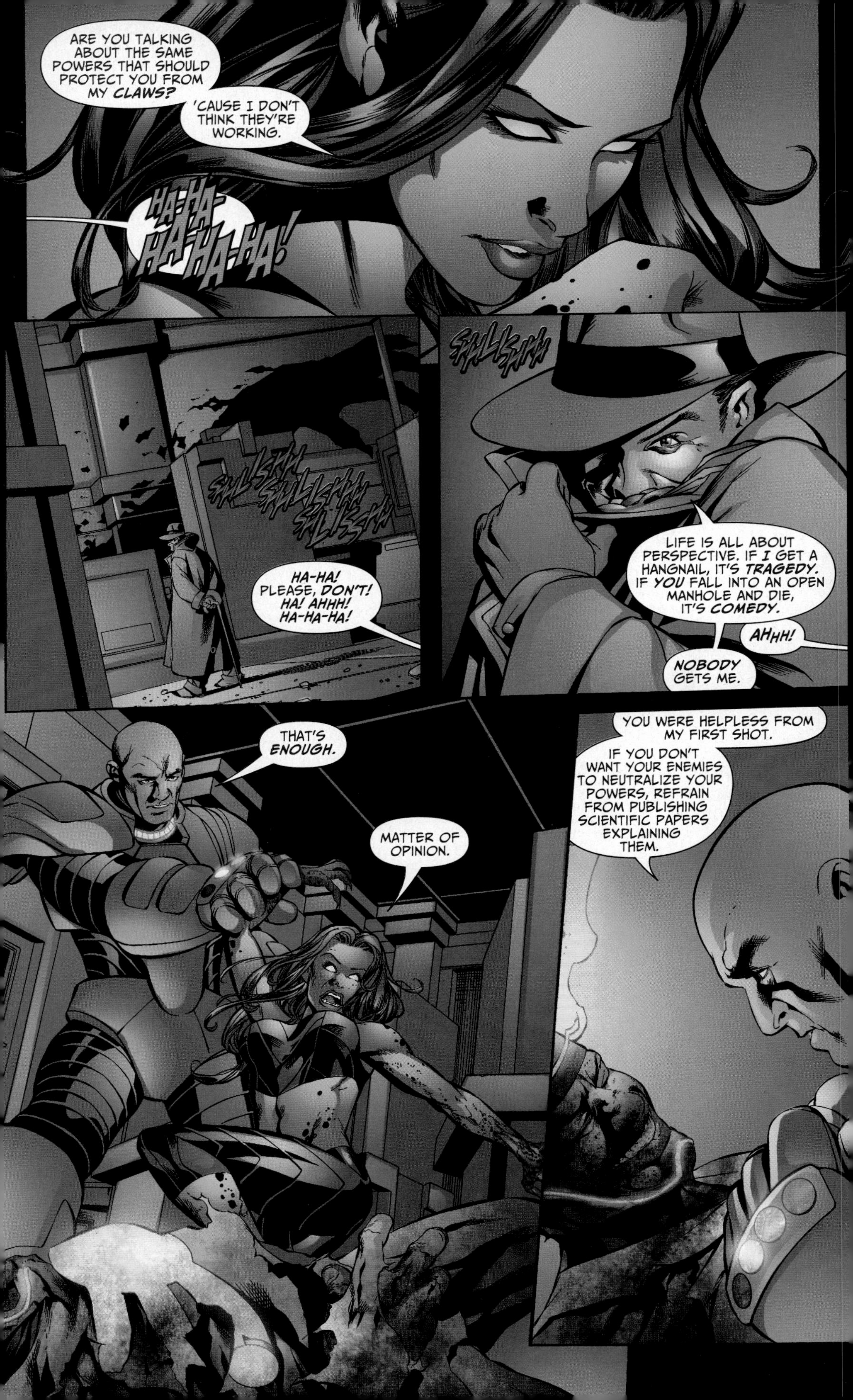

ARE YOU TALKING ABOUT THE SAME POWERS THAT SHOULD PROTECT YOU FROM MY CLAWS?
'CAUSE I DON'T THINK THEY'RE WORKING.
HA-HA-HA-HA-HA!
SHLISHHH SHLISHHH SHLISSHHH
HA-HA! PLEASE, DON'T! HA! AHHH! HA-HA-HA!
SHLISHHH
LIFE IS ALL ABOUT PERSPECTIVE. IF I GET A HANGNAIL, IT'S TRAGEDY. IF YOU FALL INTO AN OPEN MANHOLE AND DIE, IT'S COMEDY.
AHHH!
NOBODY GETS ME.
THAT'S ENOUGH.
MATTER OF OPINION.
YOU WERE HELPLESS FROM MY FIRST SHOT.
IF YOU DON'T WANT YOUR ENEMIES TO NEUTRALIZE YOUR POWERS, REFRAIN FROM PUBLISHING SCIENTIFIC PAPERS EXPLAINING THEM.

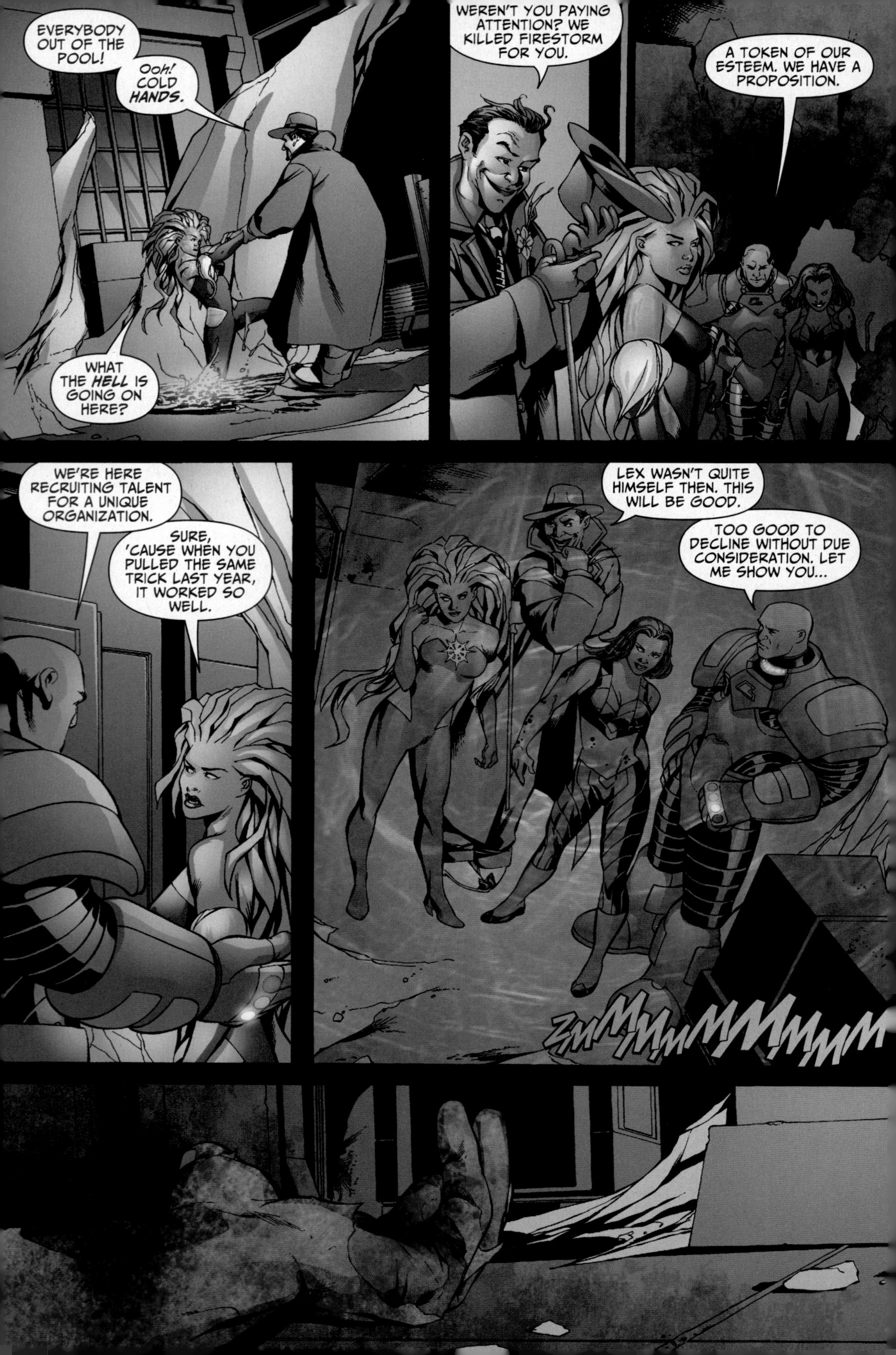

EVERYBODY OUT OF THE POOL!
Ooh! COLD HANDS.
WHAT THE HELL IS GOING ON HERE?
WEREN'T YOU PAYING ATTENTION? WE KILLED FIRESTORM FOR YOU.
A TOKEN OF OUR ESTEEM. WE HAVE A PROPOSITION.
WE'RE HERE RECRUITING TALENT FOR A UNIQUE ORGANIZATION.
SURE, 'CAUSE WHEN YOU PULLED THE SAME TRICK LAST YEAR, IT WORKED SO WELL.
LEX WASN'T QUITE HIMSELF THEN. THIS WILL BE GOOD.
TOO GOOD TO DECLINE WITHOUT DUE CONSIDERATION. LET ME SHOW YOU...
ZMMMMMMMMMMMMMMM

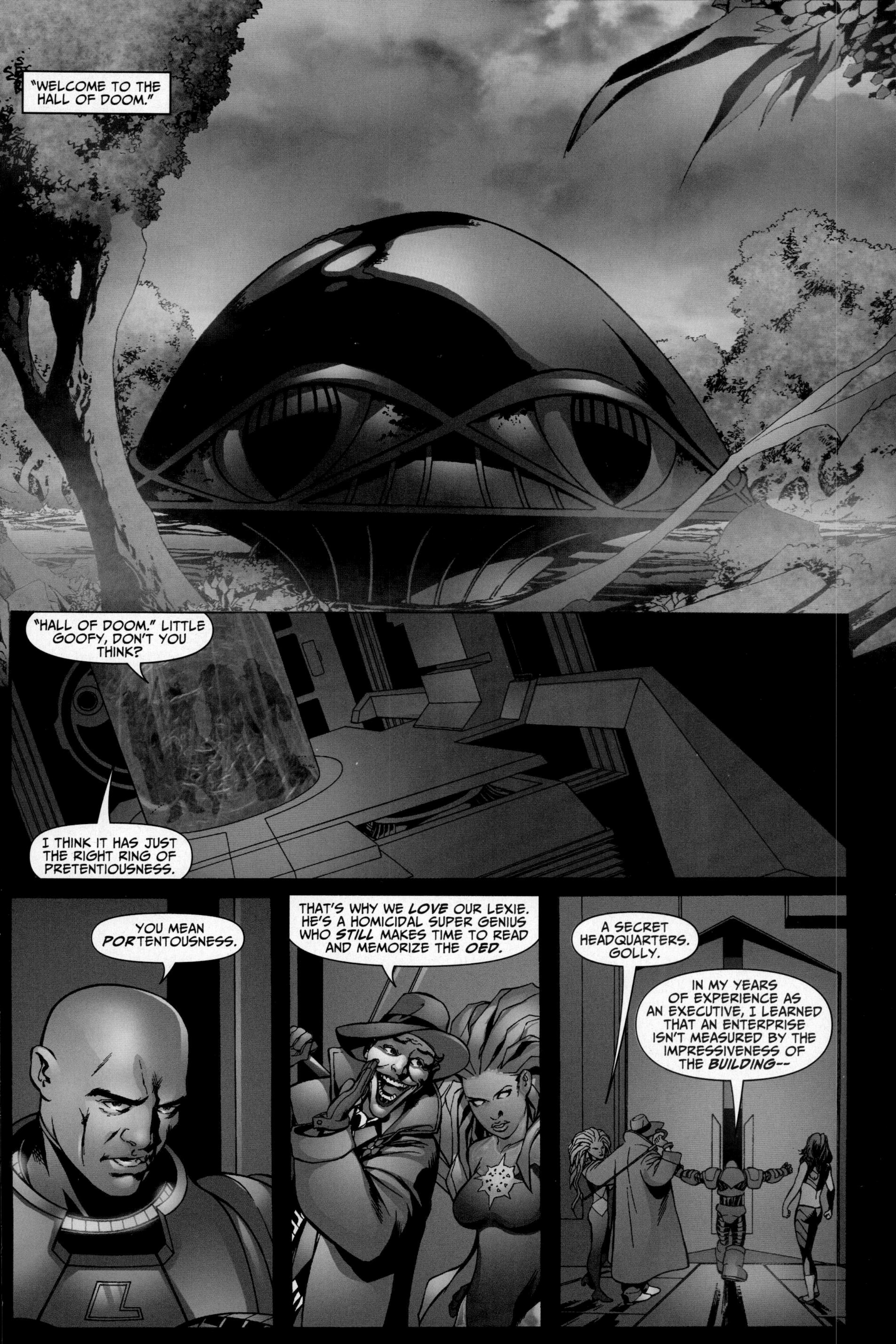
"WELCOME TO THE HALL OF DOOM."
"HALL OF DOOM." LITTLE GOOFY, DON'T YOU THINK?
I THINK IT HAS JUST THE RIGHT RING OF PRETENTIOUSNESS.
YOU MEAN ***POR***TENTOUSNESS.
THAT'S WHY WE ***LOVE*** OUR LEXIE. HE'S A HOMICIDAL SUPER GENIUS WHO ***STILL*** MAKES TIME TO READ AND MEMORIZE THE ***OED.***
A SECRET HEADQUARTERS. GOLLY.
IN MY YEARS OF EXPERIENCE AS AN EXECUTIVE, I LEARNED THAT AN ENTERPRISE ISN'T MEASURED BY THE IMPRESSIVENESS OF THE ***BUILDING--***

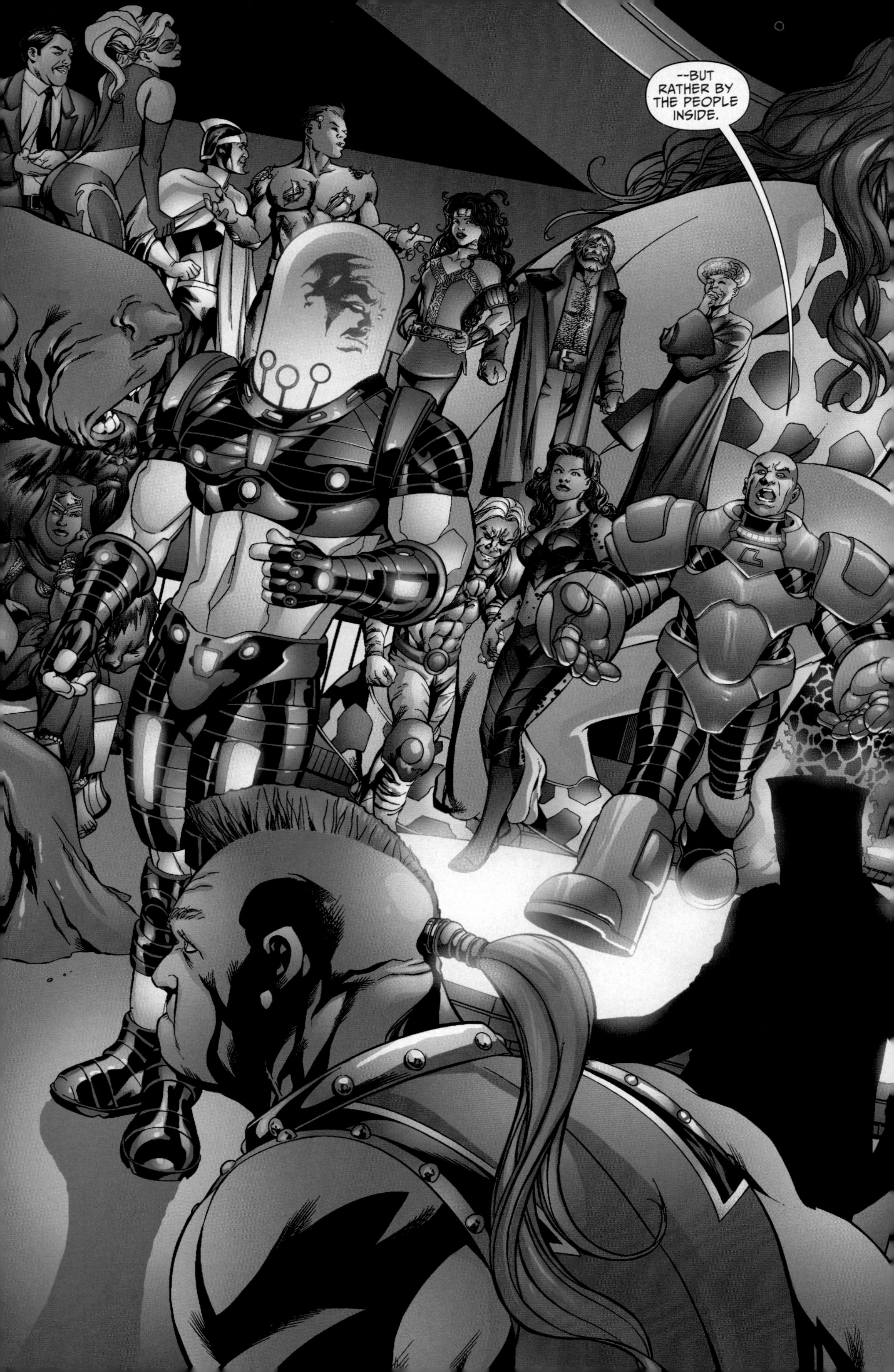
--BUT RATHER BY THE PEOPLE INSIDE.

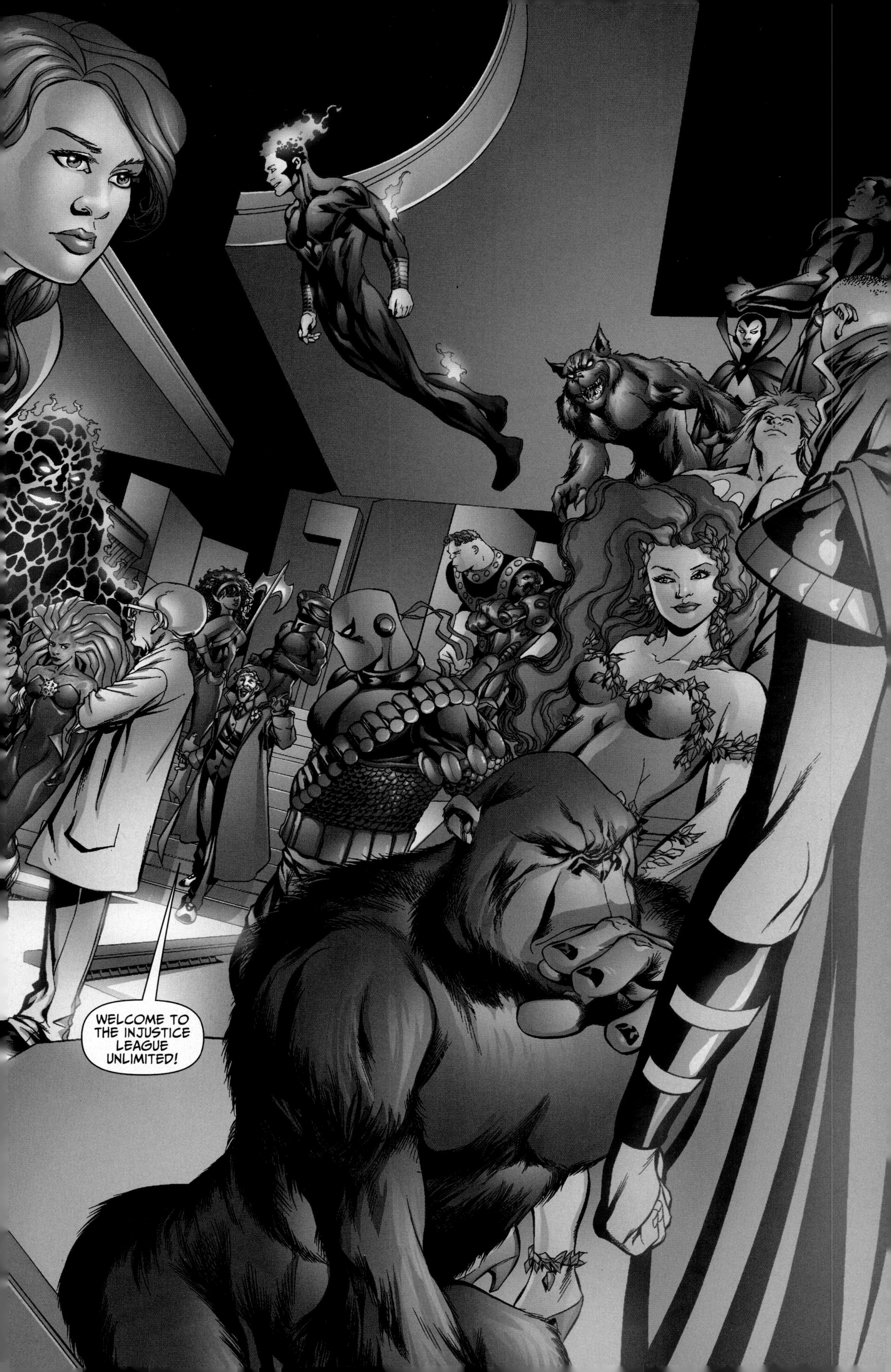
WELCOME TO THE INJUSTICE LEAGUE UNLIMITED!

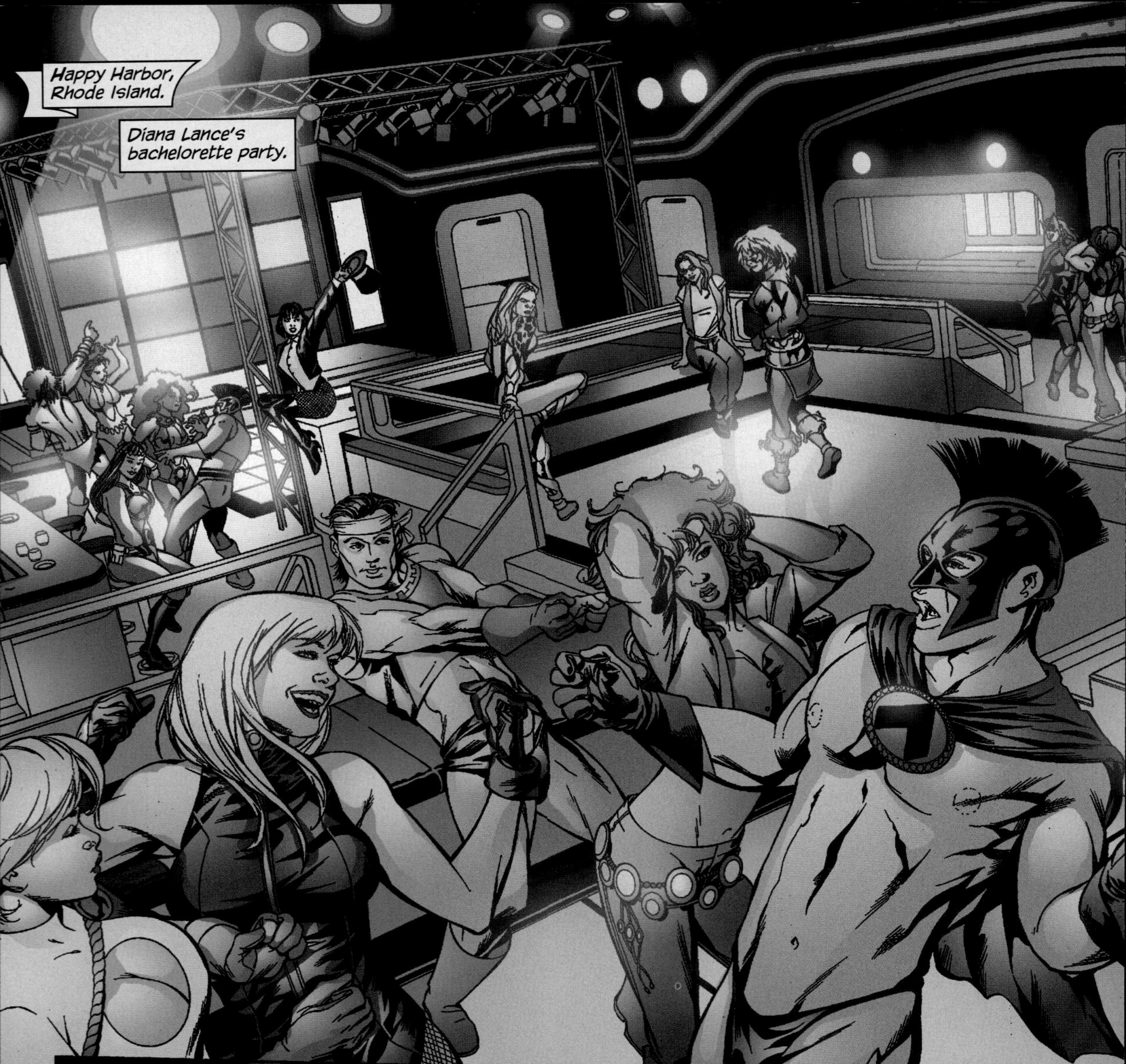
Happy Harbor, Rhode Island.
Diana Lance's bachelorette party.

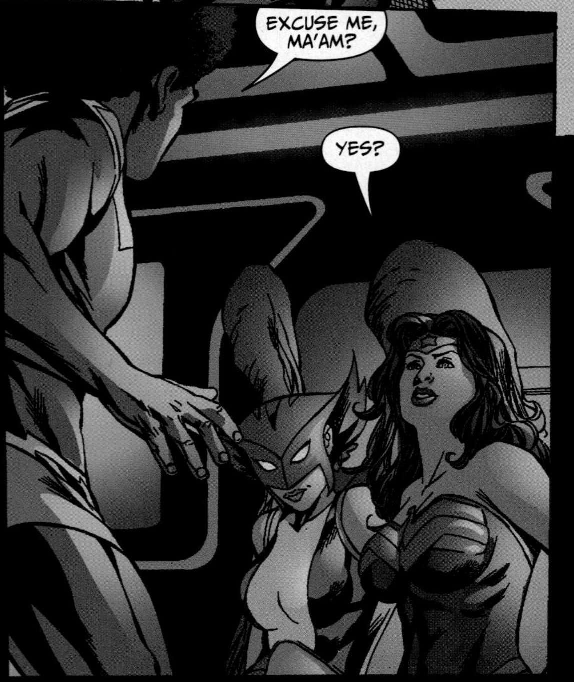
EXCUSE ME, MA'AM?
YES?

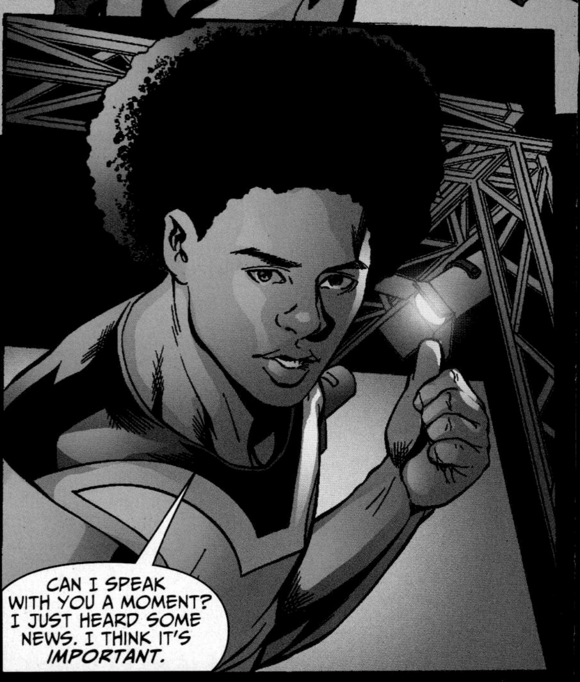
CAN I SPEAK WITH YOU A MOMENT? I JUST HEARD SOME NEWS. I THINK IT'S *IMPORTANT*.

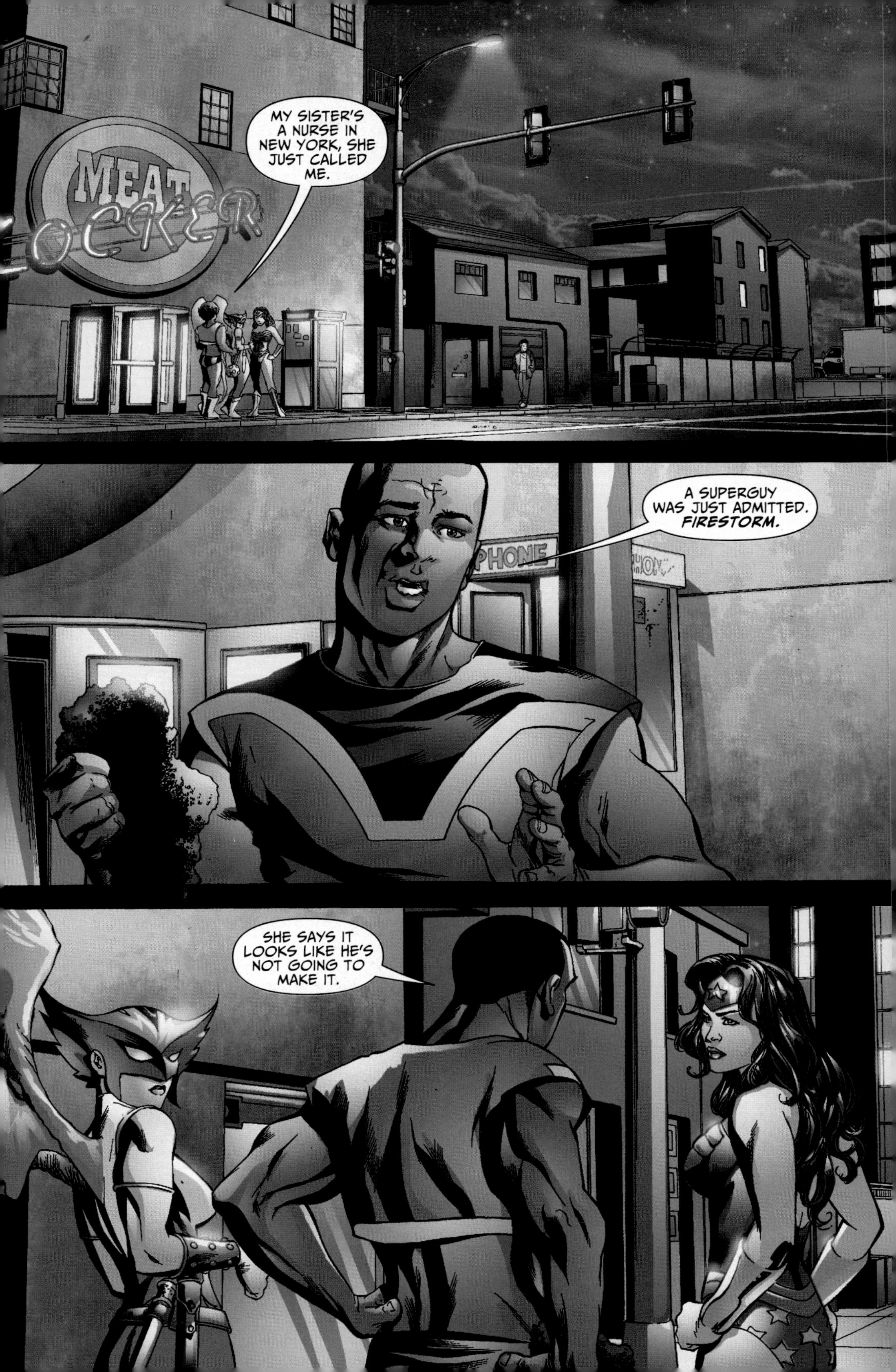
MEAT
LOCKER
MY SISTER'S A NURSE IN NEW YORK, SHE JUST CALLED ME.
PHONE
A SUPERGUY WAS JUST ADMITTED. *FIRESTORM.*
SHE SAYS IT LOOKS LIKE HE'S NOT GOING TO MAKE IT.

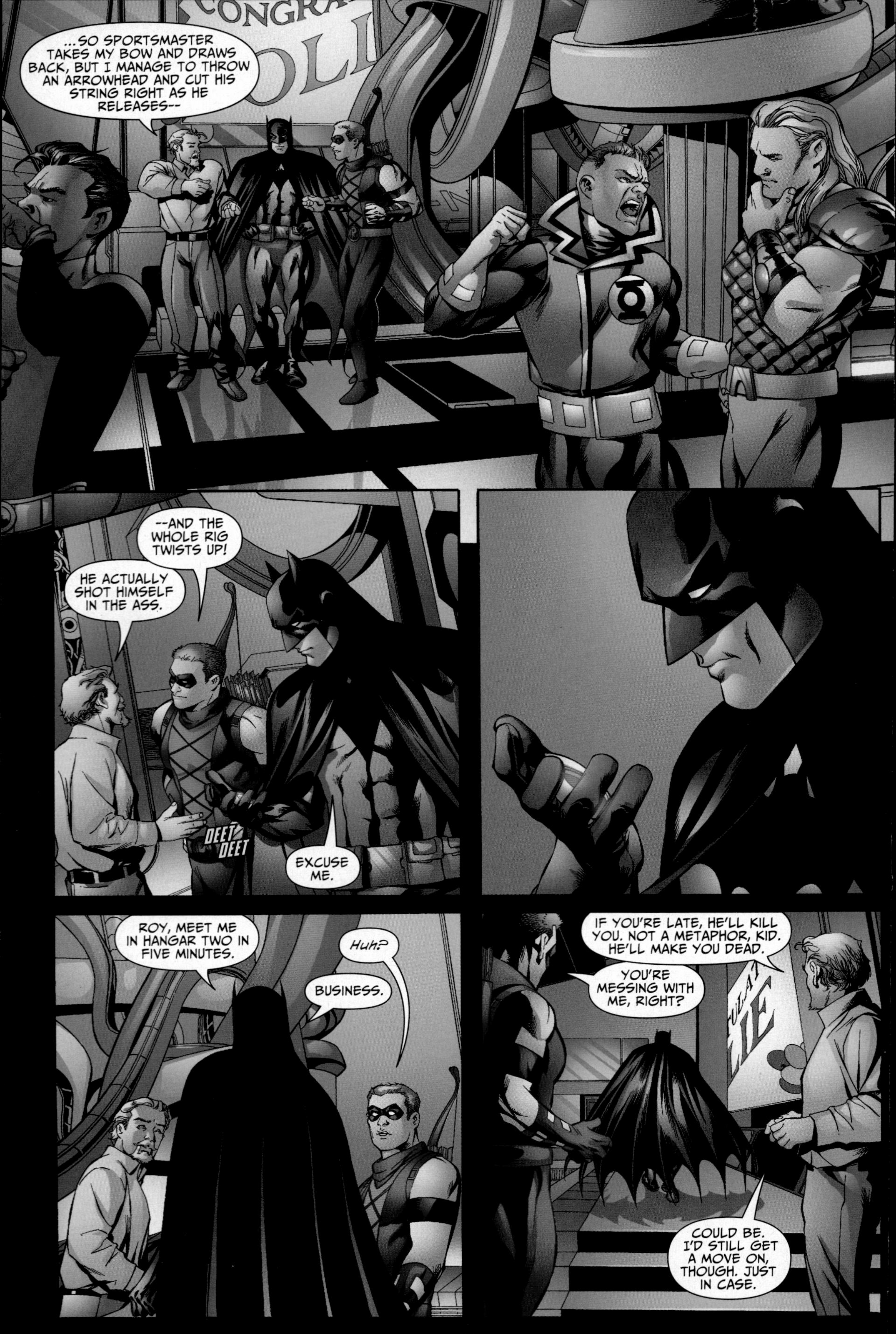
...SO SPORTSMASTER TAKES MY BOW AND DRAWS BACK, BUT I MANAGE TO THROW AN ARROWHEAD AND CUT HIS STRING RIGHT AS HE RELEASES--
CONGRA
--AND THE WHOLE RIG TWISTS UP!
HE ACTUALLY SHOT HIMSELF IN THE ASS.
DEET DEET
EXCUSE ME.
ROY, MEET ME IN HANGAR TWO IN FIVE MINUTES.
Huh?
BUSINESS.
IF YOU'RE LATE, HE'LL KILL YOU. NOT A METAPHOR, KID. HE'LL MAKE YOU DEAD.
YOU'RE MESSING WITH ME, RIGHT?
COULD BE. I'D STILL GET A MOVE ON, THOUGH. JUST IN CASE.

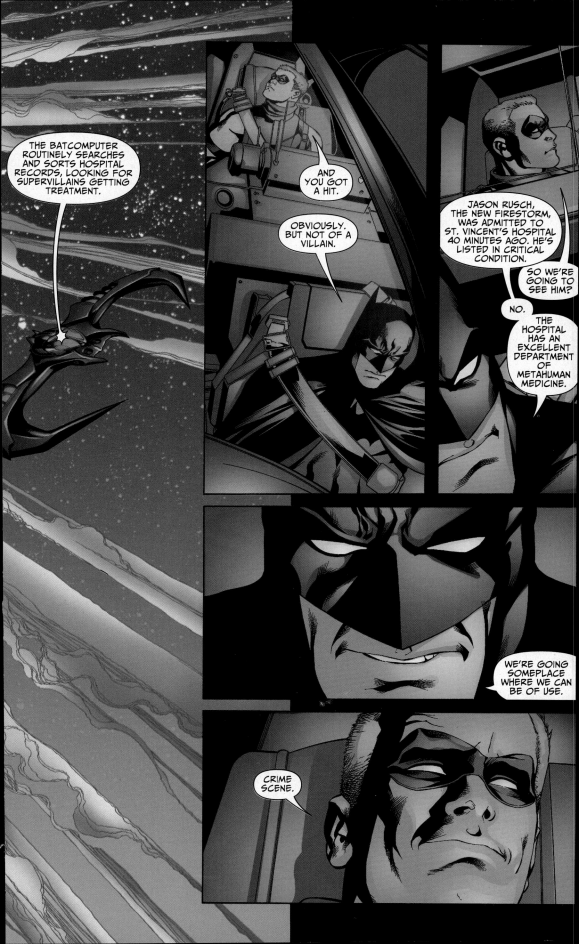

THE BATCOMPUTER ROUTINELY SEARCHES AND SORTS HOSPITAL RECORDS, LOOKING FOR SUPERVILLAINS GETTING TREATMENT.

AND YOU GOT A HIT.

OBVIOUSLY. BUT NOT OF A VILLAIN.

JASON RUSCH, THE NEW FIRESTORM, WAS ADMITTED TO ST. VINCENT'S HOSPITAL 40 MINUTES AGO. HE'S LISTED IN CRITICAL CONDITION.

SO WE'RE GOING TO SEE HIM?

NO.

THE HOSPITAL HAS AN EXCELLENT DEPARTMENT OF METAHUMAN MEDICINE.

WE'RE GOING SOMEPLACE WHERE WE CAN BE OF USE.

CRIME SCENE.

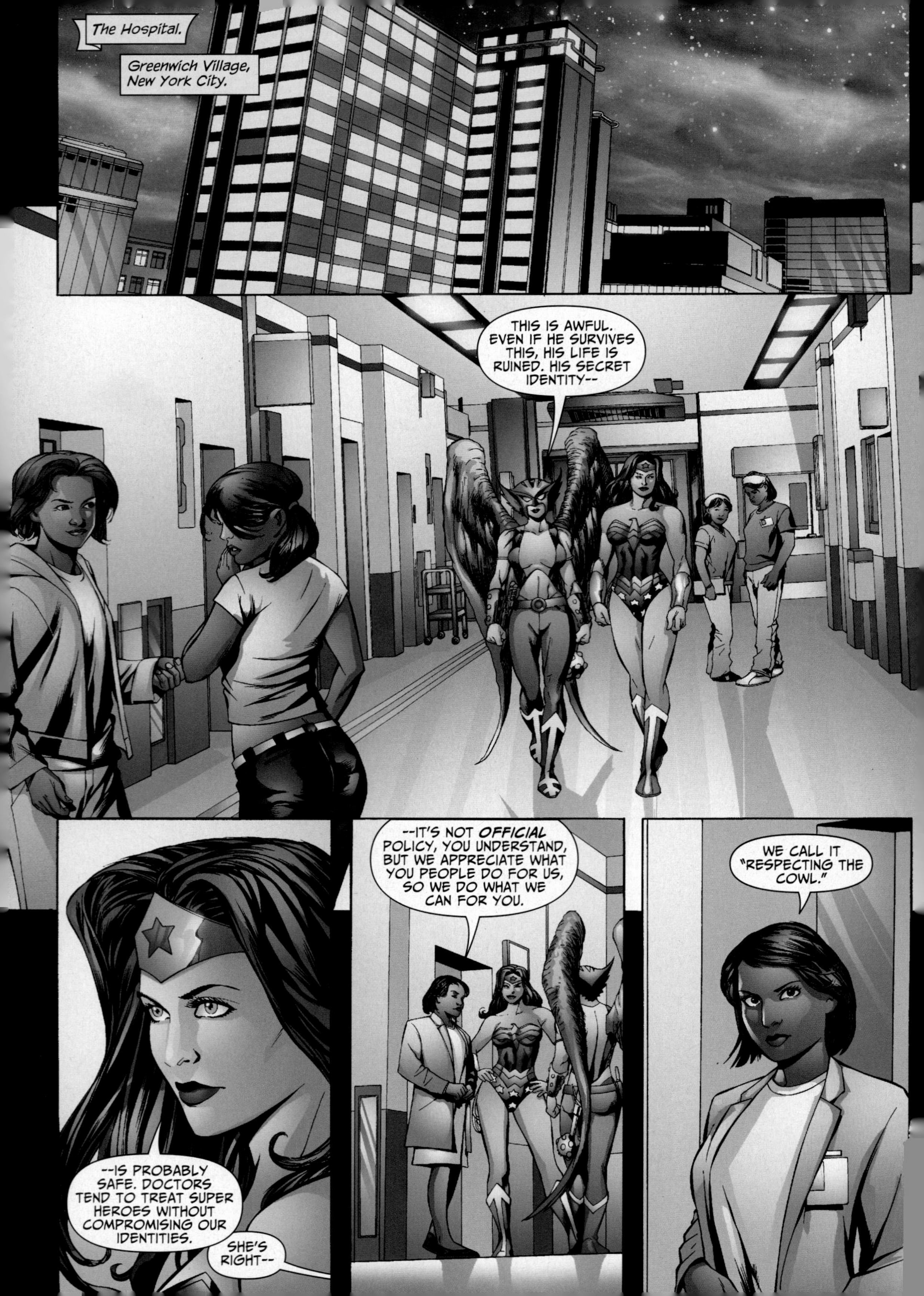
The Hospital.
Greenwich Village, New York City.
THIS IS AWFUL. EVEN IF HE SURVIVES THIS, HIS LIFE IS RUINED. HIS SECRET IDENTITY--
--IS PROBABLY SAFE. DOCTORS TEND TO TREAT SUPER HEROES WITHOUT COMPROMISING OUR IDENTITIES.
SHE'S RIGHT--
--IT'S NOT OFFICIAL POLICY, YOU UNDERSTAND, BUT WE APPRECIATE WHAT YOU PEOPLE DO FOR US, SO WE DO WHAT WE CAN FOR YOU.
WE CALL IT "RESPECTING THE COWL."

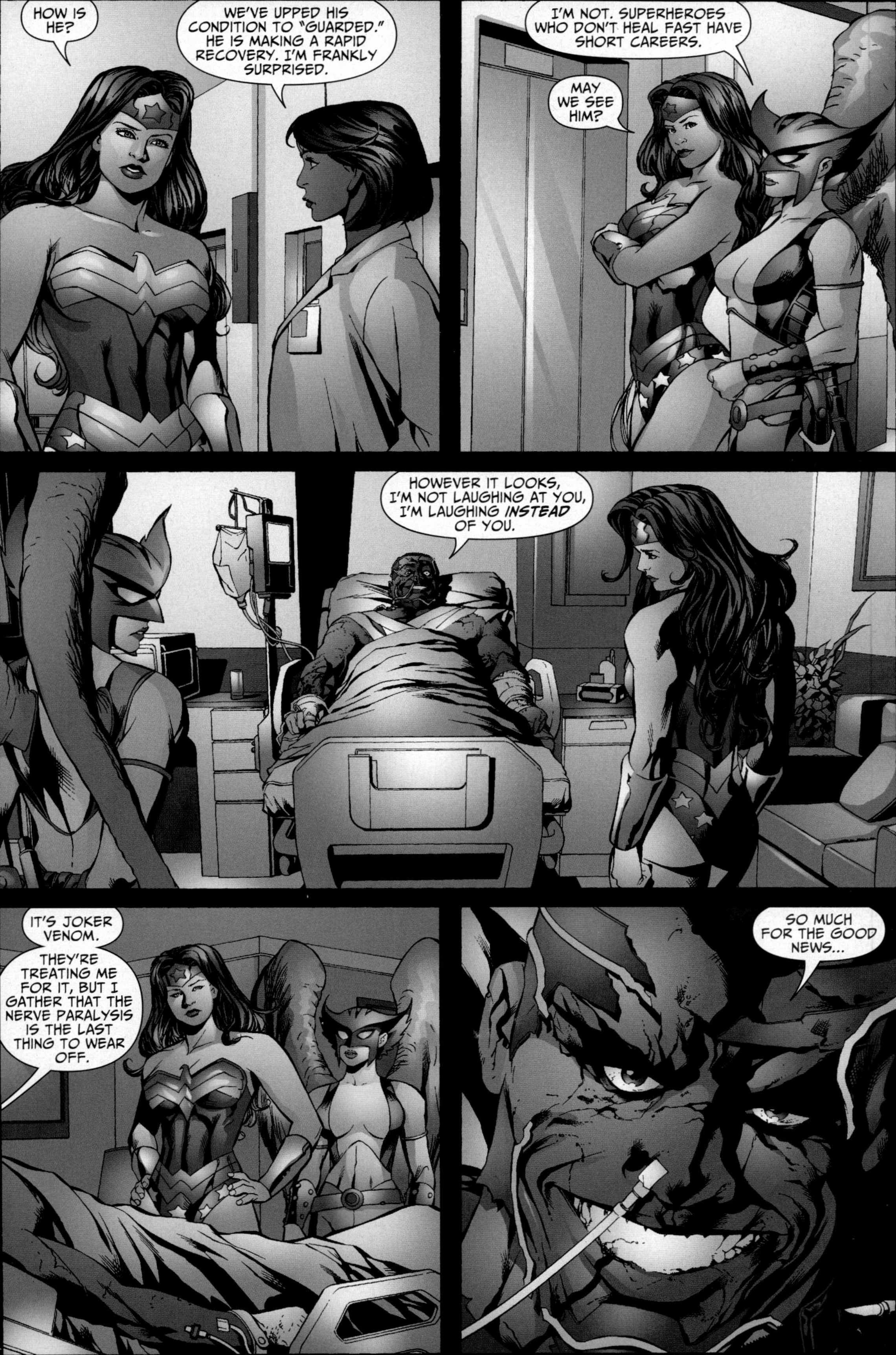
HOW IS HE?
WE'VE UPPED HIS CONDITION TO "GUARDED." HE IS MAKING A RAPID RECOVERY. I'M FRANKLY SURPRISED.
I'M NOT. SUPERHEROES WHO DON'T HEAL FAST HAVE SHORT CAREERS.
MAY WE SEE HIM?
HOWEVER IT LOOKS, I'M NOT LAUGHING AT YOU, I'M LAUGHING INSTEAD OF YOU.
IT'S JOKER VENOM.
THEY'RE TREATING ME FOR IT, BUT I GATHER THAT THE NERVE PARALYSIS IS THE LAST THING TO WEAR OFF.
SO MUCH FOR THE GOOD NEWS...

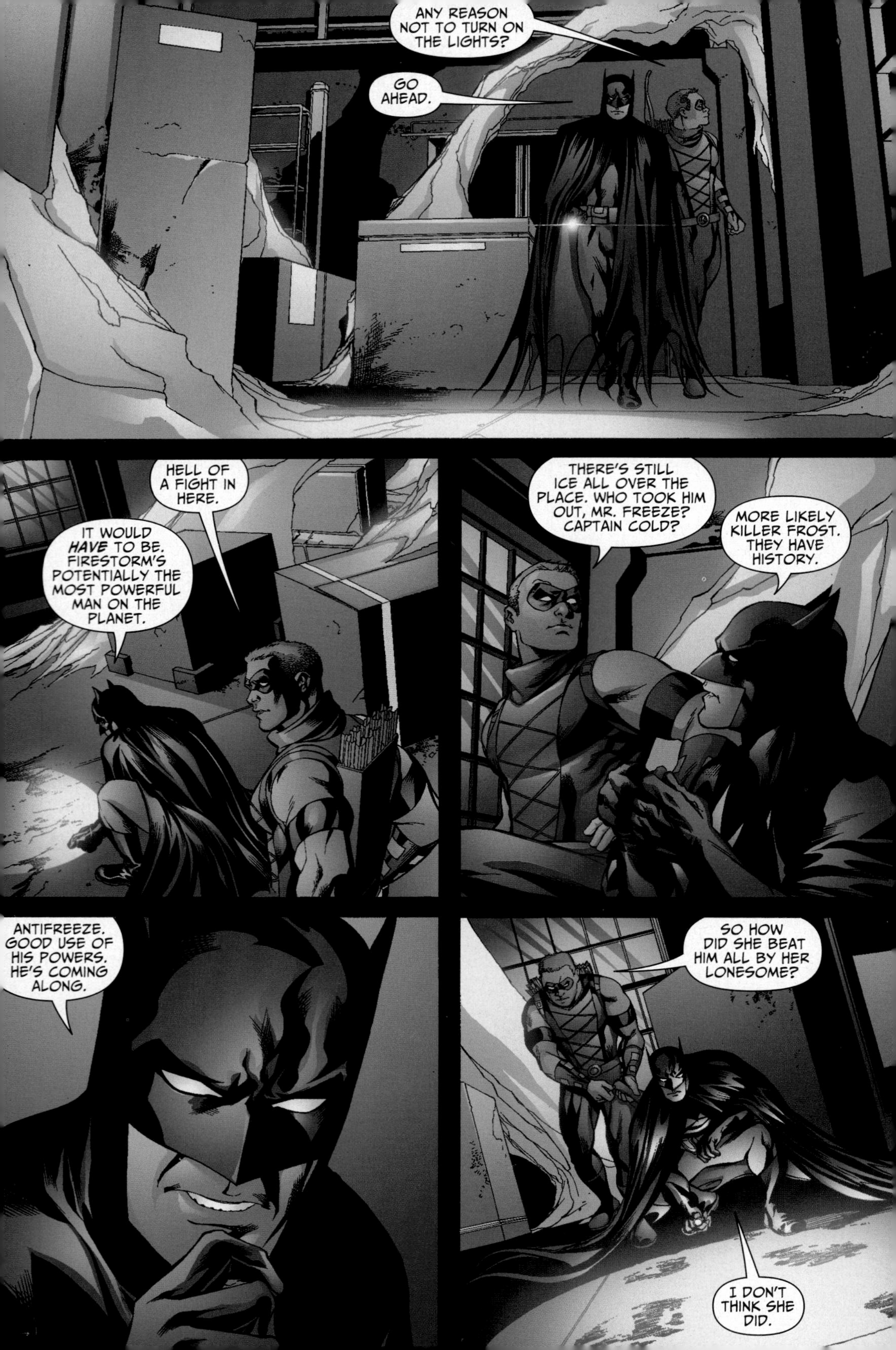
ANY REASON NOT TO TURN ON THE LIGHTS?
GO AHEAD.
HELL OF A FIGHT IN HERE.
IT WOULD *HAVE* TO BE. FIRESTORM'S POTENTIALLY THE MOST POWERFUL MAN ON THE PLANET.
THERE'S STILL ICE ALL OVER THE PLACE. WHO TOOK HIM OUT, MR. FREEZE? CAPTAIN COLD?
MORE LIKELY KILLER FROST. THEY HAVE HISTORY.
ANTIFREEZE. GOOD USE OF HIS POWERS. HE'S COMING ALONG.
SO HOW DID SHE BEAT HIM ALL BY HER LONESOME?
I DON'T THINK SHE DID.

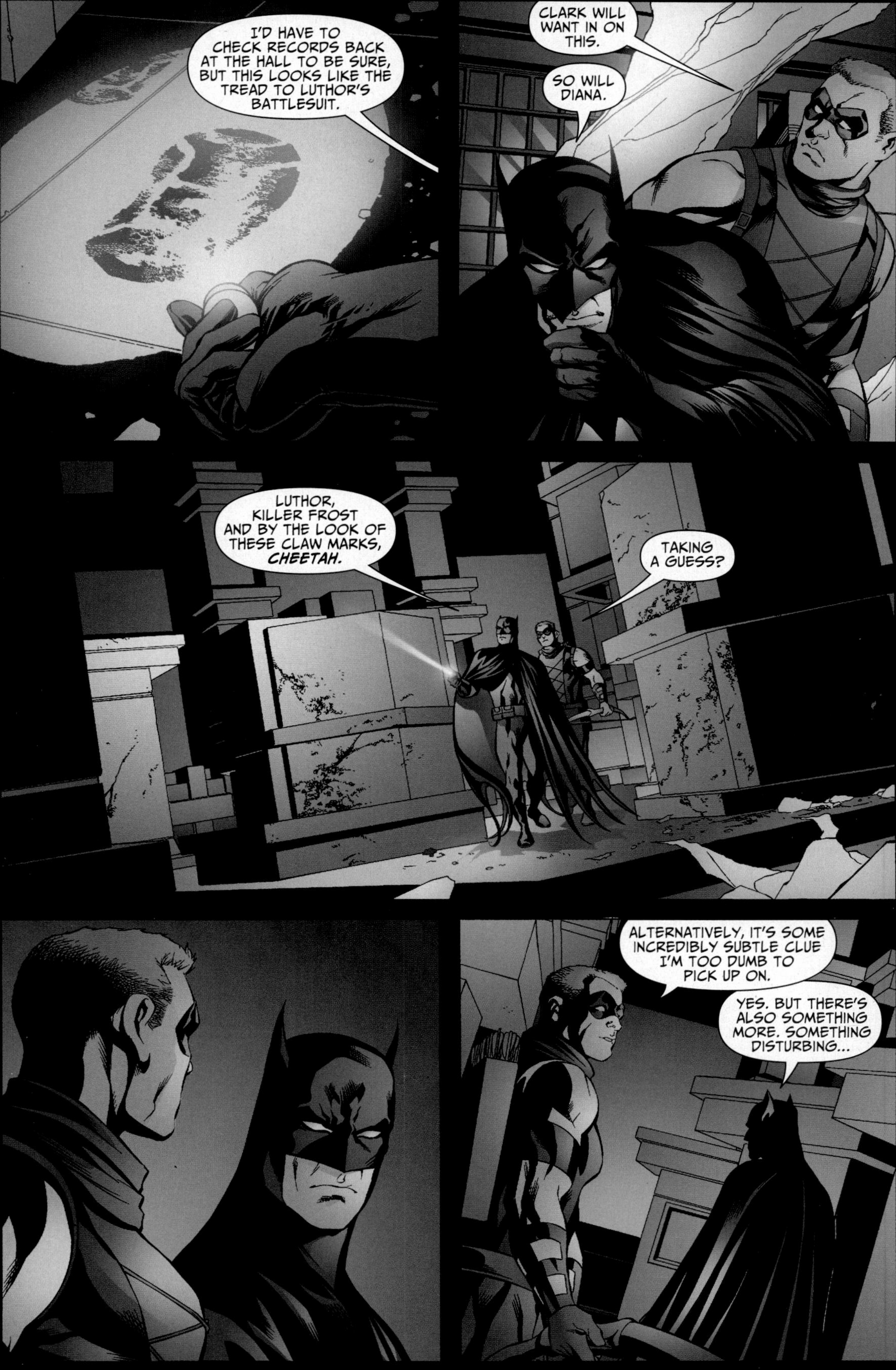
I'D HAVE TO CHECK RECORDS BACK AT THE HALL TO BE SURE, BUT THIS LOOKS LIKE THE TREAD TO LUTHOR'S BATTLESUIT.
CLARK WILL WANT IN ON THIS.
SO WILL DIANA.
LUTHOR, KILLER FROST AND BY THE LOOK OF THESE CLAW MARKS, CHEETAH.
TAKING A GUESS?
ALTERNATIVELY, IT'S SOME INCREDIBLY SUBTLE CLUE I'M TOO DUMB TO PICK UP ON.
YES. BUT THERE'S ALSO SOMETHING MORE. SOMETHING DISTURBING...

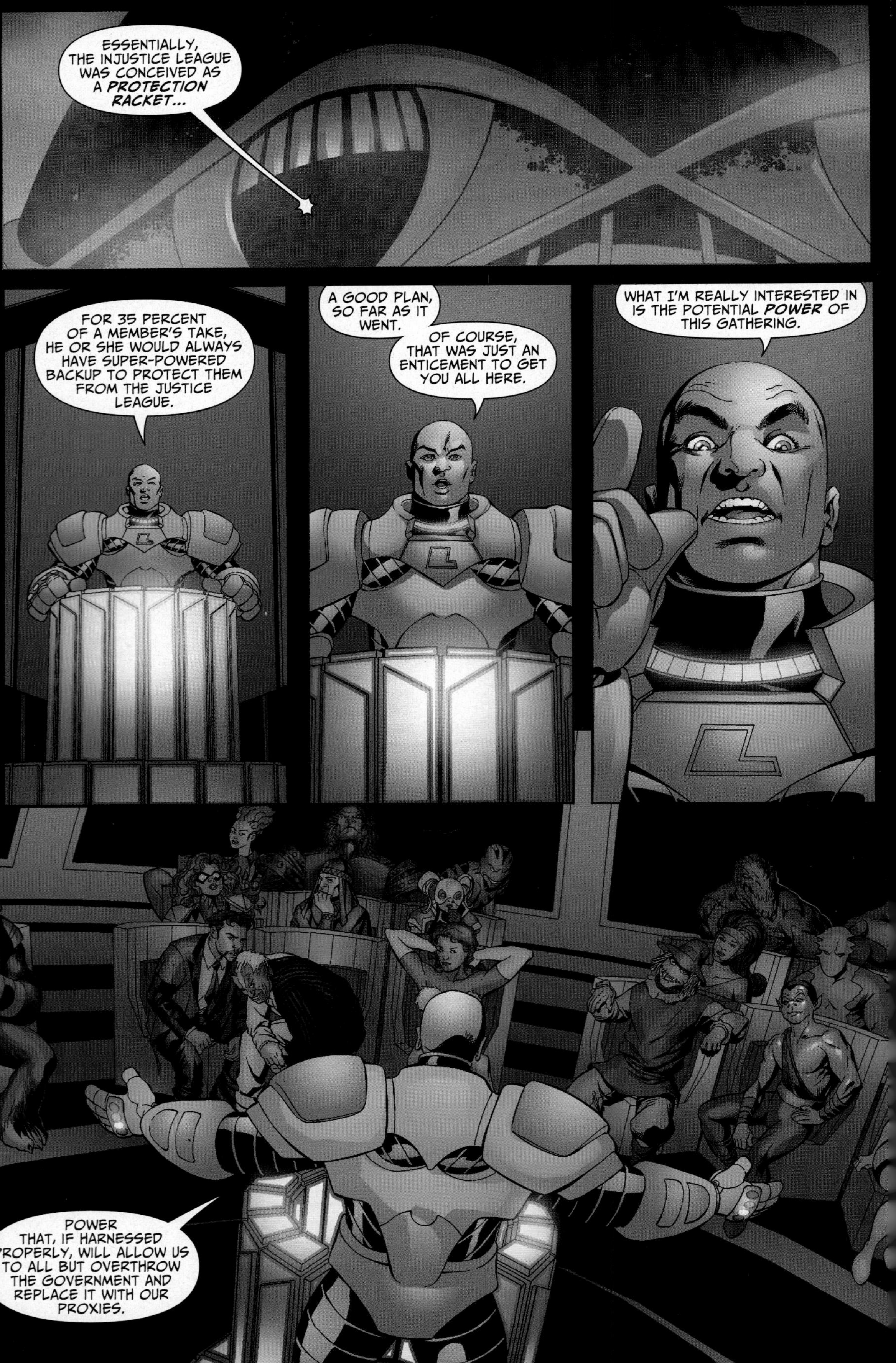
ESSENTIALLY, THE INJUSTICE LEAGUE WAS CONCEIVED AS A *PROTECTION RACKET...*
FOR 35 PERCENT OF A MEMBER'S TAKE, HE OR SHE WOULD ALWAYS HAVE SUPER-POWERED BACKUP TO PROTECT THEM FROM THE JUSTICE LEAGUE.
A GOOD PLAN, SO FAR AS IT WENT.
OF COURSE, THAT WAS JUST AN ENTICEMENT TO GET YOU ALL HERE.
WHAT I'M REALLY INTERESTED IN IS THE POTENTIAL *POWER* OF THIS GATHERING.
POWER THAT, IF HARNESSED PROPERLY, WILL ALLOW US TO ALL BUT OVERTHROW THE GOVERNMENT AND REPLACE IT WITH OUR PROXIES.

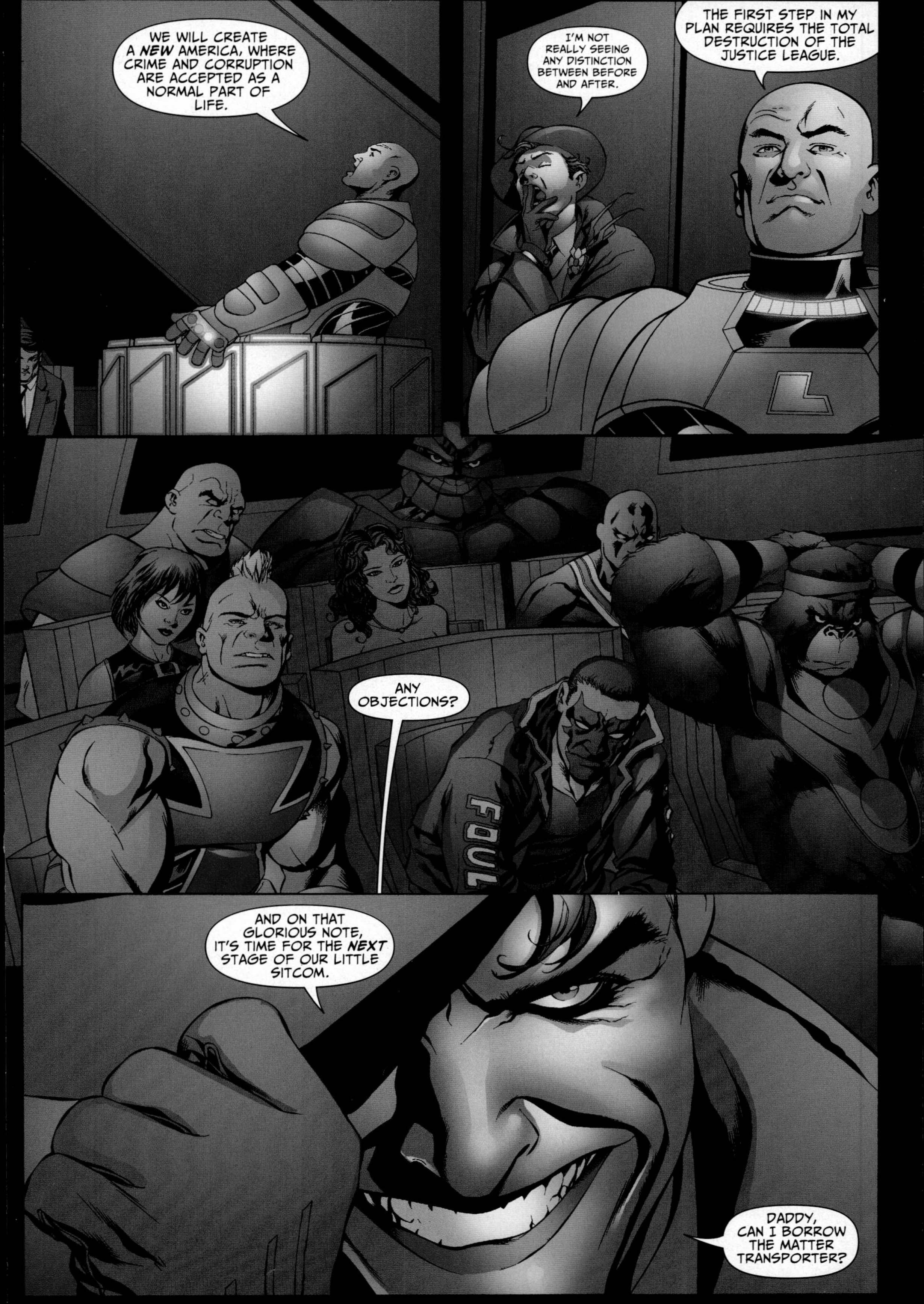
WE WILL CREATE A NEW AMERICA, WHERE CRIME AND CORRUPTION ARE ACCEPTED AS A NORMAL PART OF LIFE.
I'M NOT REALLY SEEING ANY DISTINCTION BETWEEN BEFORE AND AFTER.
THE FIRST STEP IN MY PLAN REQUIRES THE TOTAL DESTRUCTION OF THE JUSTICE LEAGUE.
ANY OBJECTIONS?
FOUL
AND ON THAT GLORIOUS NOTE, IT'S TIME FOR THE NEXT STAGE OF OUR LITTLE SITCOM.
DADDY, CAN I BORROW THE MATTER TRANSPORTER?

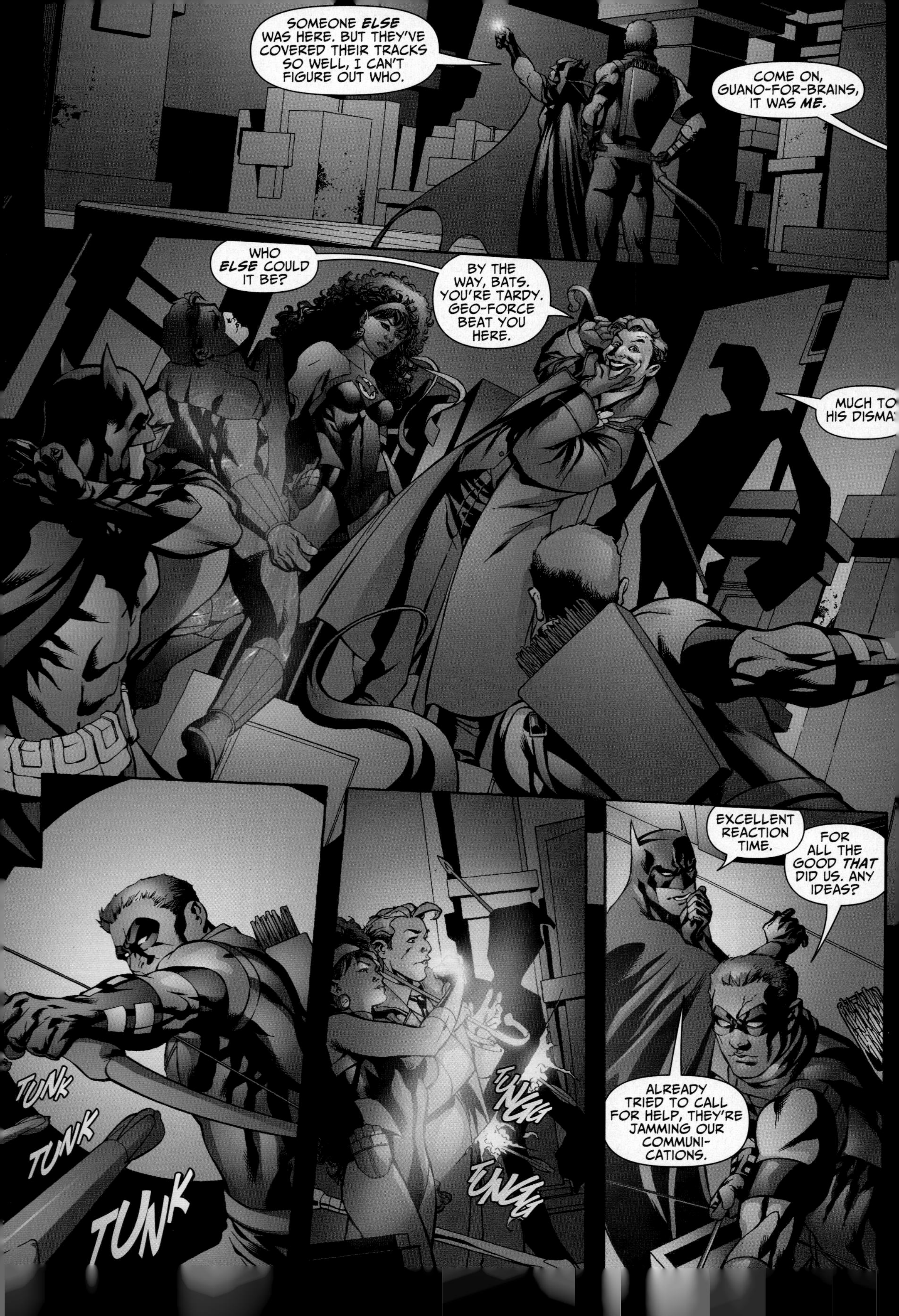
SOMEONE ELSE WAS HERE. BUT THEY'VE COVERED THEIR TRACKS SO WELL, I CAN'T FIGURE OUT WHO.
COME ON, GUANO-FOR-BRAINS, IT WAS ME.
WHO ELSE COULD IT BE?
BY THE WAY, BATS. YOU'RE TARDY. GEO-FORCE BEAT YOU HERE.
MUCH TO HIS DISMA
TUNK
TUNK
TUNK
TUNGG
TUNGG
EXCELLENT REACTION TIME.
FOR ALL THE GOOD THAT DID US. ANY IDEAS?
ALREADY TRIED TO CALL FOR HELP, THEY'RE JAMMING OUR COMMUNI-CATIONS.

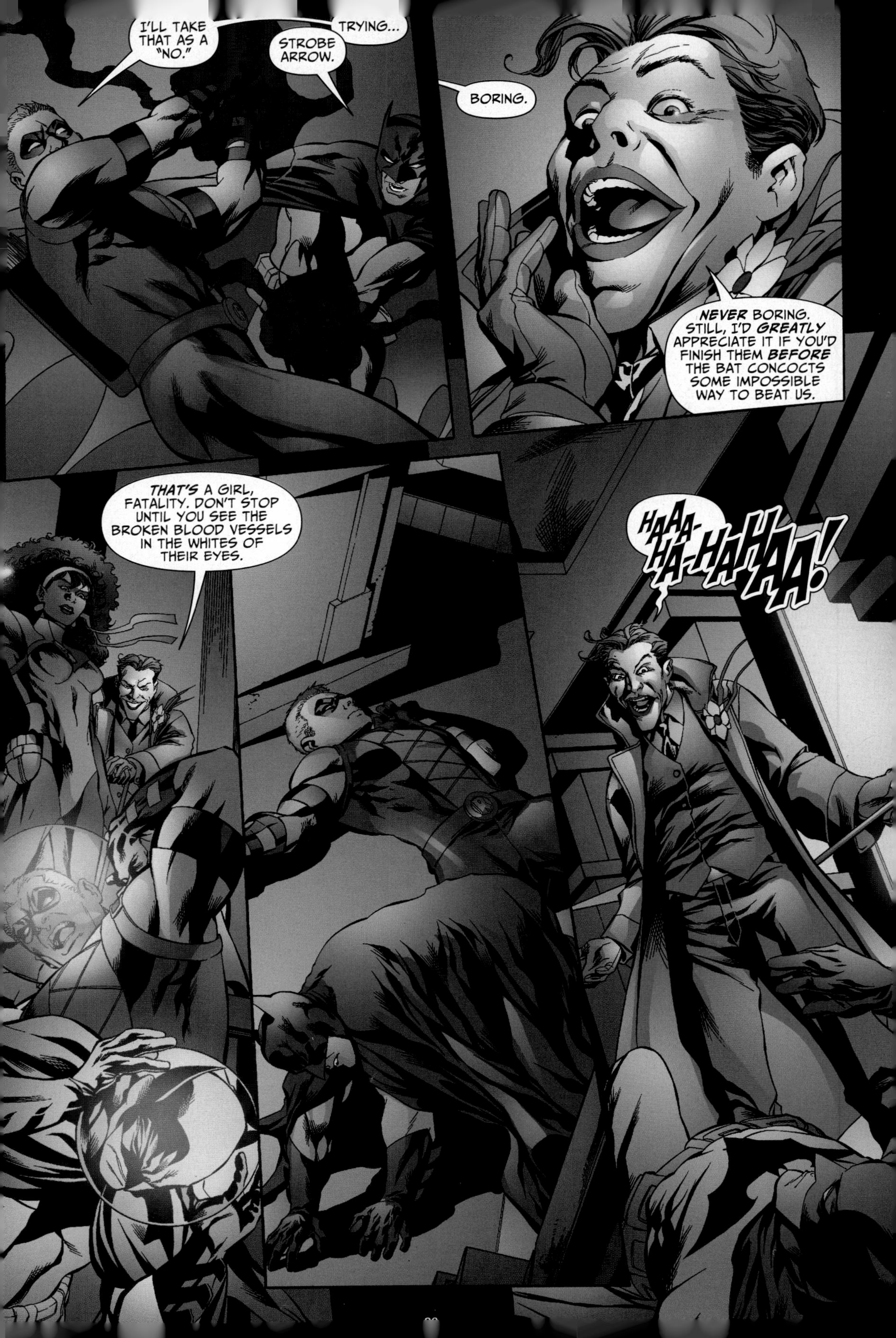
I'LL TAKE THAT AS A "NO."
TRYING...
STROBE ARROW.
BORING.
NEVER BORING. STILL, I'D *GREATLY* APPRECIATE IT IF YOU'D FINISH THEM *BEFORE* THE BAT CONCOCTS SOME IMPOSSIBLE WAY TO BEAT US.
THAT'S A GIRL, FATALITY. DON'T STOP UNTIL YOU SEE THE BROKEN BLOOD VESSELS IN THE WHITES OF THEIR EYES.
HAAAA-HA-HAHAAA!

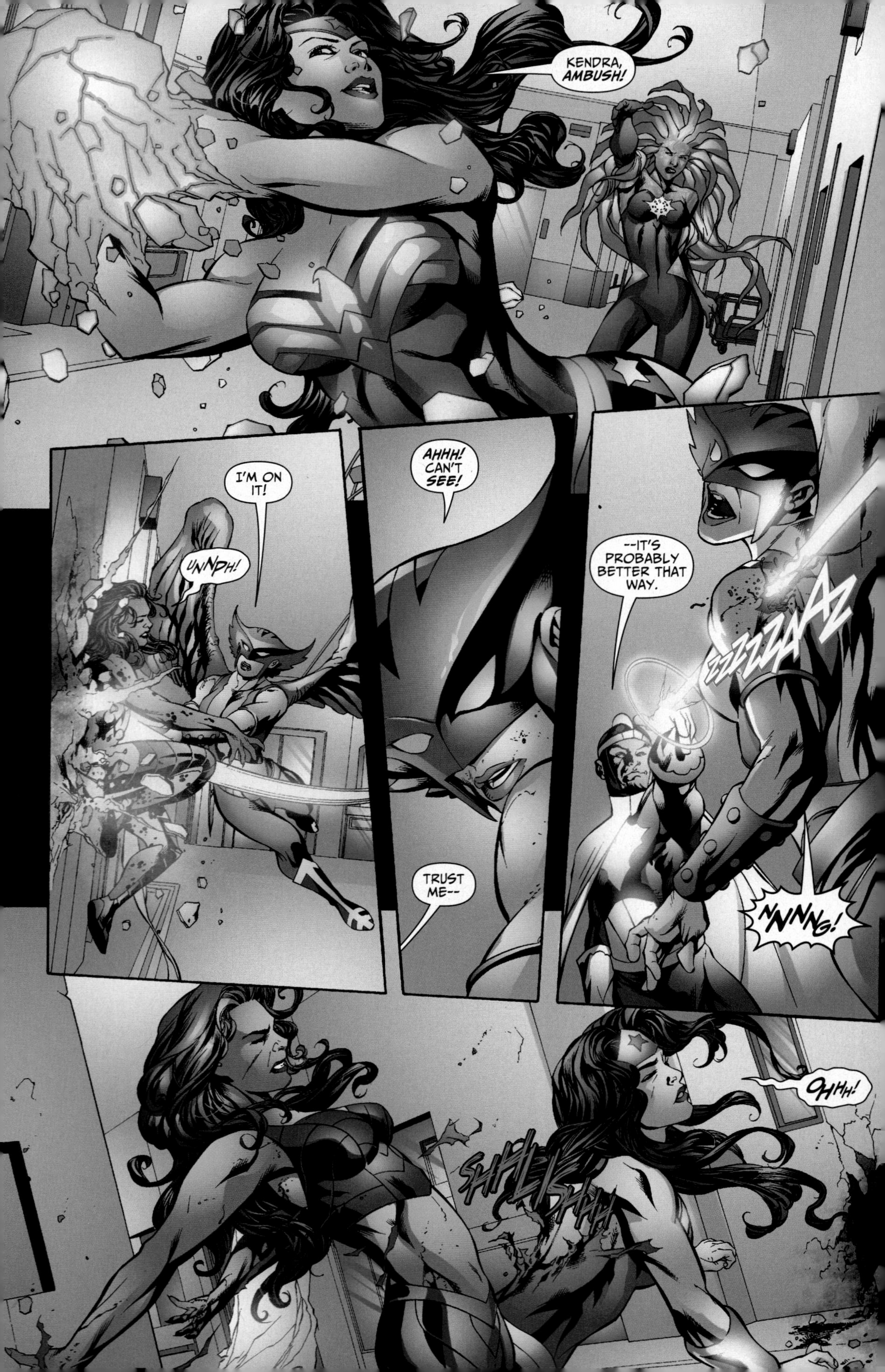
KENDRA, AMBUSH!
I'M ON IT!
UNNPH!
AHHH! CAN'T SEE!
TRUST ME--
--IT'S PROBABLY BETTER THAT WAY.
ZZZZZZAAAZ
NNNNG!
OHHH!
SHHLISHHH

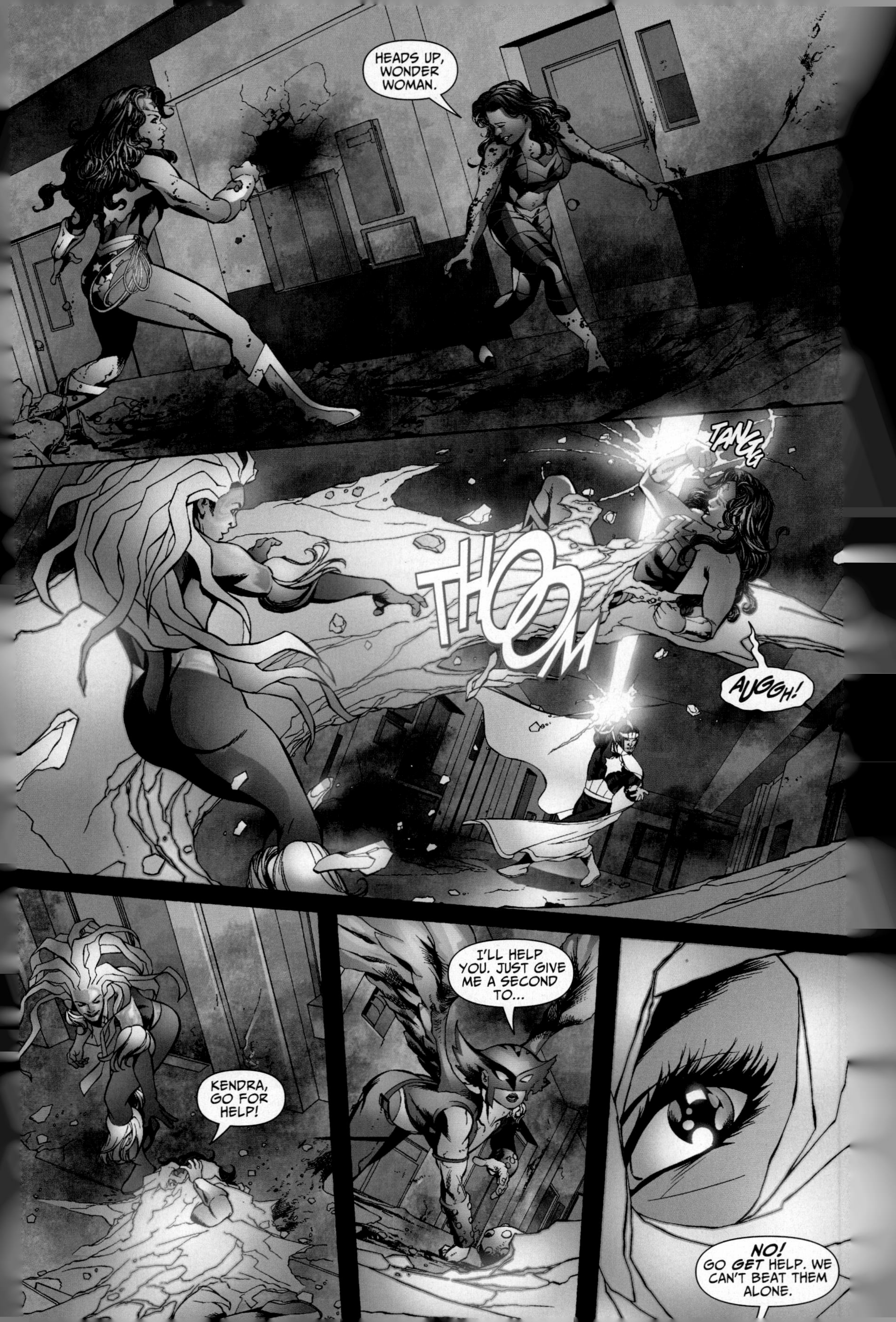
HEADS UP, WONDER WOMAN.
TANGG
THOOM
AUGGH!
KENDRA, GO FOR HELP!
I'LL HELP YOU. JUST GIVE ME A SECOND TO...
NO! GO GET HELP. WE CAN'T BEAT THEM ALONE.

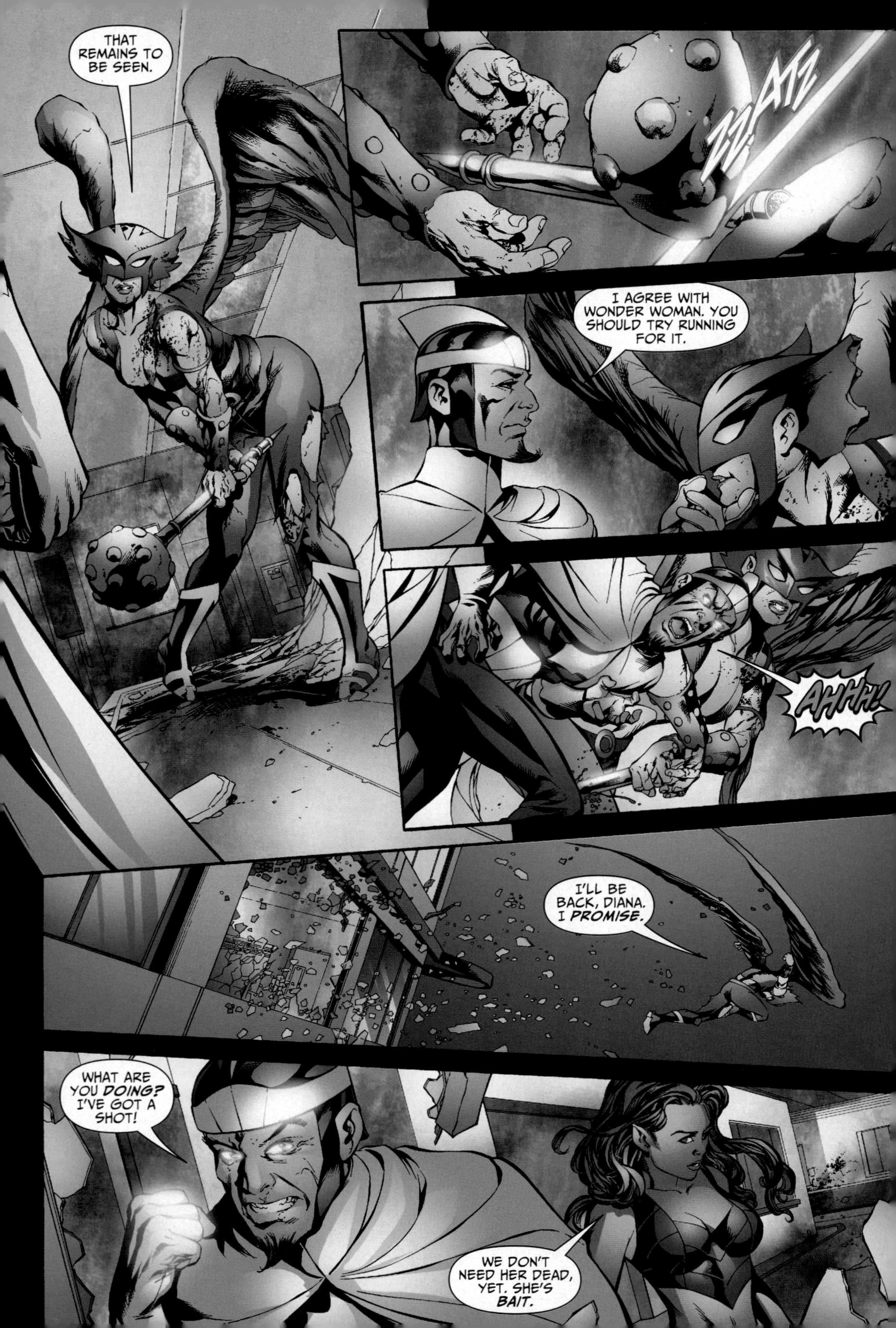
THAT REMAINS TO BE SEEN.
ZZAAZZ
I AGREE WITH WONDER WOMAN. YOU SHOULD TRY RUNNING FOR IT.
AHHH!
I'LL BE BACK, DIANA. I PROMISE.
WHAT ARE YOU DOING? I'VE GOT A SHOT!
WE DON'T NEED HER DEAD, YET. SHE'S BAIT.

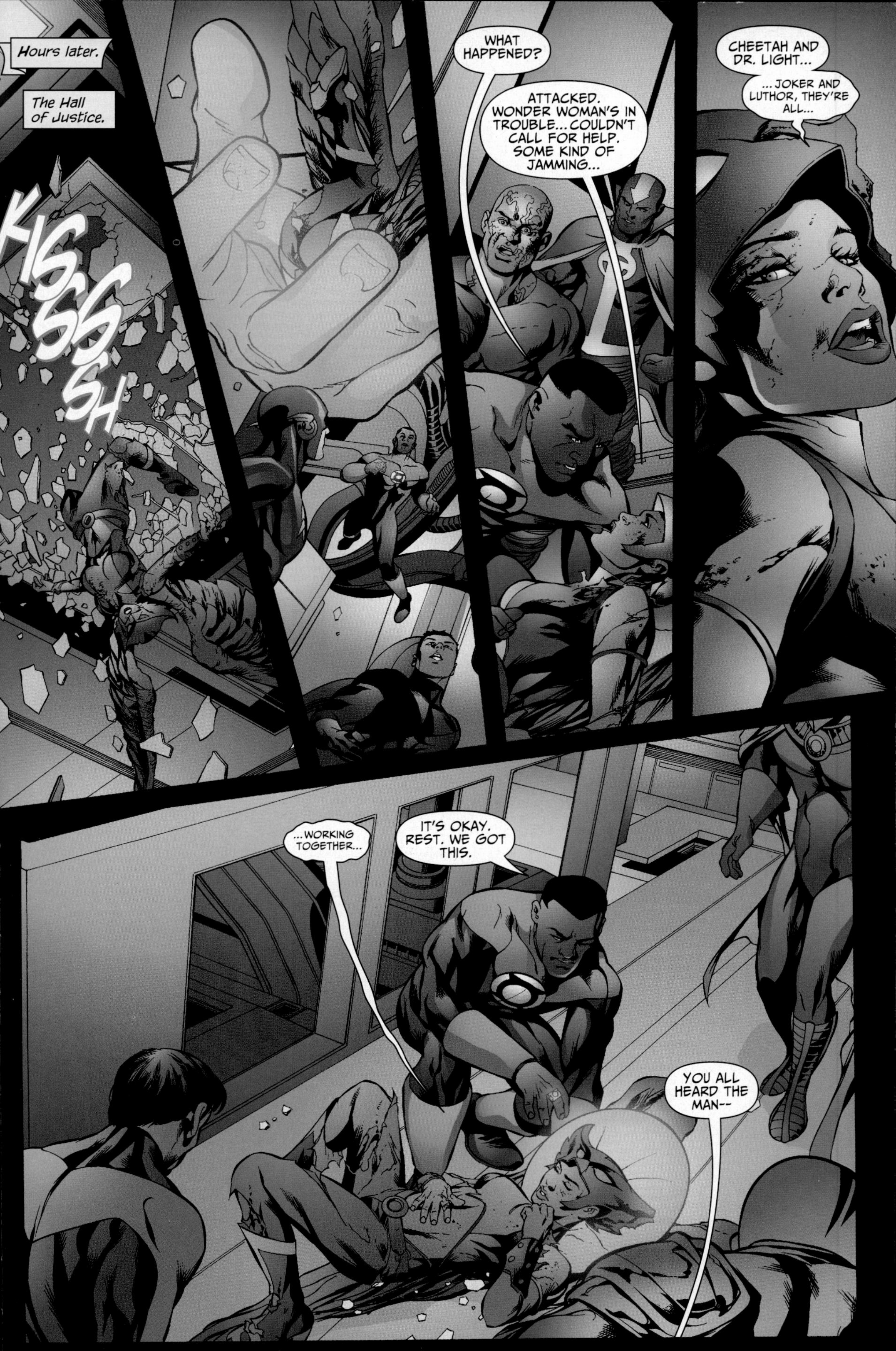
Hours later.
The Hall of Justice.
KISSSSSH
WHAT HAPPENED?
ATTACKED. WONDER WOMAN'S IN TROUBLE...COULDN'T CALL FOR HELP. SOME KIND OF JAMMING...
CHEETAH AND DR. LIGHT...
...JOKER AND LUTHOR, THEY'RE ALL...
...WORKING TOGETHER...
IT'S OKAY. REST. WE GOT THIS.
YOU ALL HEARD THE MAN--

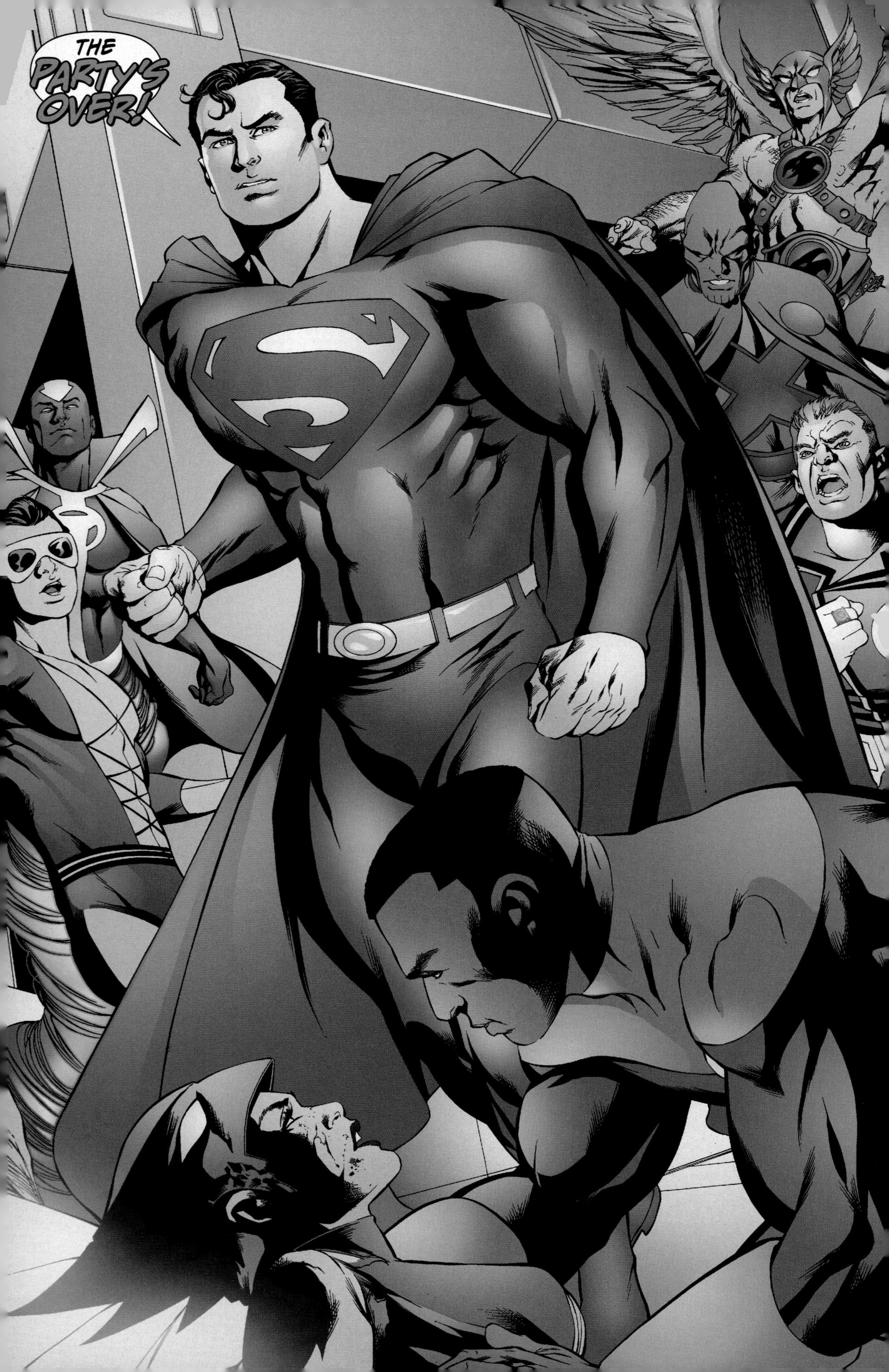
THE PARTY'S OVER!

JUSTICE LEAGUE of AMERICA

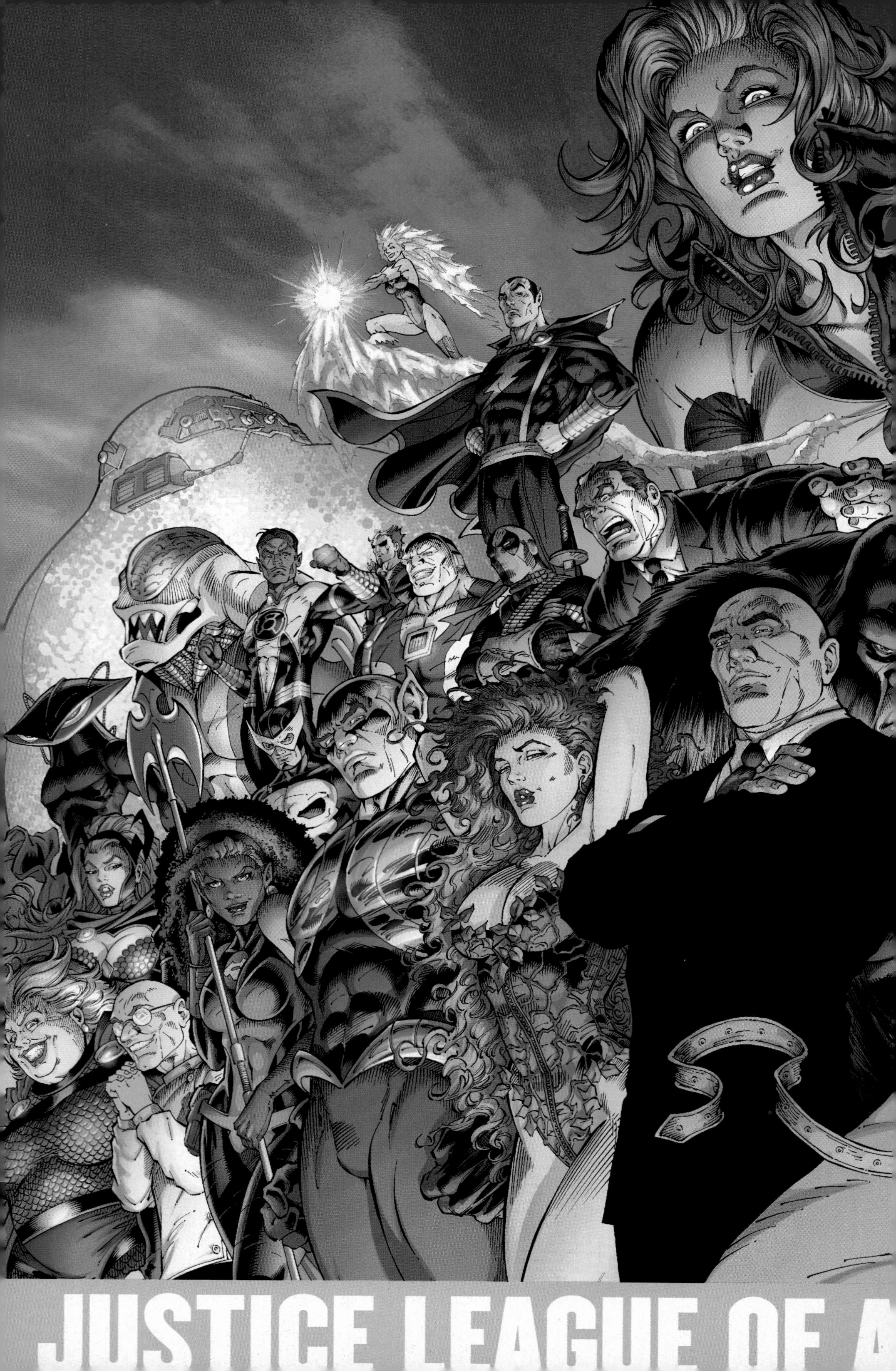
JUSTICE LEAGUE OF

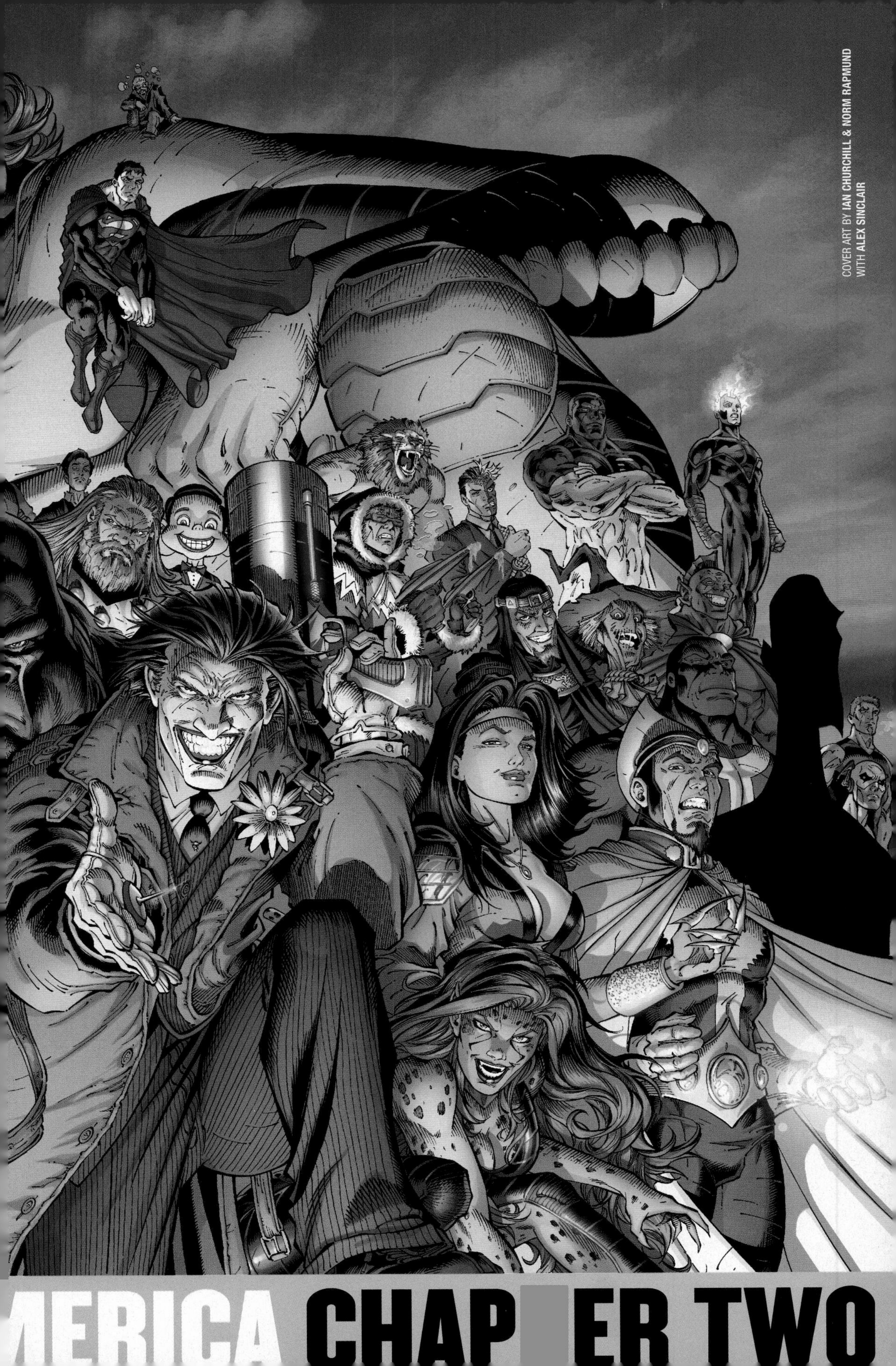
COVER ART BY IAN CHURCHILL & NORM RAPMUND
WITH ALEX SINCLAIR
ERICA CHAP ER TWO

"I don't know how to thank you. I—"

"Start by being honest with your teammates."

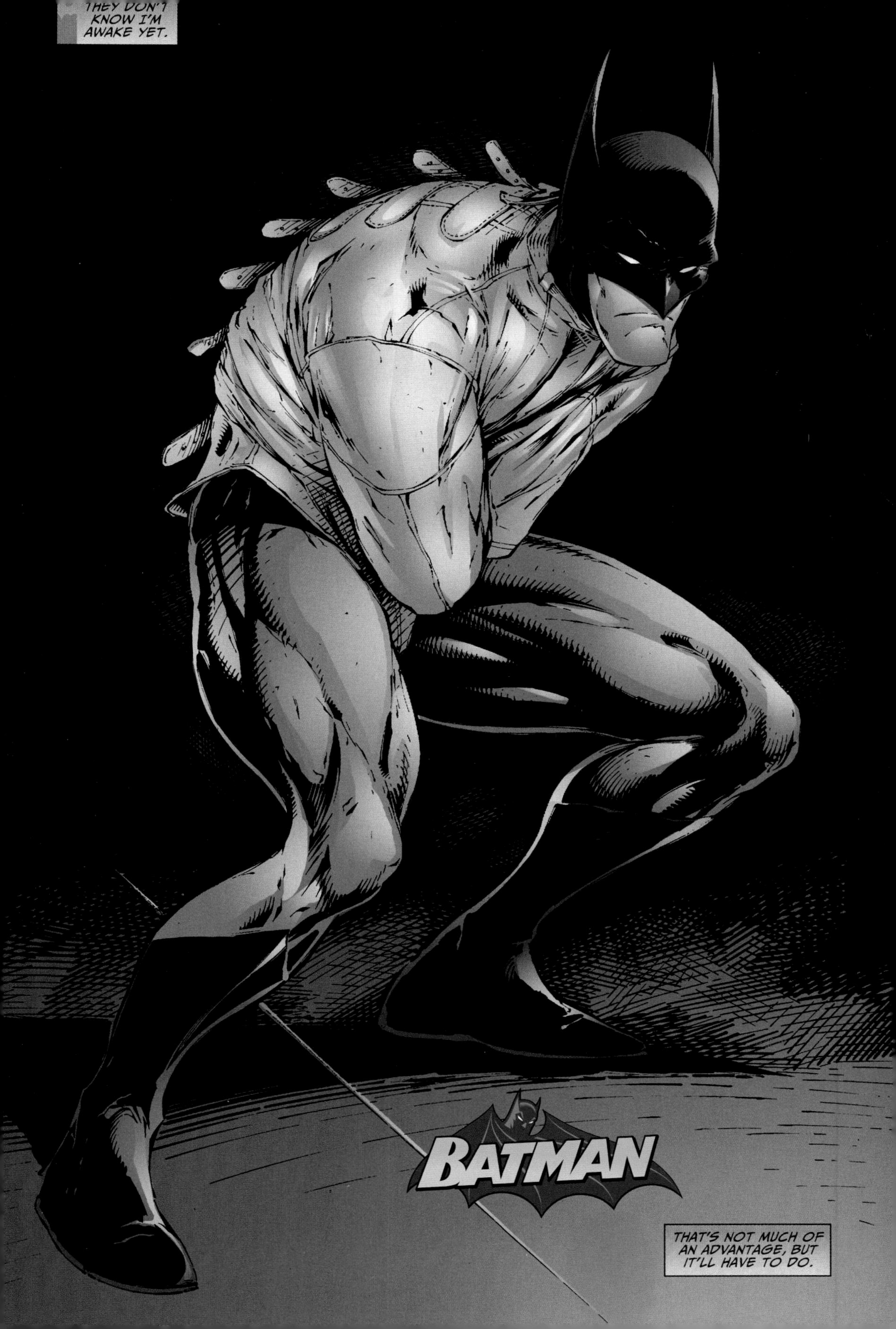

THEY DON'T KNOW I'M AWAKE YET.
BATMAN
THAT'S NOT MUCH OF AN ADVANTAGE, BUT IT'LL HAVE TO DO.

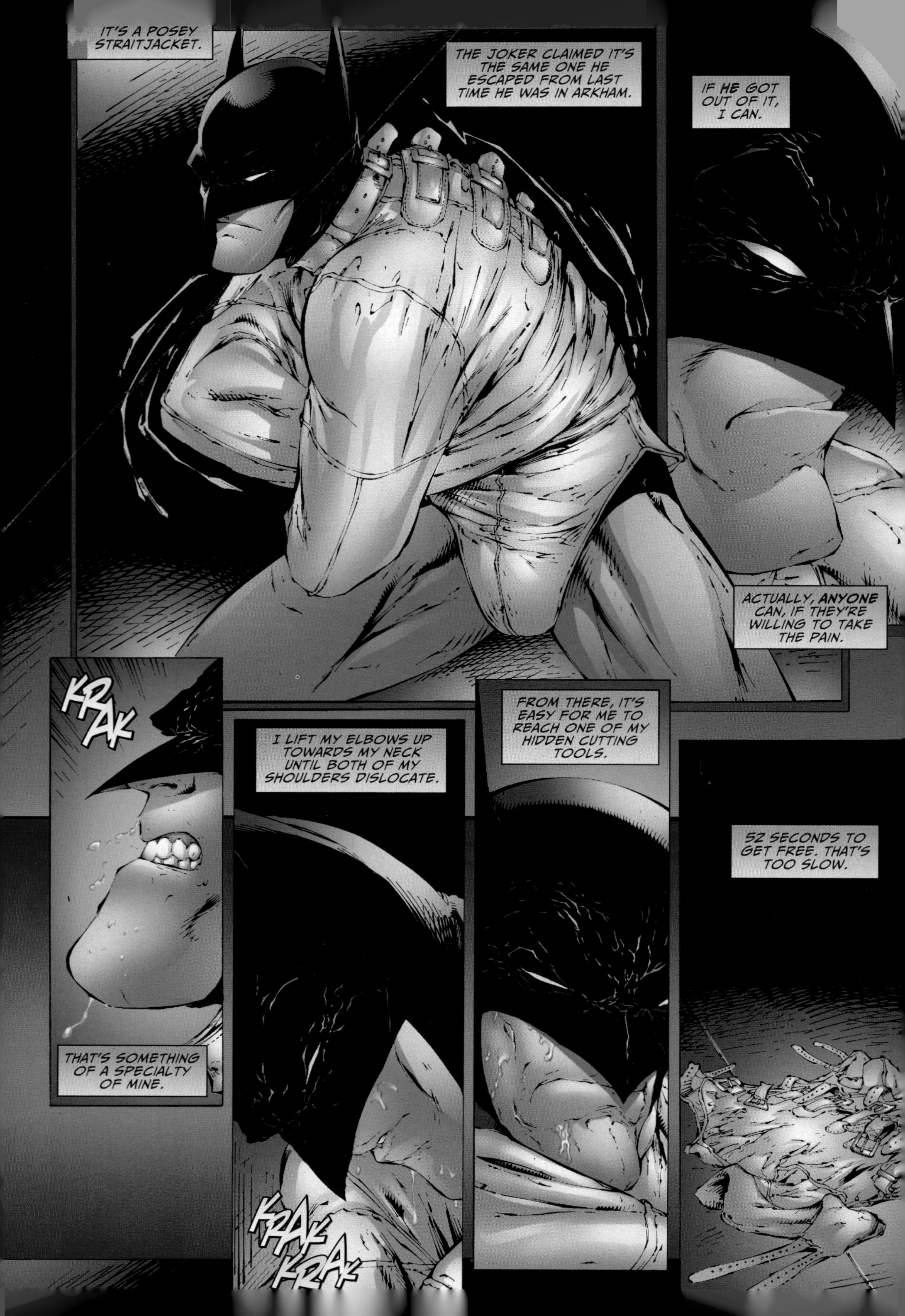

IT'S A POSEY STRAITJACKET.
THE JOKER CLAIMED IT'S THE SAME ONE HE ESCAPED FROM LAST TIME HE WAS IN ARKHAM.
IF HE GOT OUT OF IT, I CAN.
ACTUALLY, ANYONE CAN, IF THEY'RE WILLING TO TAKE THE PAIN.
KRAK
THAT'S SOMETHING OF A SPECIALTY OF MINE.
I LIFT MY ELBOWS UP TOWARDS MY NECK UNTIL BOTH OF MY SHOULDERS DISLOCATE.
KRAK KRAK
FROM THERE, IT'S EASY FOR ME TO REACH ONE OF MY HIDDEN CUTTING TOOLS.
52 SECONDS TO GET FREE. THAT'S TOO SLOW.

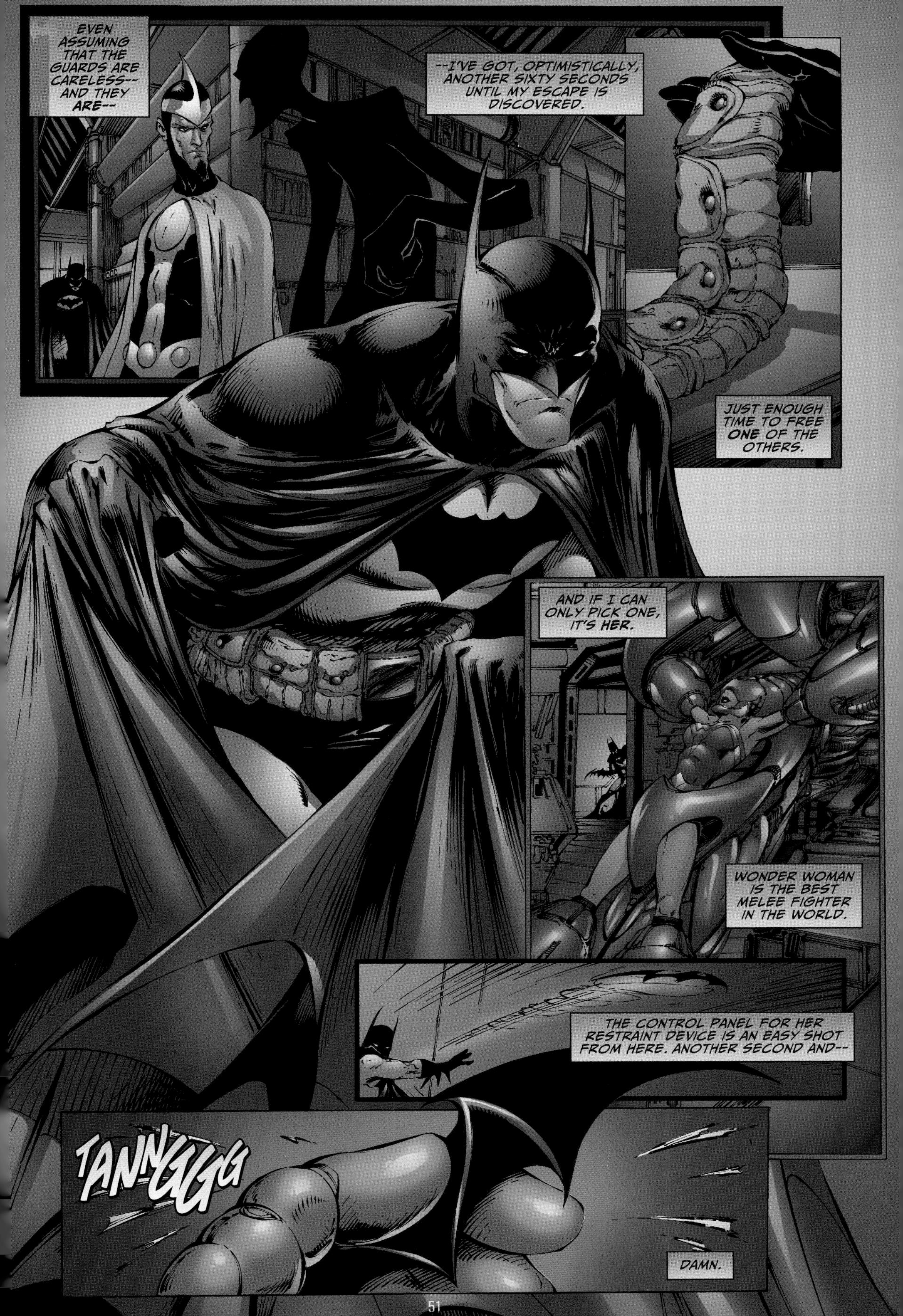
EVEN ASSUMING THAT THE GUARDS ARE CARELESS-- AND THEY ARE--
--I'VE GOT, OPTIMISTICALLY, ANOTHER SIXTY SECONDS UNTIL MY ESCAPE IS DISCOVERED.
JUST ENOUGH TIME TO FREE ONE OF THE OTHERS.
AND IF I CAN ONLY PICK ONE, IT'S HER.
WONDER WOMAN IS THE BEST MELEE FIGHTER IN THE WORLD.
THE CONTROL PANEL FOR HER RESTRAINT DEVICE IS AN EASY SHOT FROM HERE. ANOTHER SECOND AND--
TANNGGG
DAMN.

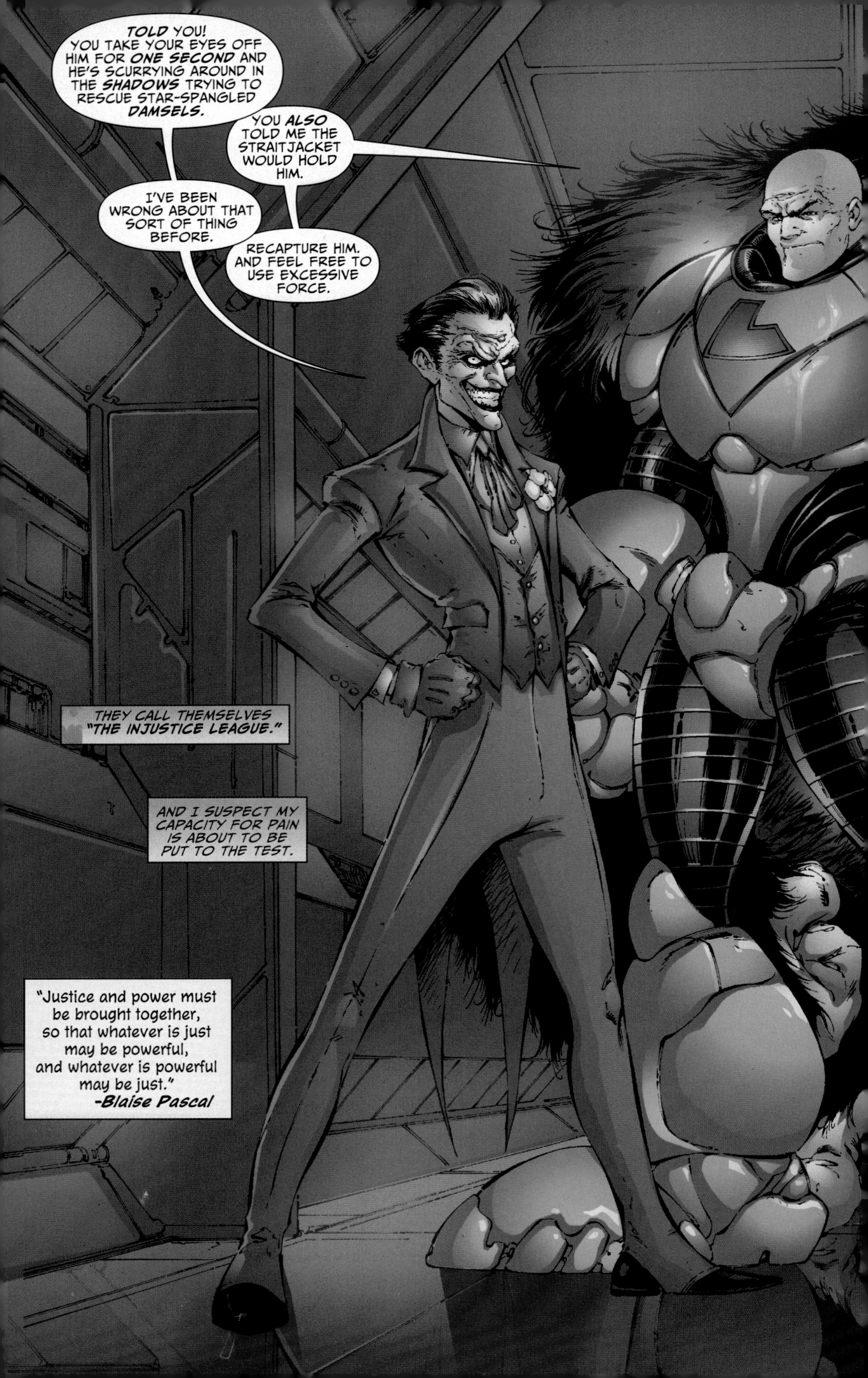

TOLD YOU! YOU TAKE YOUR EYES OFF HIM FOR ONE SECOND AND HE'S SCURRYING AROUND IN THE SHADOWS TRYING TO RESCUE STAR-SPANGLED DAMSELS.
YOU ALSO TOLD ME THE STRAITJACKET WOULD HOLD HIM.
I'VE BEEN WRONG ABOUT THAT SORT OF THING BEFORE.
RECAPTURE HIM. AND FEEL FREE TO USE EXCESSIVE FORCE.
THEY CALL THEMSELVES "THE INJUSTICE LEAGUE."
AND I SUSPECT MY CAPACITY FOR PAIN IS ABOUT TO BE PUT TO THE TEST.
"Justice and power must be brought together, so that whatever is just may be powerful, and whatever is powerful may be just." -Blaise Pascal

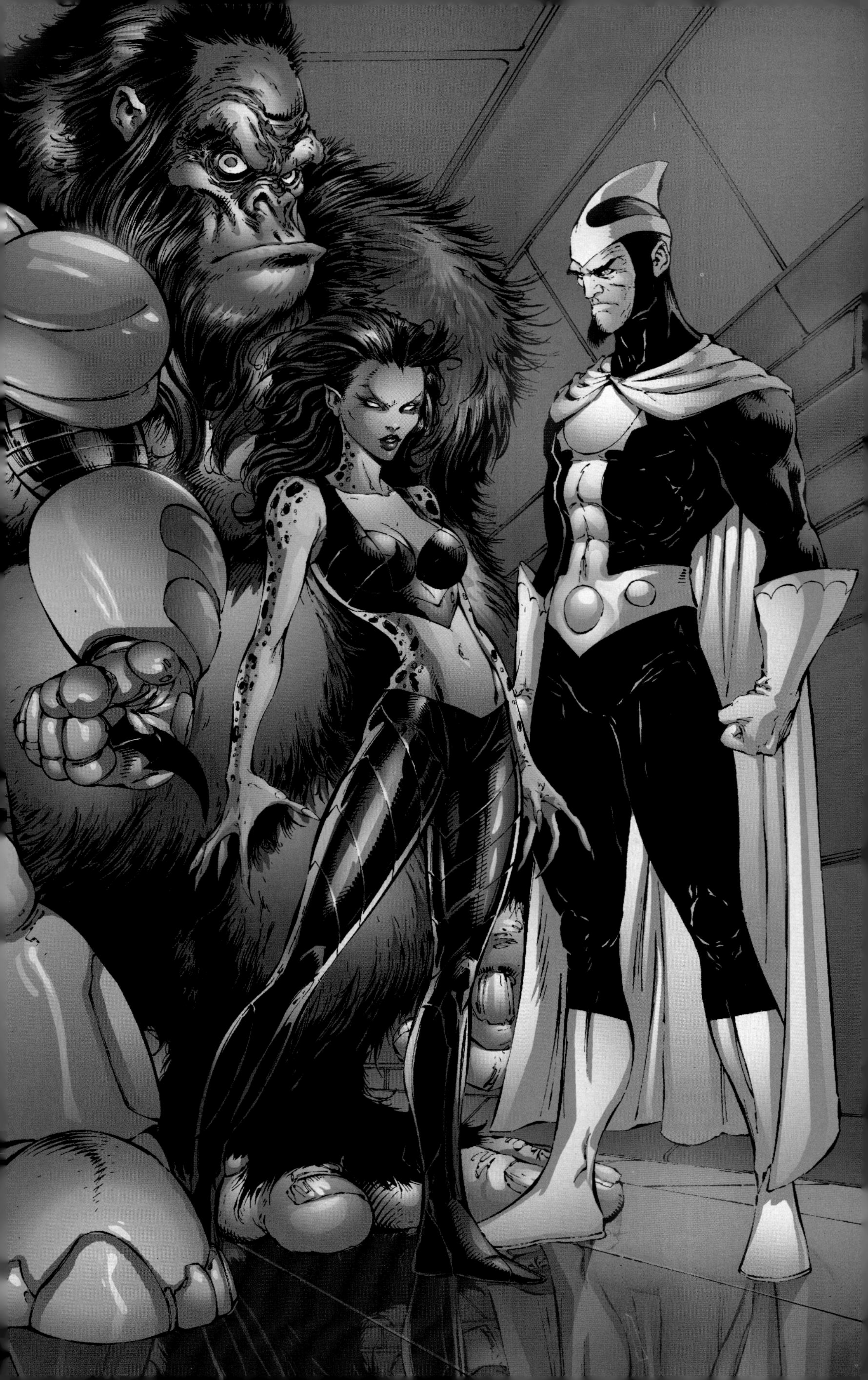

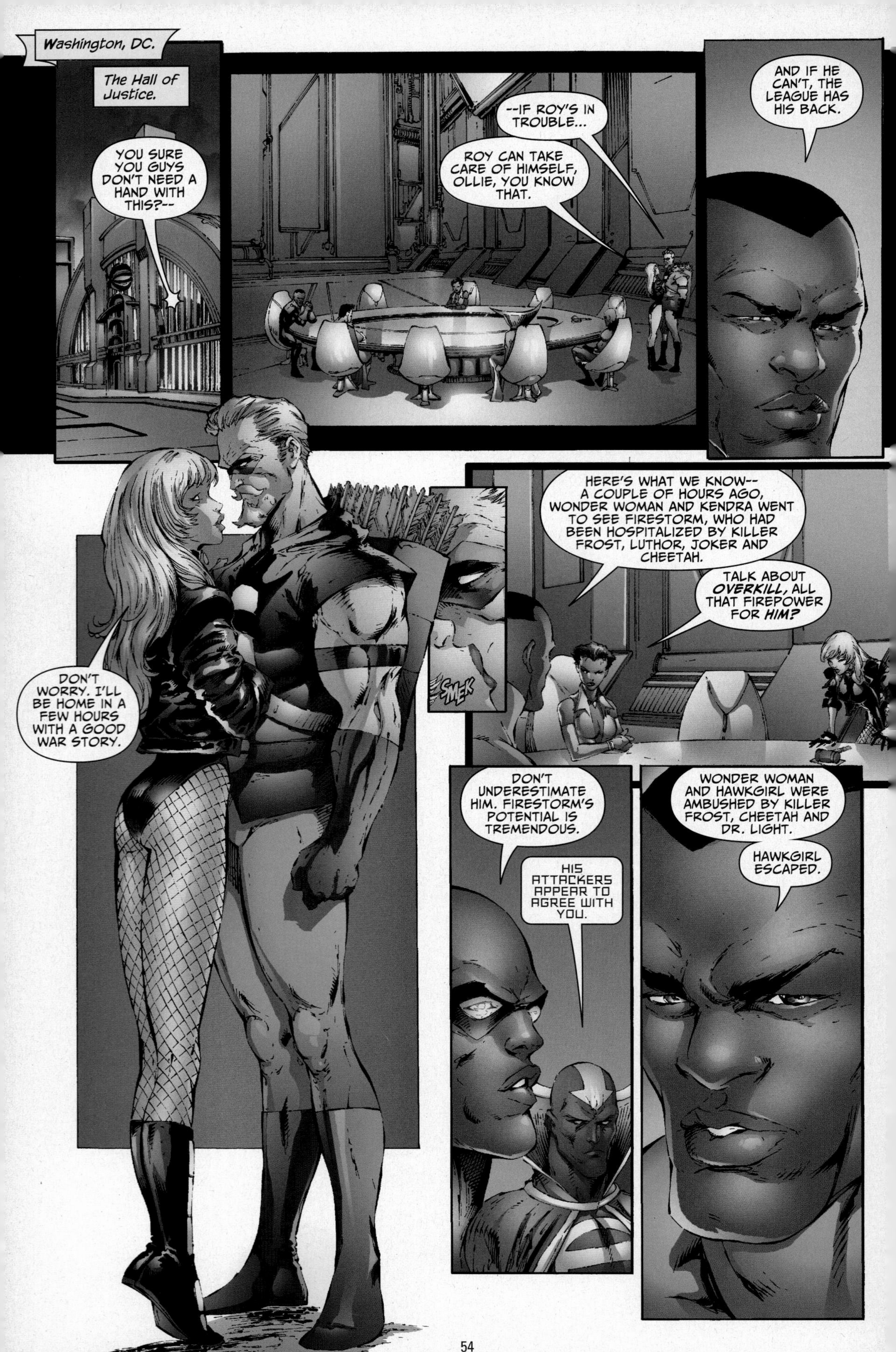

Washington, DC.
The Hall of Justice.
YOU SURE YOU GUYS DON'T NEED A HAND WITH THIS?--
--IF ROY'S IN TROUBLE...
ROY CAN TAKE CARE OF HIMSELF, OLLIE, YOU KNOW THAT.
AND IF HE CAN'T, THE LEAGUE HAS HIS BACK.
DON'T WORRY. I'LL BE HOME IN A FEW HOURS WITH A GOOD WAR STORY.
SMEK
HERE'S WHAT WE KNOW-- A COUPLE OF HOURS AGO, WONDER WOMAN AND KENDRA WENT TO SEE FIRESTORM, WHO HAD BEEN HOSPITALIZED BY KILLER FROST, LUTHOR, JOKER AND CHEETAH.
TALK ABOUT *OVERKILL*, ALL THAT FIREPOWER FOR *HIM?*
DON'T UNDERESTIMATE HIM. FIRESTORM'S POTENTIAL IS TREMENDOUS.
HIS ATTACKERS APPEAR TO AGREE WITH YOU.
WONDER WOMAN AND HAWKGIRL WERE AMBUSHED BY KILLER FROST, CHEETAH AND DR. LIGHT.
HAWKGIRL ESCAPED.

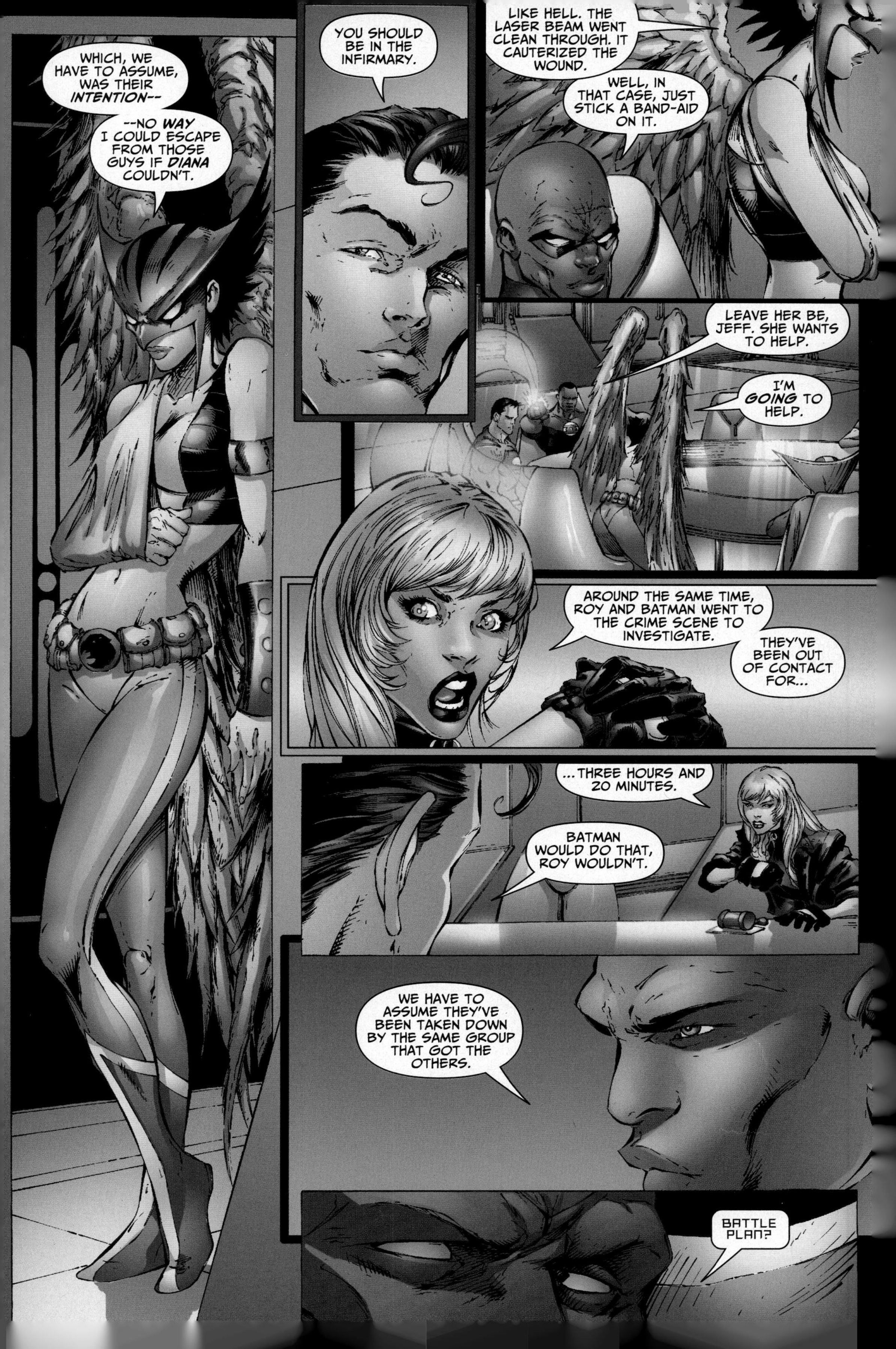
WHICH, WE HAVE TO ASSUME, WAS THEIR *INTENTION*--
--NO *WAY* I COULD ESCAPE FROM THOSE GUYS IF *DIANA* COULDN'T.
YOU SHOULD BE IN THE INFIRMARY.
LIKE HELL. THE LASER BEAM WENT CLEAN THROUGH. IT CAUTERIZED THE WOUND.
WELL, IN THAT CASE, JUST STICK A BAND-AID ON IT.
LEAVE HER BE, JEFF. SHE WANTS TO HELP.
I'M *GOING* TO HELP.
AROUND THE SAME TIME, ROY AND BATMAN WENT TO THE CRIME SCENE TO INVESTIGATE.
THEY'VE BEEN OUT OF CONTACT FOR...
...THREE HOURS AND 20 MINUTES.
BATMAN WOULD DO THAT, ROY WOULDN'T.
WE HAVE TO ASSUME THEY'VE BEEN TAKEN DOWN BY THE SAME GROUP THAT GOT THE OTHERS.
BATTLE PLAN?

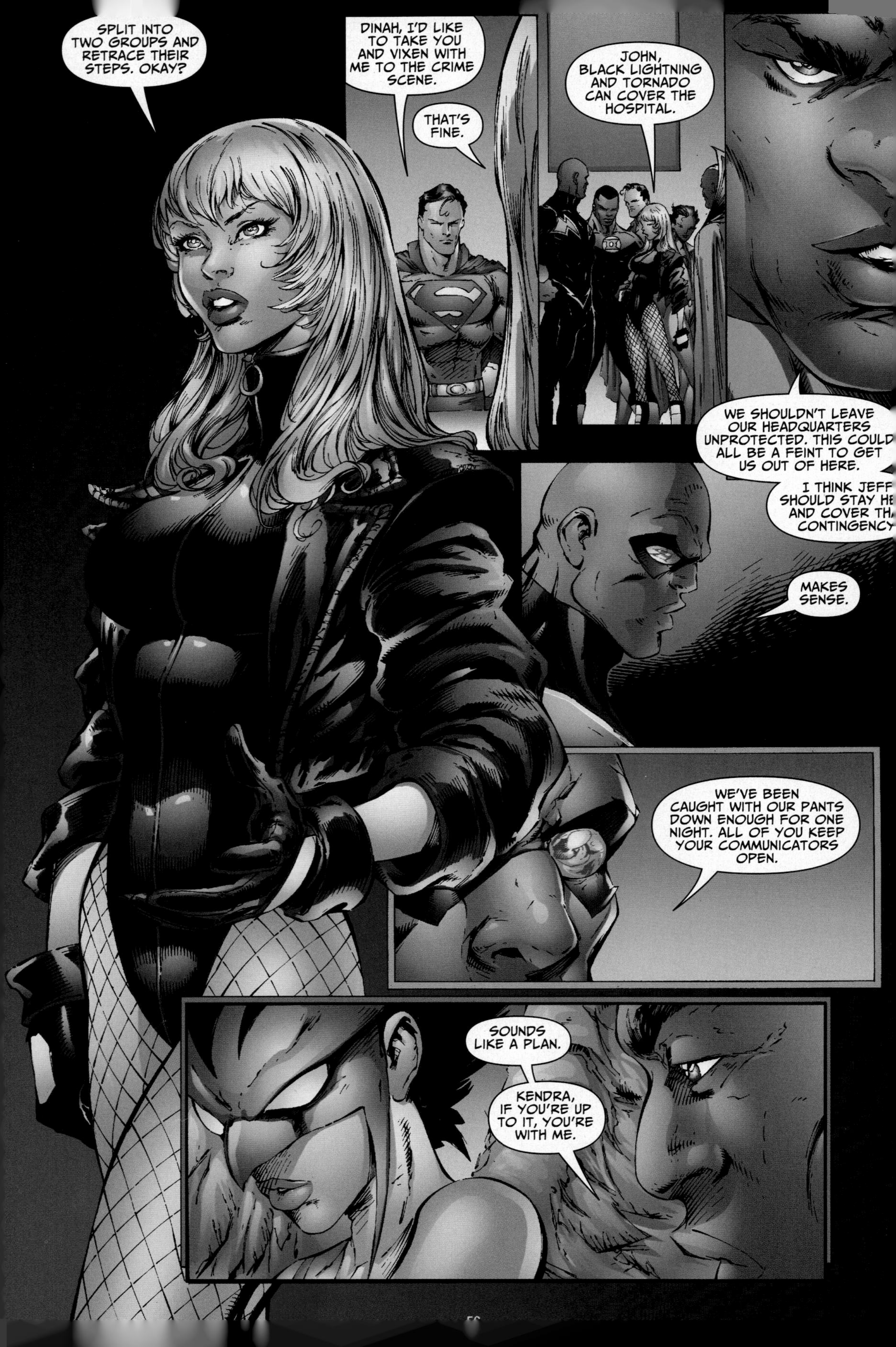
SPLIT INTO TWO GROUPS AND RETRACE THEIR STEPS. OKAY?
DINAH, I'D LIKE TO TAKE YOU AND VIXEN WITH ME TO THE CRIME SCENE.
THAT'S FINE.
JOHN, BLACK LIGHTNING AND TORNADO CAN COVER THE HOSPITAL.
WE SHOULDN'T LEAVE OUR HEADQUARTERS UNPROTECTED. THIS COULD ALL BE A FEINT TO GET US OUT OF HERE.
I THINK JEFF SHOULD STAY HE AND COVER TH CONTINGENCY
MAKES SENSE.
WE'VE BEEN CAUGHT WITH OUR PANTS DOWN ENOUGH FOR ONE NIGHT. ALL OF YOU KEEP YOUR COMMUNICATORS OPEN.
SOUNDS LIKE A PLAN.
KENDRA, IF YOU'RE UP TO IT, YOU'RE WITH ME.

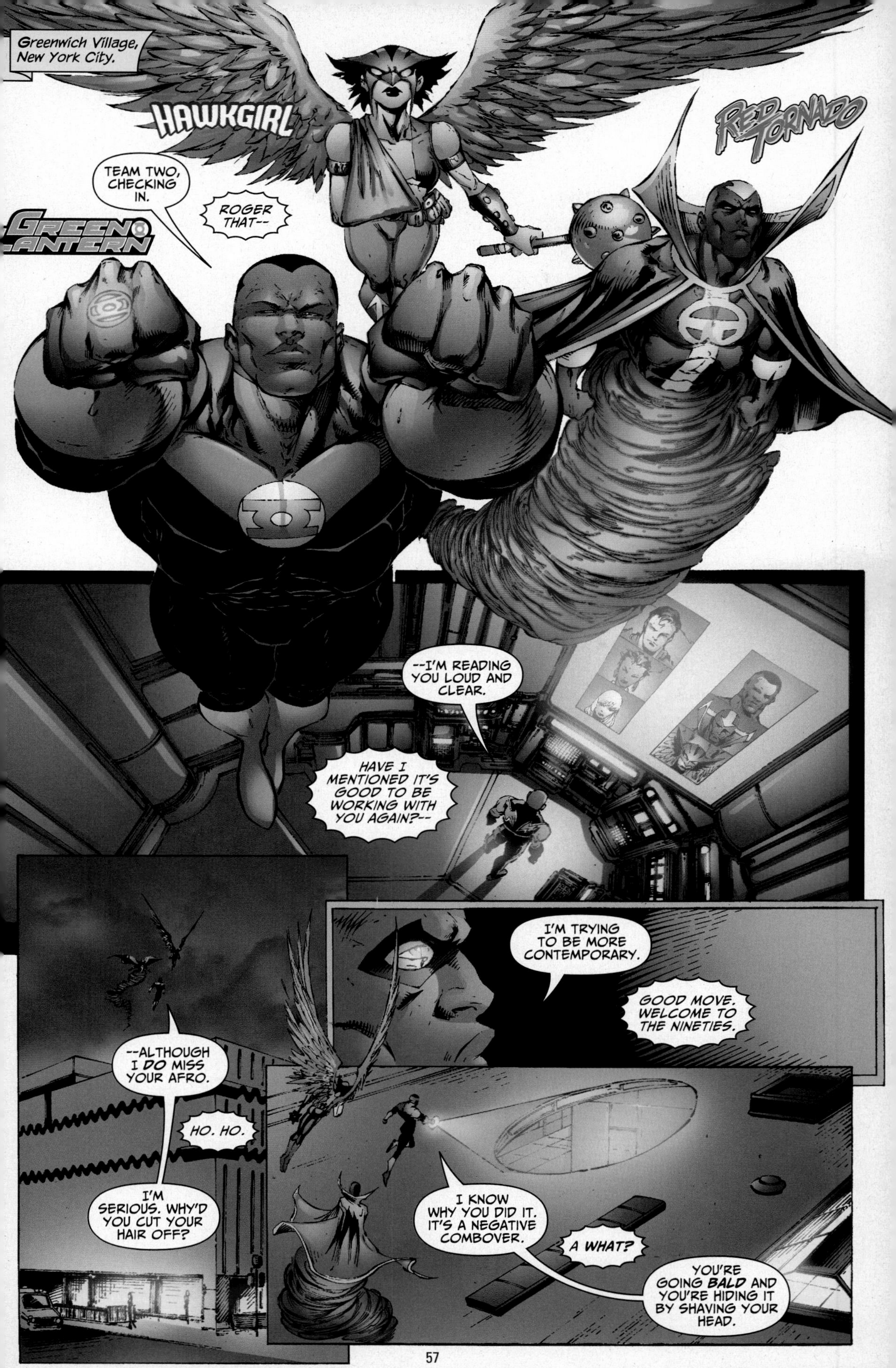

Greenwich Village, New York City.
HAWKGIRL
RED TORNADO
GREEN LANTERN
TEAM TWO, CHECKING IN.
ROGER THAT--
--I'M READING YOU LOUD AND CLEAR.
HAVE I MENTIONED IT'S GOOD TO BE WORKING WITH YOU AGAIN?--
--ALTHOUGH I *DO* MISS YOUR AFRO.
HO. HO.
I'M SERIOUS. WHY'D YOU CUT YOUR HAIR OFF?
I'M TRYING TO BE MORE CONTEMPORARY.
GOOD MOVE. WELCOME TO THE NINETIES.
I KNOW WHY YOU DID IT. IT'S A NEGATIVE COMBOVER.
A *WHAT?*
YOU'RE GOING *BALD* AND YOU'RE HIDING IT BY SHAVING YOUR HEAD.

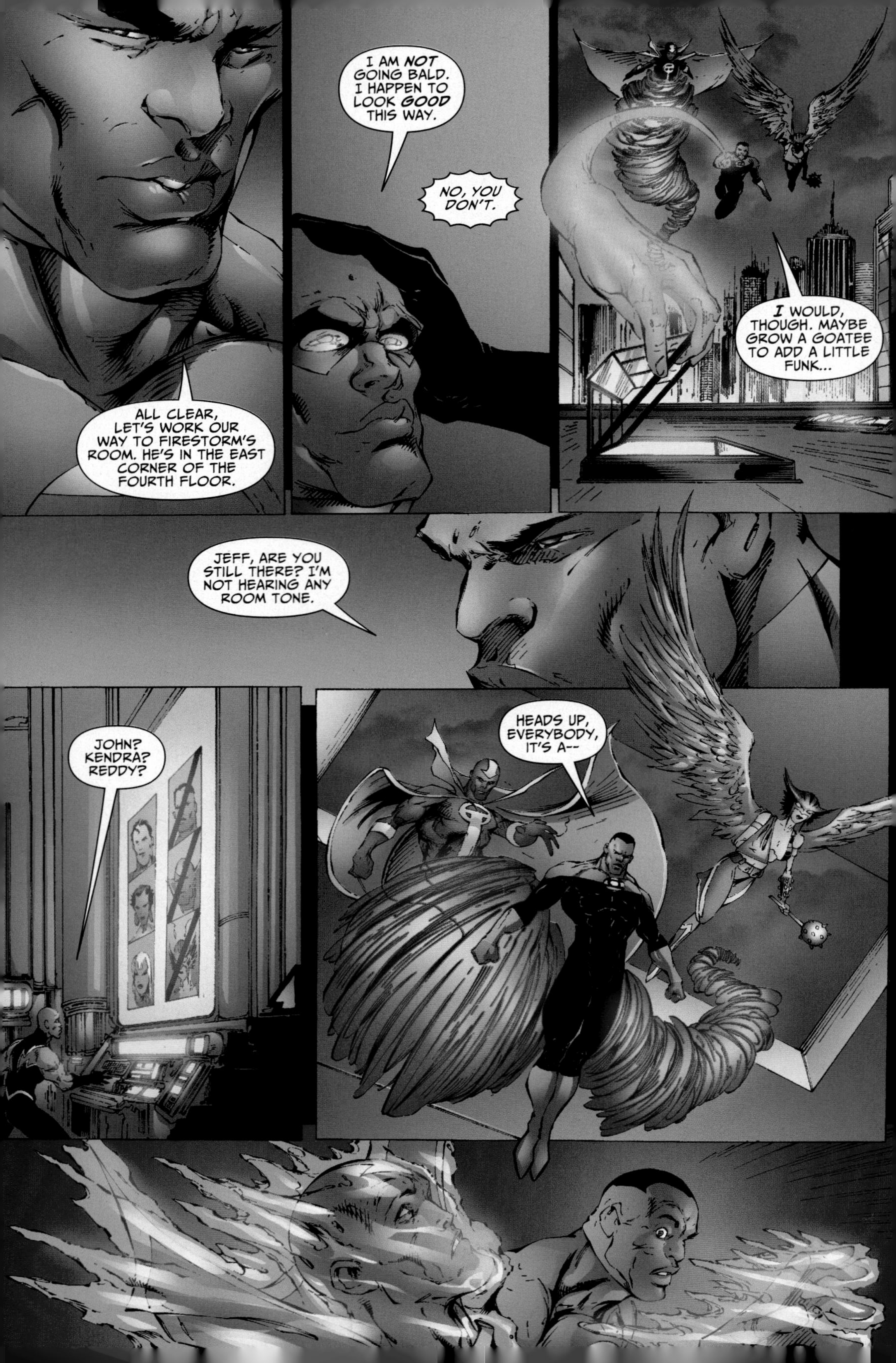
ALL CLEAR, LET'S WORK OUR WAY TO FIRESTORM'S ROOM. HE'S IN THE EAST CORNER OF THE FOURTH FLOOR.
I AM NOT GOING BALD. I HAPPEN TO LOOK GOOD THIS WAY.
NO, YOU DON'T.
I WOULD, THOUGH. MAYBE GROW A GOATEE TO ADD A LITTLE FUNK...
JEFF, ARE YOU STILL THERE? I'M NOT HEARING ANY ROOM TONE.
JOHN? KENDRA? REDDY?
HEADS UP, EVERYBODY, IT'S A--

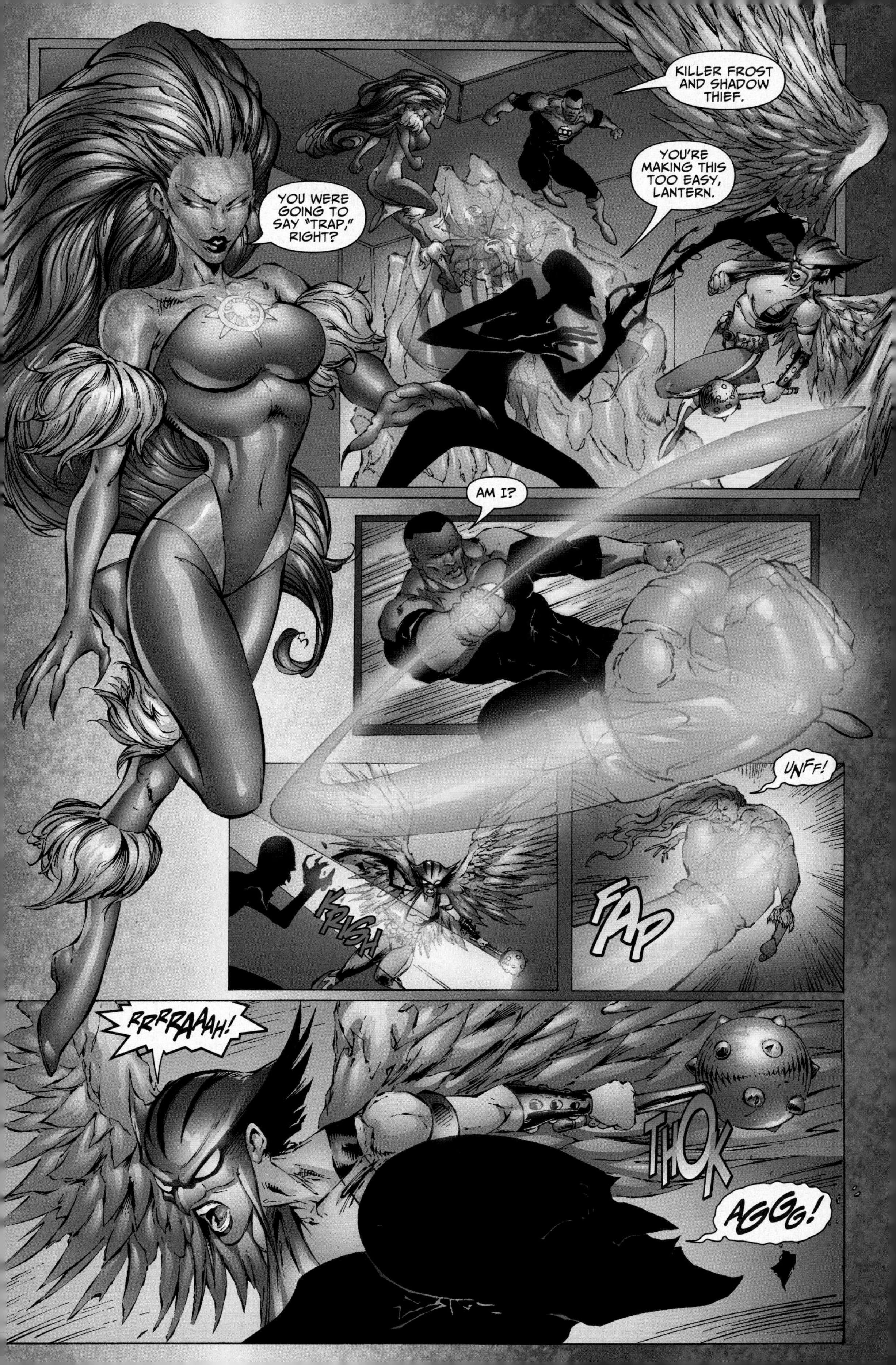

KILLER FROST AND SHADOW THIEF.
YOU WERE GOING TO SAY "TRAP," RIGHT?
YOU'RE MAKING THIS TOO EASY, LANTERN.
AM I?
UNFF!
KRISH
FAP
RRRRAAAH!
THOK
AGGG!

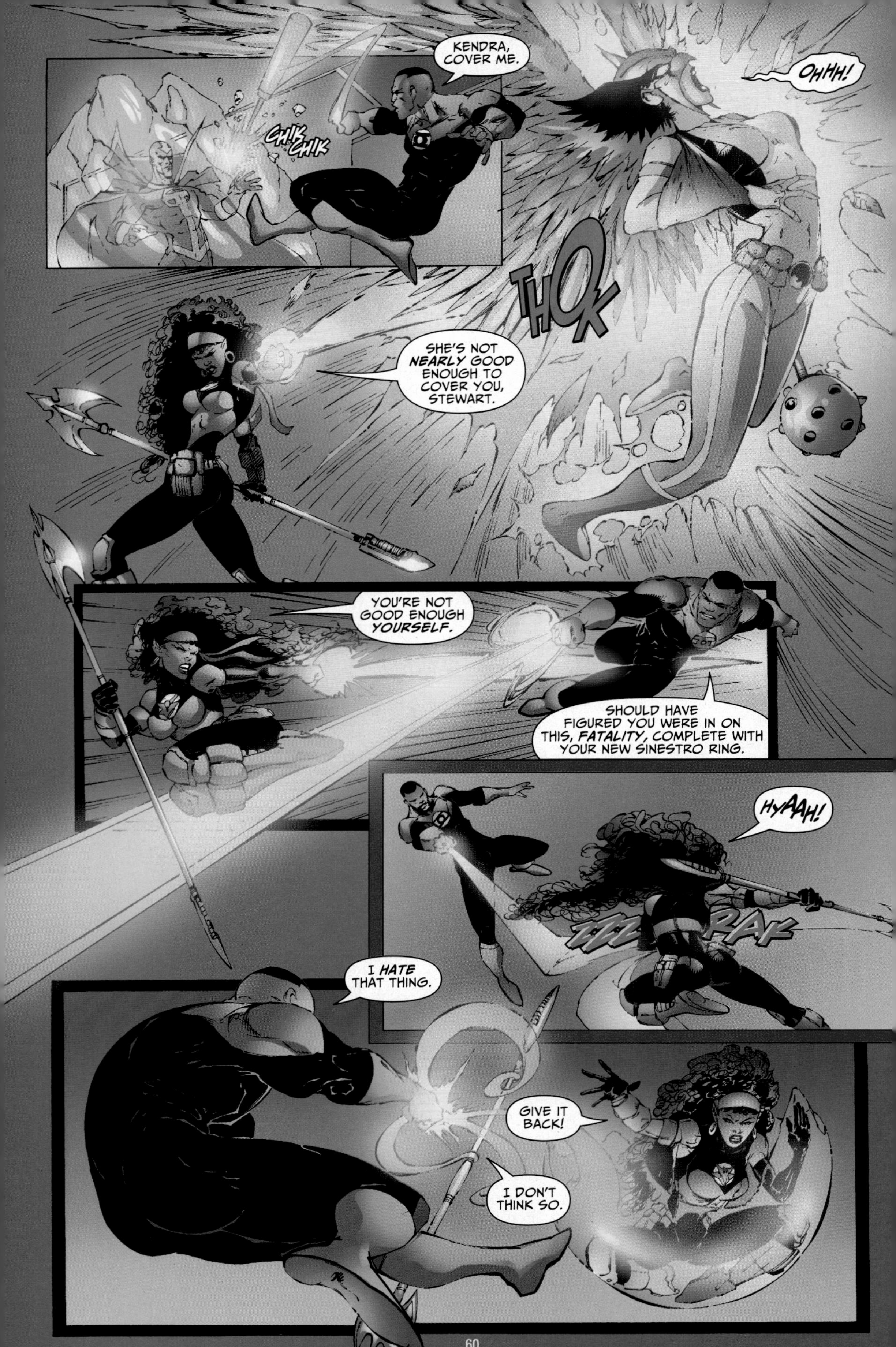
KENDRA, COVER ME.
CHIK CHIK
OHHH!
THOK
SHE'S NOT NEARLY GOOD ENOUGH TO COVER YOU, STEWART.
YOU'RE NOT GOOD ENOUGH YOURSELF.
SHOULD HAVE FIGURED YOU WERE IN ON THIS, FATALITY, COMPLETE WITH YOUR NEW SINESTRO RING.
HYAAH!
ZZZRAK
I HATE THAT THING.
GIVE IT BACK!
I DON'T THINK SO.

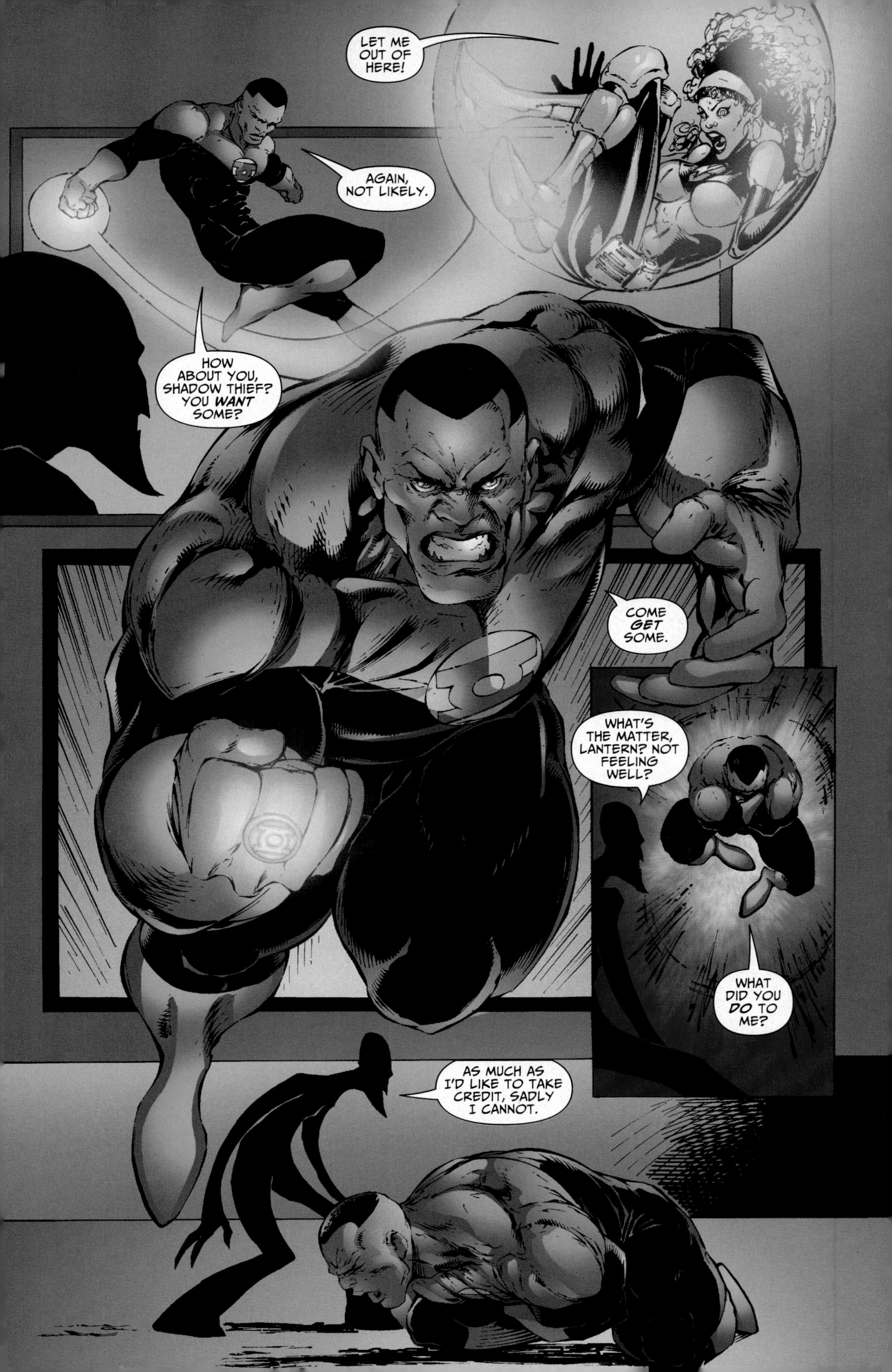
LET ME OUT OF HERE!
AGAIN, NOT LIKELY.
HOW ABOUT YOU, SHADOW THIEF? YOU *WANT* SOME?
COME *GET* SOME.
WHAT'S THE MATTER, LANTERN? NOT FEELING WELL?
WHAT DID YOU *DO* TO ME?
AS MUCH AS I'D LIKE TO TAKE CREDIT, SADLY I CANNOT.

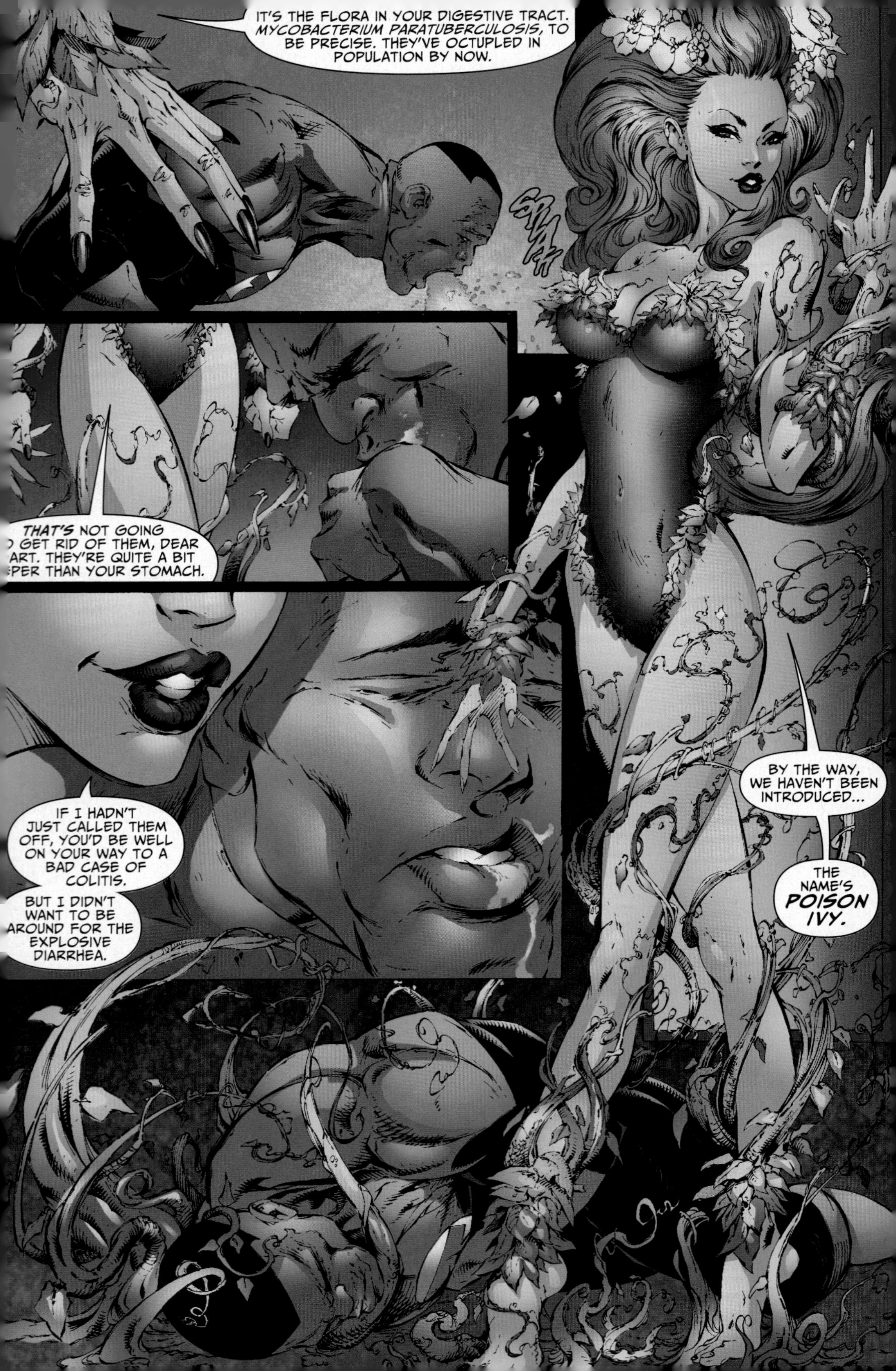
IT'S THE FLORA IN YOUR DIGESTIVE TRACT. *MYCOBACTERIUM PARATUBERCULOSIS*, TO BE PRECISE. THEY'VE OCTUPLED IN POPULATION BY NOW.
THAT'S NOT GOING O GET RID OF THEM, DEAR ART. THEY'RE QUITE A BIT EPER THAN YOUR STOMACH.
IF I HADN'T JUST CALLED THEM OFF, YOU'D BE WELL ON YOUR WAY TO A BAD CASE OF COLITIS.
BUT I DIDN'T WANT TO BE AROUND FOR THE EXPLOSIVE DIARRHEA.
BY THE WAY, WE HAVEN'T BEEN INTRODUCED...
THE NAME'S ***POISON IVY.***

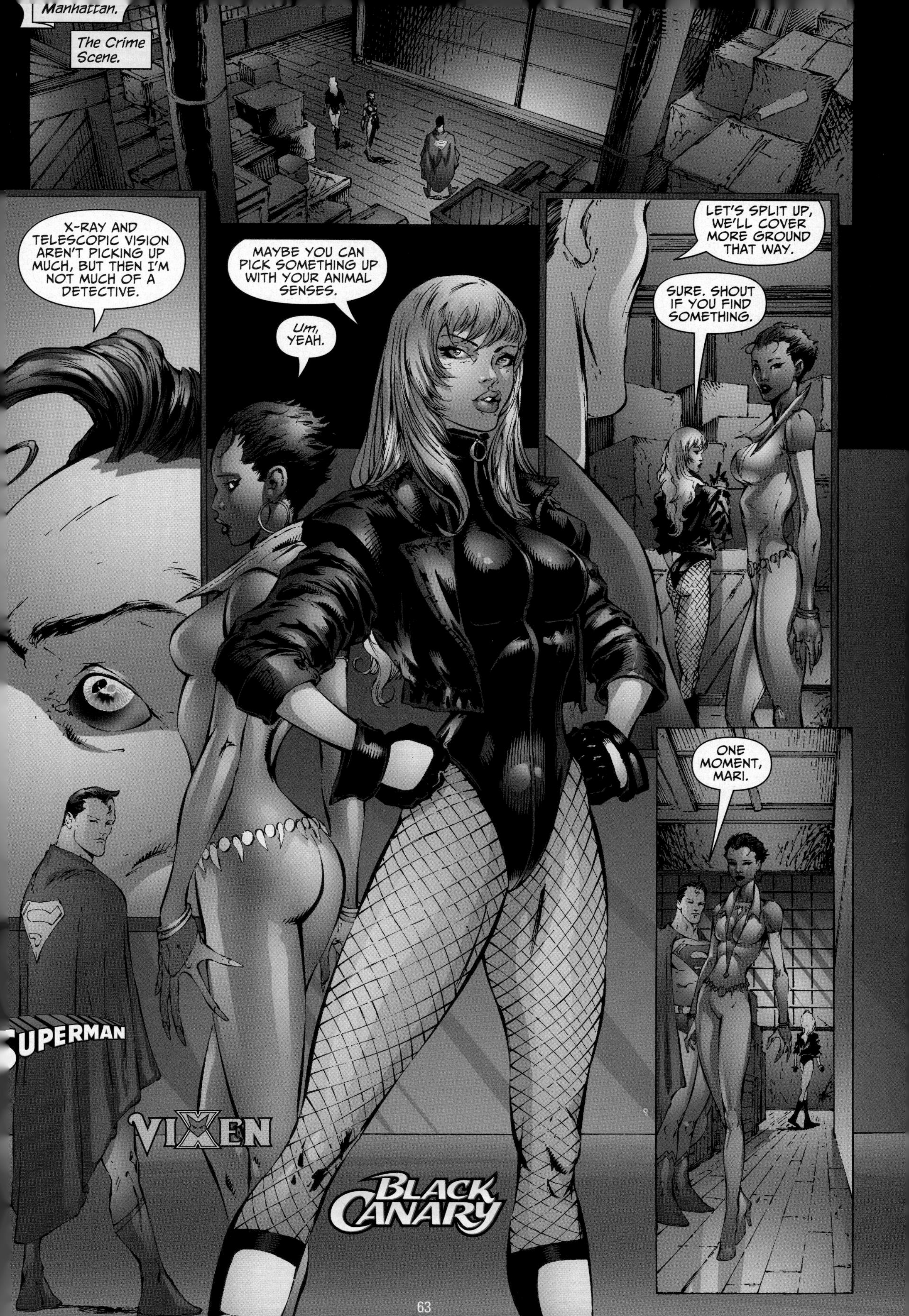
Manhattan.
The Crime Scene.
X-RAY AND TELESCOPIC VISION AREN'T PICKING UP MUCH, BUT THEN I'M NOT MUCH OF A DETECTIVE.
MAYBE YOU CAN PICK SOMETHING UP WITH YOUR ANIMAL SENSES.
Um, YEAH.
LET'S SPLIT UP, WE'LL COVER MORE GROUND THAT WAY.
SURE. SHOUT IF YOU FIND SOMETHING.
ONE MOMENT, MARI.
SUPERMAN
VIXEN
BLACK CANARY

I DIDN'T WANT TO TALK IN FRONT OF DINAH.

I MEAN, I THINK YOU SHOULD TELL EVERYONE, BUT I ALSO THINK THAT'S YOUR DECISION TO MAKE.

I DON'T KNOW WHAT YOU'RE TALKING ABOUT.

SURE YOU DO. YOUR POWERS AREN'T WORKING PROPERLY.

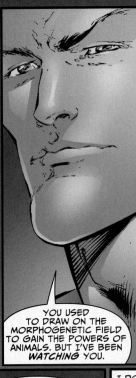

YOU USED TO DRAW ON THE MORPHOGENETIC FIELD TO GAIN THE POWERS OF ANIMALS. BUT I'VE BEEN *WATCHING* YOU.

YOU DON'T, OR *CAN'T* DO THAT ANYMORE.

CAN'T. NOT FOR WEEKS.

BUT PEOPLE ARE ANIMALS TOO, SO YOU'VE BEEN DRAWING ON THE POWERS OF YOUR FELLOW JUSTICE LEAGUERS.

I WOULD NEVER DO ANYTHING TO HURT ANY OF YOU.

I KNOW. THAT'S WHY I PICKED YOU FOR MY TEAM.

I FIGURED IF YOU'RE GOING TO BE SIPHONING SUPERPOWERS, THEY MIGHT AS WELL BE FROM ME.

I DON'T KNOW HOW TO THANK YOU, I--

START BY BEING HONEST WITH YOUR TEAMMATES.

BETWEEN US ALL, IF THERE *IS* A WAY TO CURE YOU, WE'LL FIND IT.

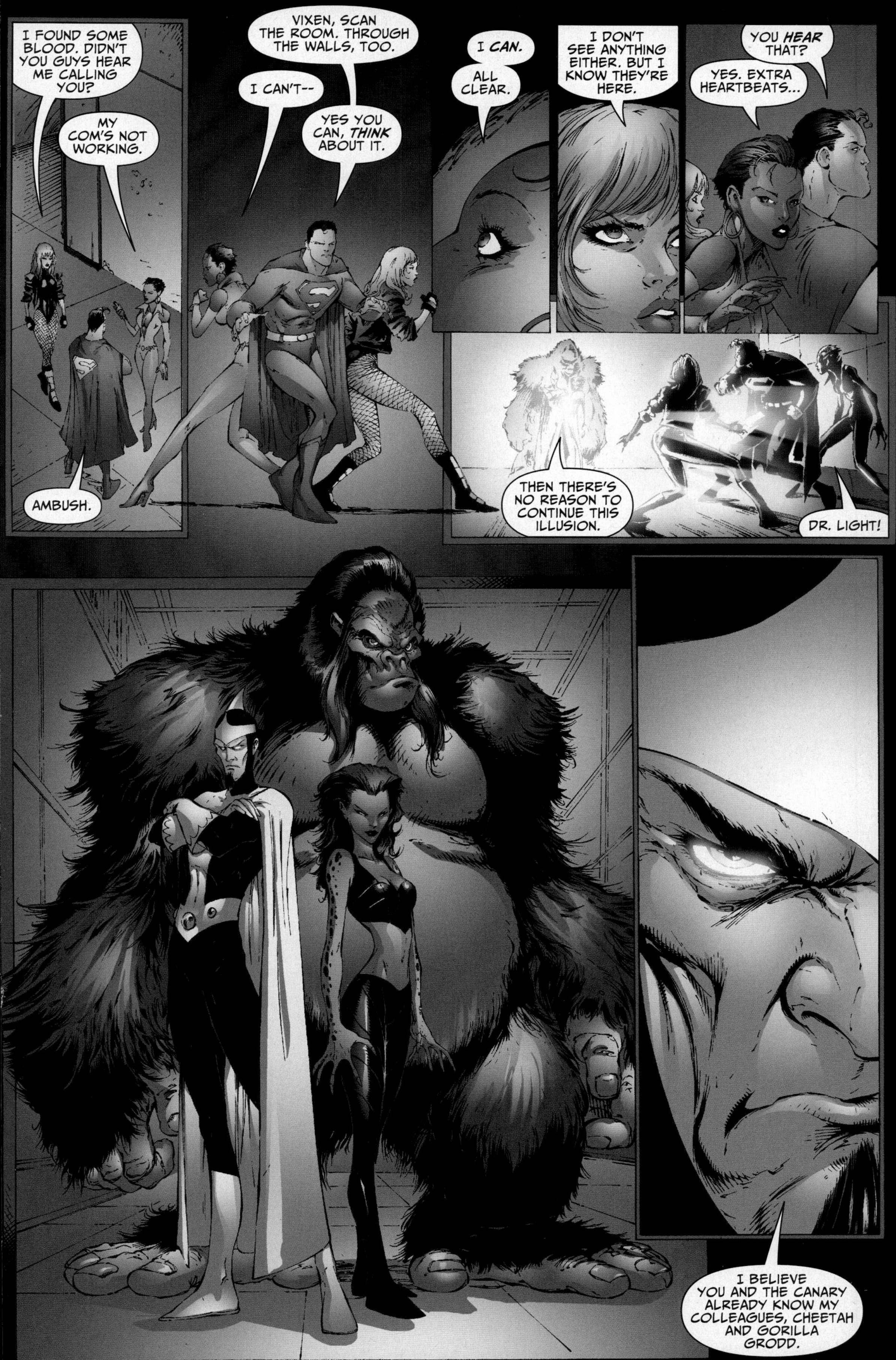
I FOUND SOME BLOOD. DIDN'T YOU GUYS HEAR ME CALLING YOU?
MY COM'S NOT WORKING.
AMBUSH.
VIXEN, SCAN THE ROOM. THROUGH THE WALLS, TOO.
I CAN'T--
YES YOU CAN, THINK ABOUT IT.
I CAN.
ALL CLEAR.
I DON'T SEE ANYTHING EITHER. BUT I KNOW THEY'RE HERE.
YOU HEAR THAT?
YES. EXTRA HEARTBEATS...
THEN THERE'S NO REASON TO CONTINUE THIS ILLUSION.
DR. LIGHT!
I BELIEVE YOU AND THE CANARY ALREADY KNOW MY COLLEAGUES, CHEETAH AND GORILLA GRODD.

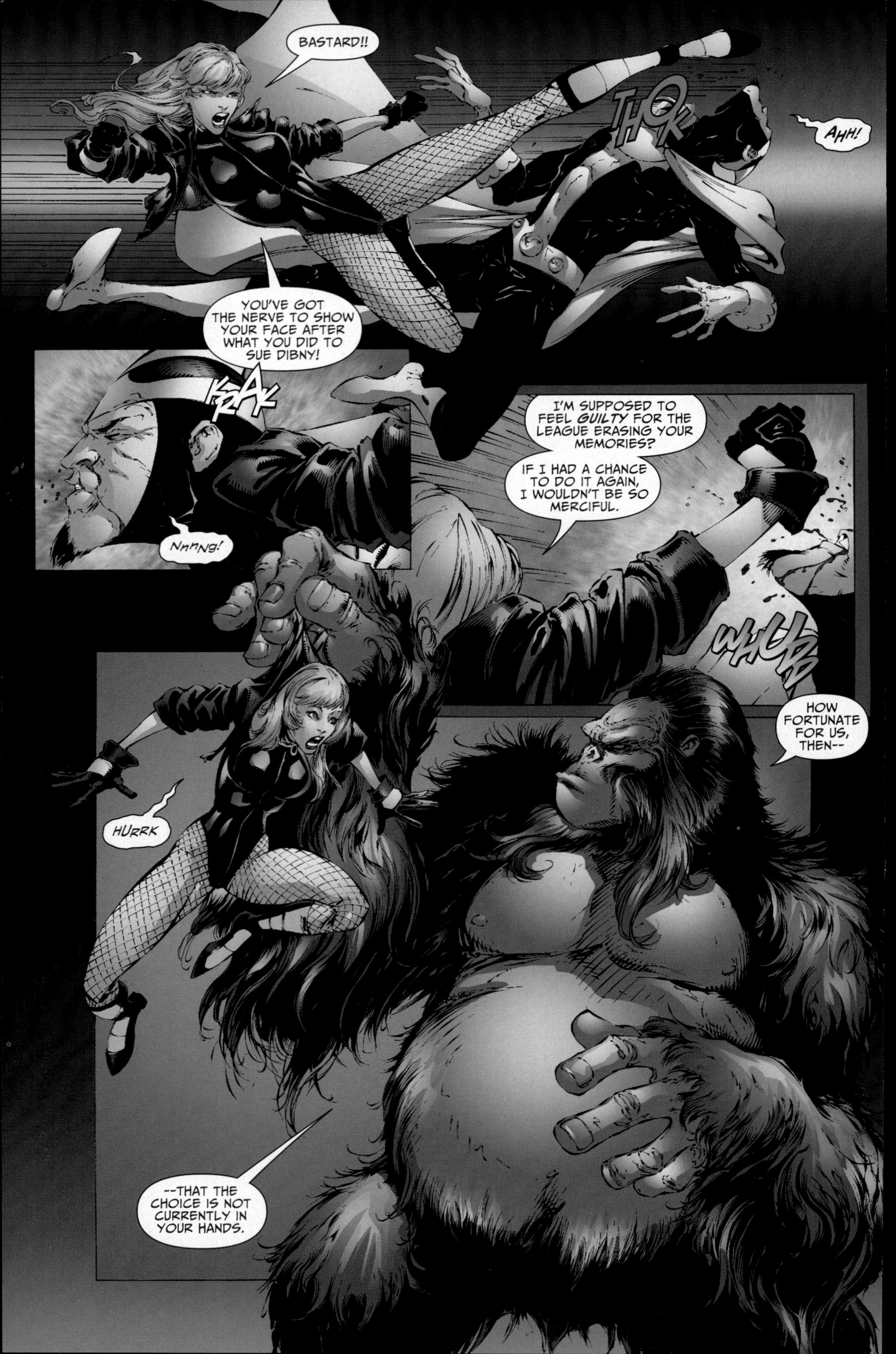
BASTARD!!
THOK
AHH!
YOU'VE GOT THE NERVE TO SHOW YOUR FACE AFTER WHAT YOU DID TO SUE DIBNY!
KRAK
NnnNg!
I'M SUPPOSED TO FEEL GUILTY FOR THE LEAGUE ERASING YOUR MEMORIES?
IF I HAD A CHANCE TO DO IT AGAIN, I WOULDN'T BE SO MERCIFUL.
WHUD
HOW FORTUNATE FOR US, THEN--
HURRK
--THAT THE CHOICE IS NOT CURRENTLY IN YOUR HANDS.

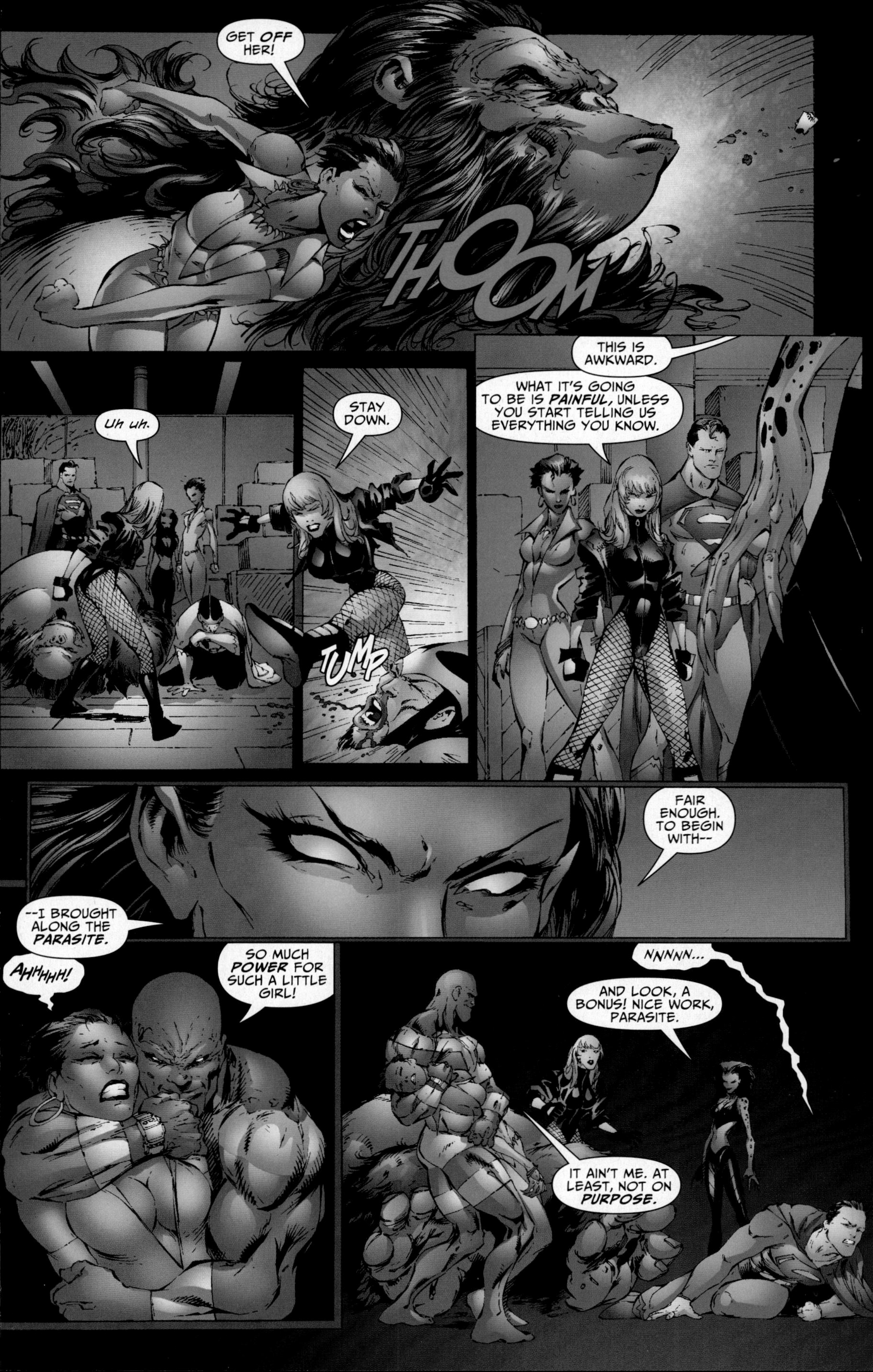
GET OFF HER!
THOOM
Uh uh.
STAY DOWN.
TUMP
THIS IS AWKWARD.
WHAT IT'S GOING TO BE IS PAINFUL, UNLESS YOU START TELLING US EVERYTHING YOU KNOW.
FAIR ENOUGH. TO BEGIN WITH--
--I BROUGHT ALONG THE PARASITE.
AHHHHH!
SO MUCH POWER FOR SUCH A LITTLE GIRL!
NNNNN...
AND LOOK, A BONUS! NICE WORK, PARASITE.
IT AIN'T ME. AT LEAST, NOT ON PURPOSE.

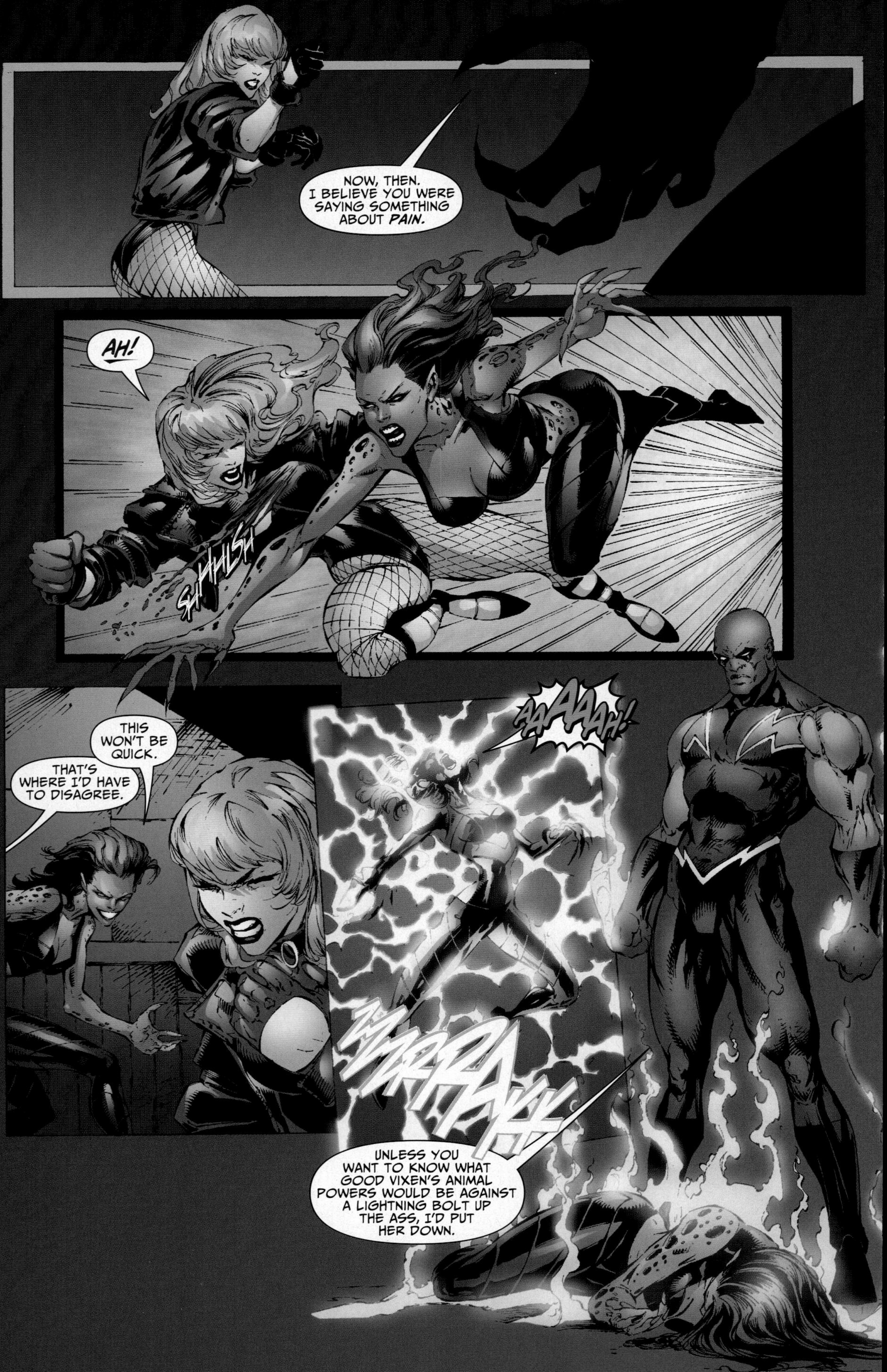
NOW, THEN. I BELIEVE YOU WERE SAYING SOMETHING ABOUT *PAIN.*
AH!
SHHHLSH
THIS WON'T BE QUICK.
THAT'S WHERE I'D HAVE TO DISAGREE.
UNLESS YOU WANT TO KNOW WHAT GOOD VIXEN'S ANIMAL POWERS WOULD BE AGAINST A LIGHTNING BOLT UP THE ASS, I'D PUT HER DOWN.

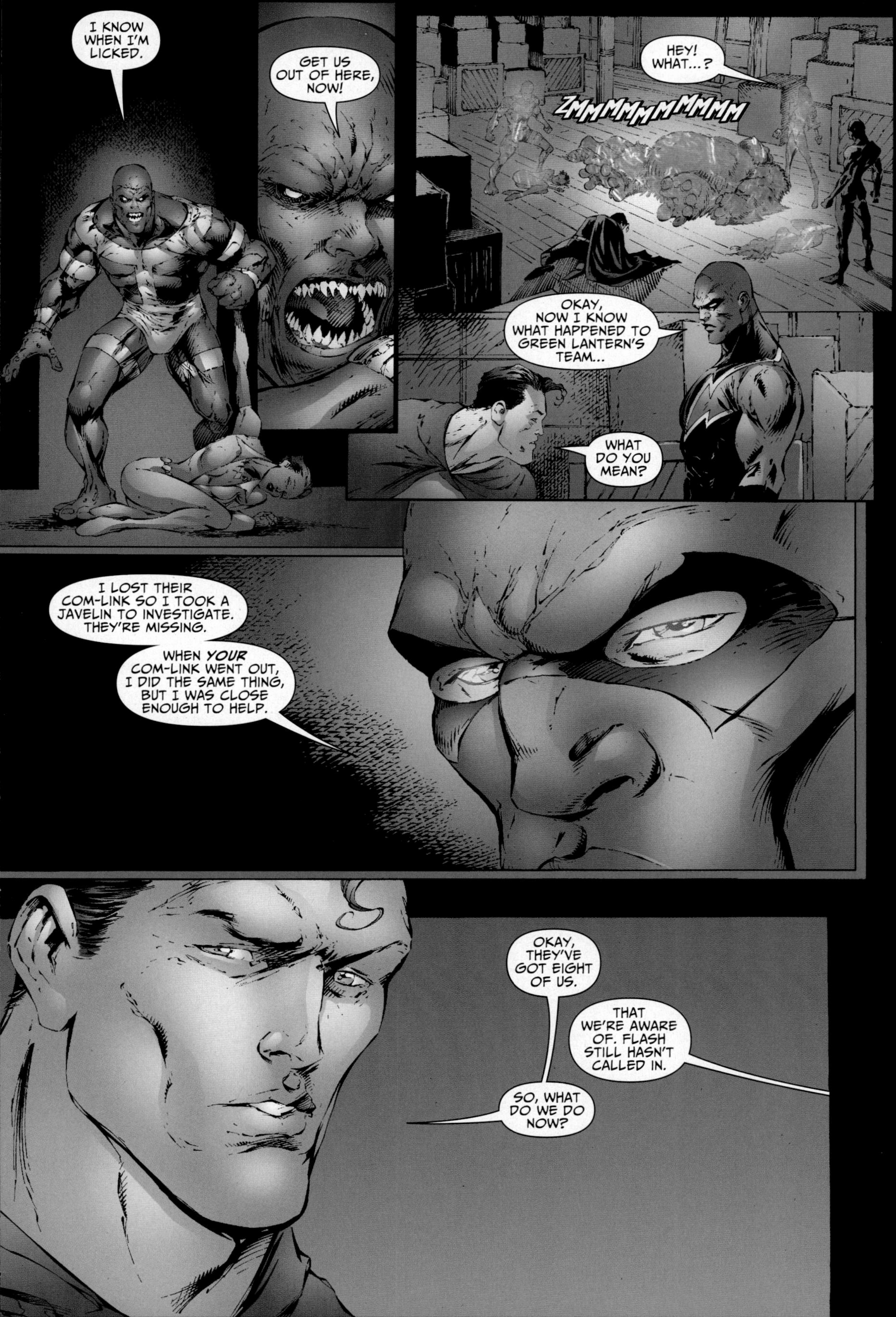
I KNOW WHEN I'M LICKED.
GET US OUT OF HERE, NOW!
HEY! WHAT...?
ZMMMMMMMMMM
OKAY, NOW I KNOW WHAT HAPPENED TO GREEN LANTERN'S TEAM...
WHAT DO YOU MEAN?
I LOST THEIR COM-LINK SO I TOOK A JAVELIN TO INVESTIGATE. THEY'RE MISSING.
WHEN YOUR COM-LINK WENT OUT, I DID THE SAME THING, BUT I WAS CLOSE ENOUGH TO HELP.
OKAY, THEY'VE GOT EIGHT OF US.
THAT WE'RE AWARE OF. FLASH STILL HASN'T CALLED IN.
SO, WHAT DO WE DO NOW?

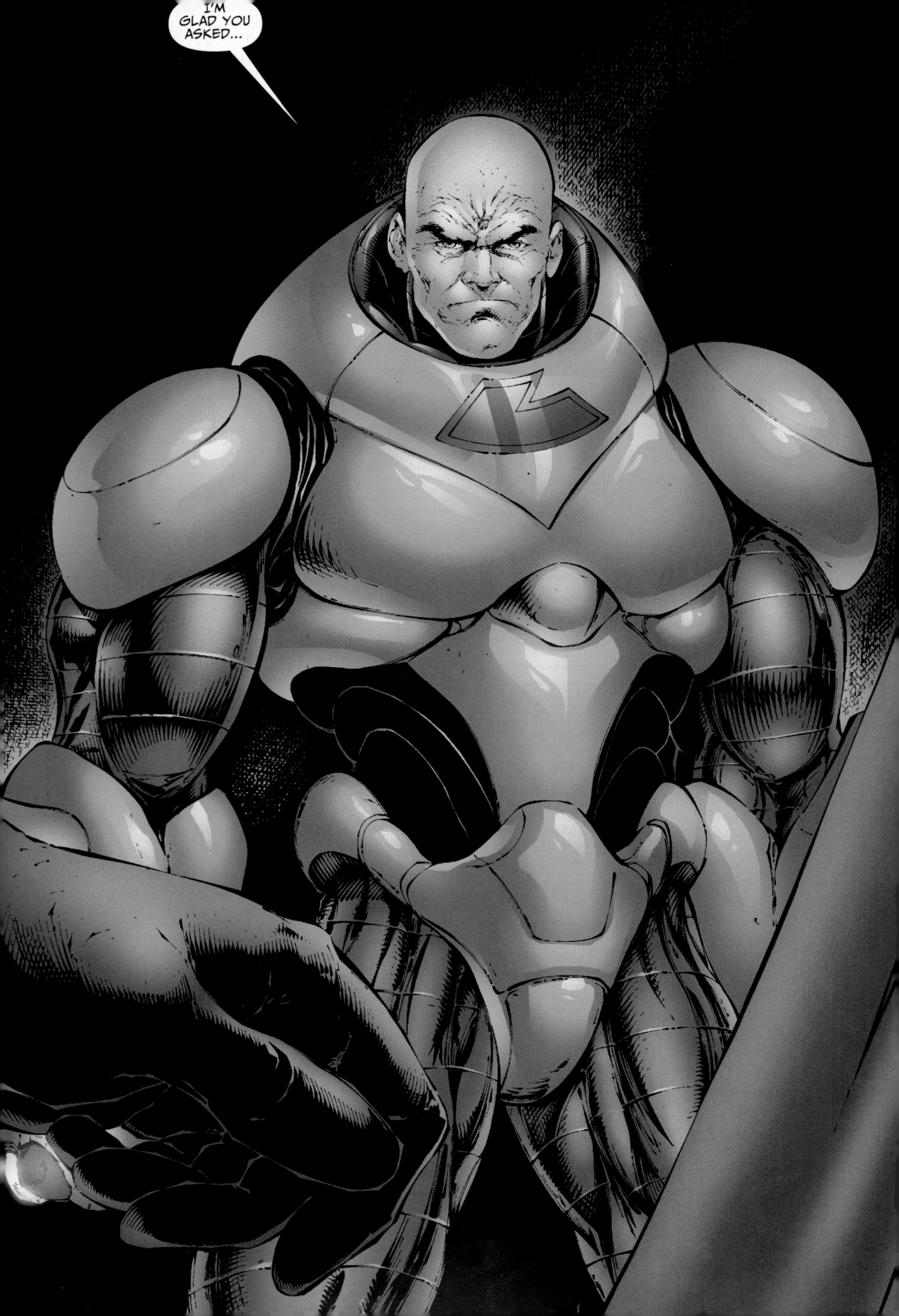
I'M GLAD YOU ASKED...

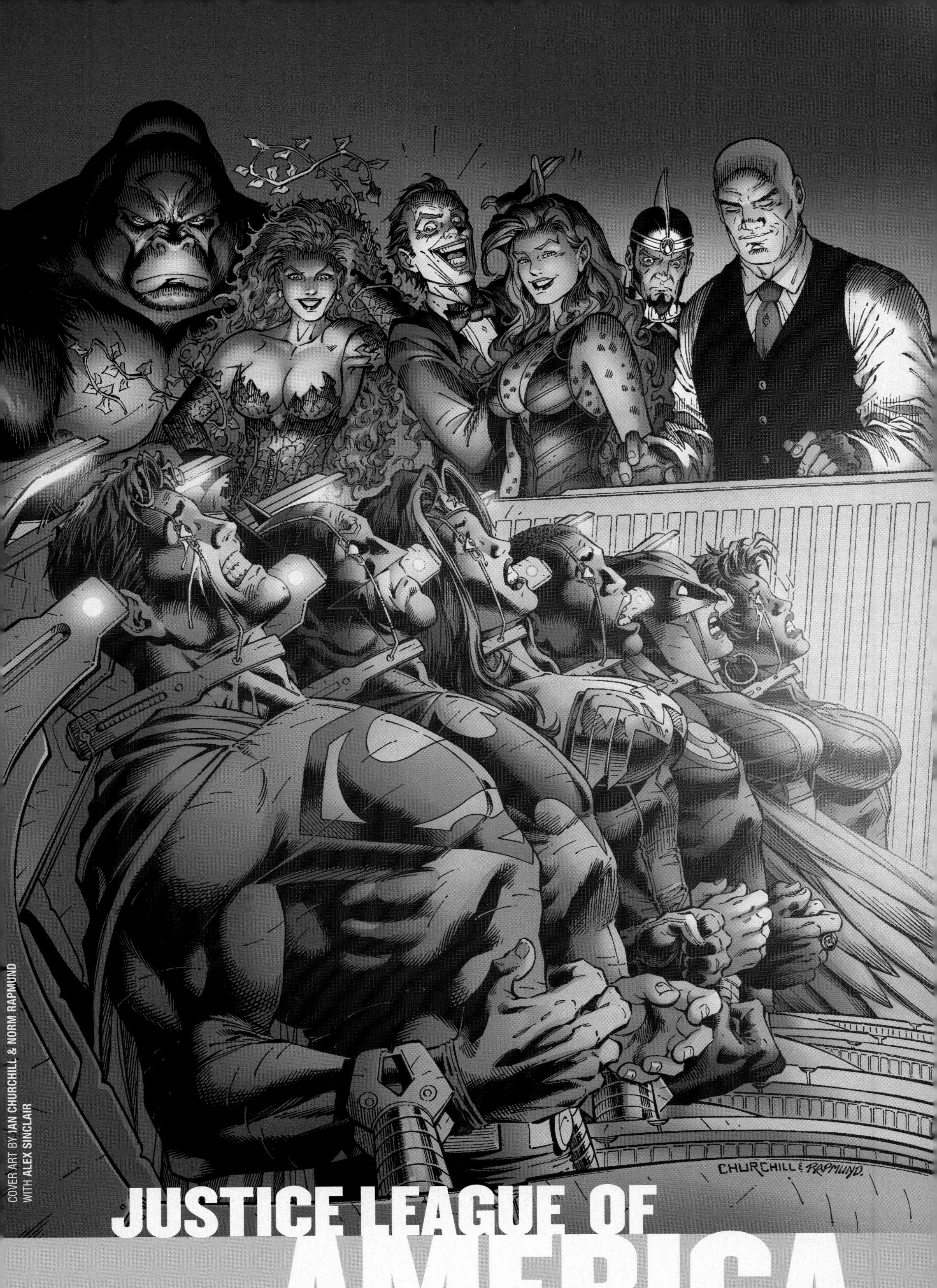
CHURCHILL & RAPMUND.

COVER ART BY IAN CHURCHILL & NORM RAPMUND
WITH ALEX SINCLAIR

JUSTICE LEAGUE OF AMERICA

CHAPTER THREE

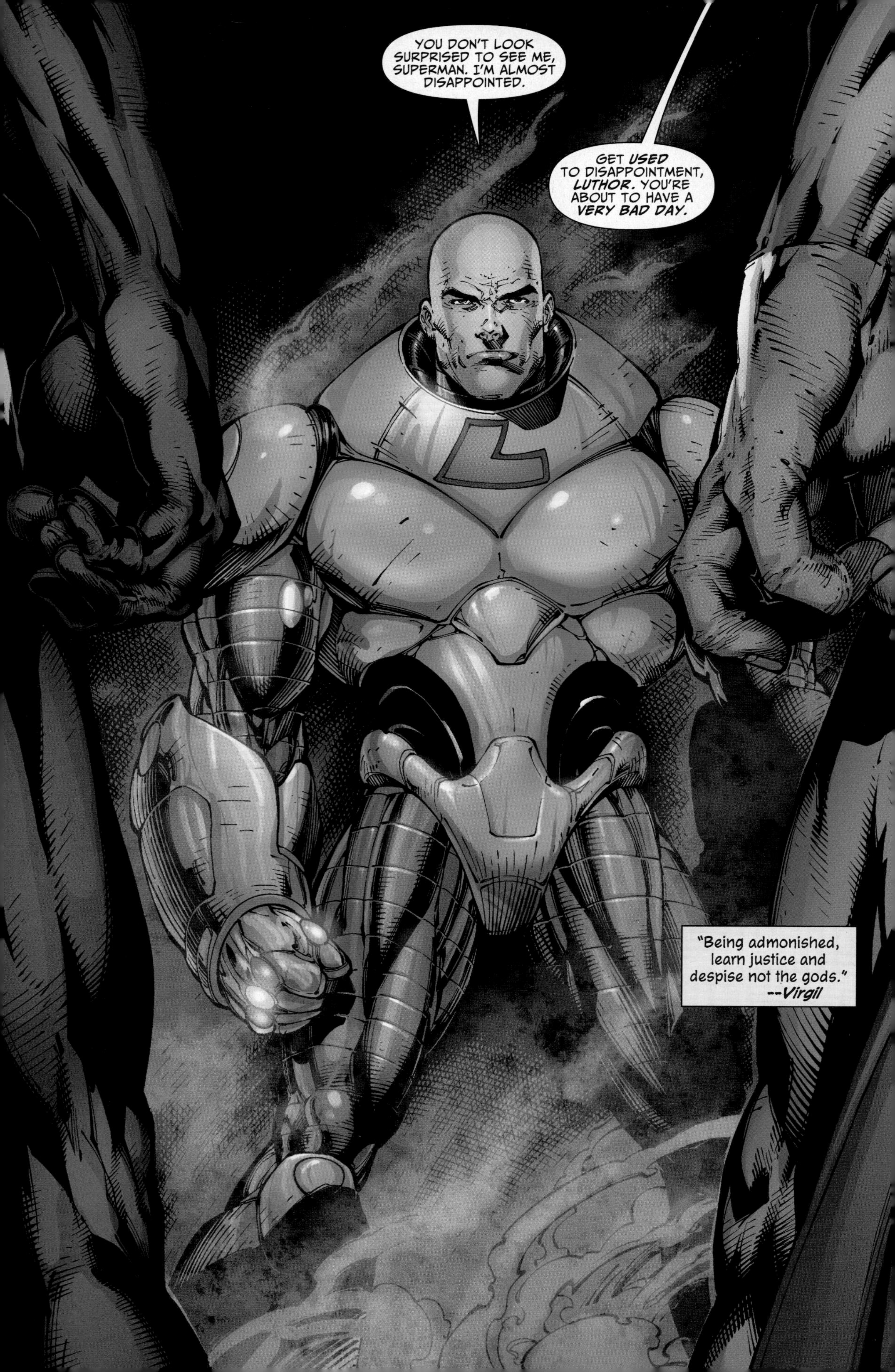
YOU DON'T LOOK SURPRISED TO SEE ME, SUPERMAN. I'M ALMOST DISAPPOINTED.
GET USED TO DISAPPOINTMENT, LUTHOR. YOU'RE ABOUT TO HAVE A VERY BAD DAY.
"Being admonished, learn justice and despise not the gods." --Virgil

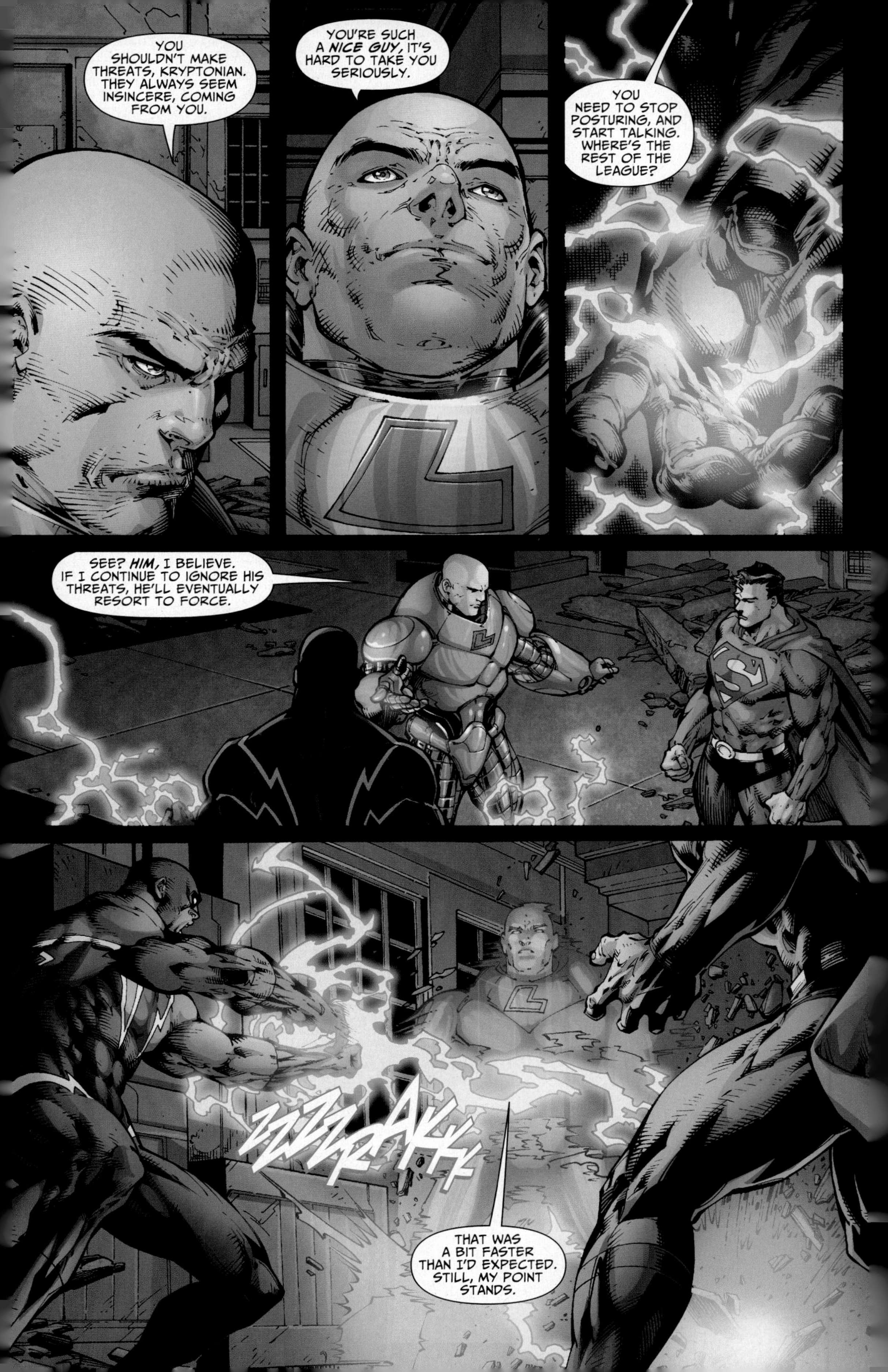

YOU SHOULDN'T MAKE THREATS, KRYPTONIAN. THEY ALWAYS SEEM INSINCERE, COMING FROM YOU.
YOU'RE SUCH A NICE GUY, IT'S HARD TO TAKE YOU SERIOUSLY.
YOU NEED TO STOP POSTURING, AND START TALKING. WHERE'S THE REST OF THE LEAGUE?
SEE? HIM, I BELIEVE. IF I CONTINUE TO IGNORE HIS THREATS, HE'LL EVENTUALLY RESORT TO FORCE.
ZZZZRAKK
THAT WAS A BIT FASTER THAN I'D EXPECTED. STILL, MY POINT STANDS.

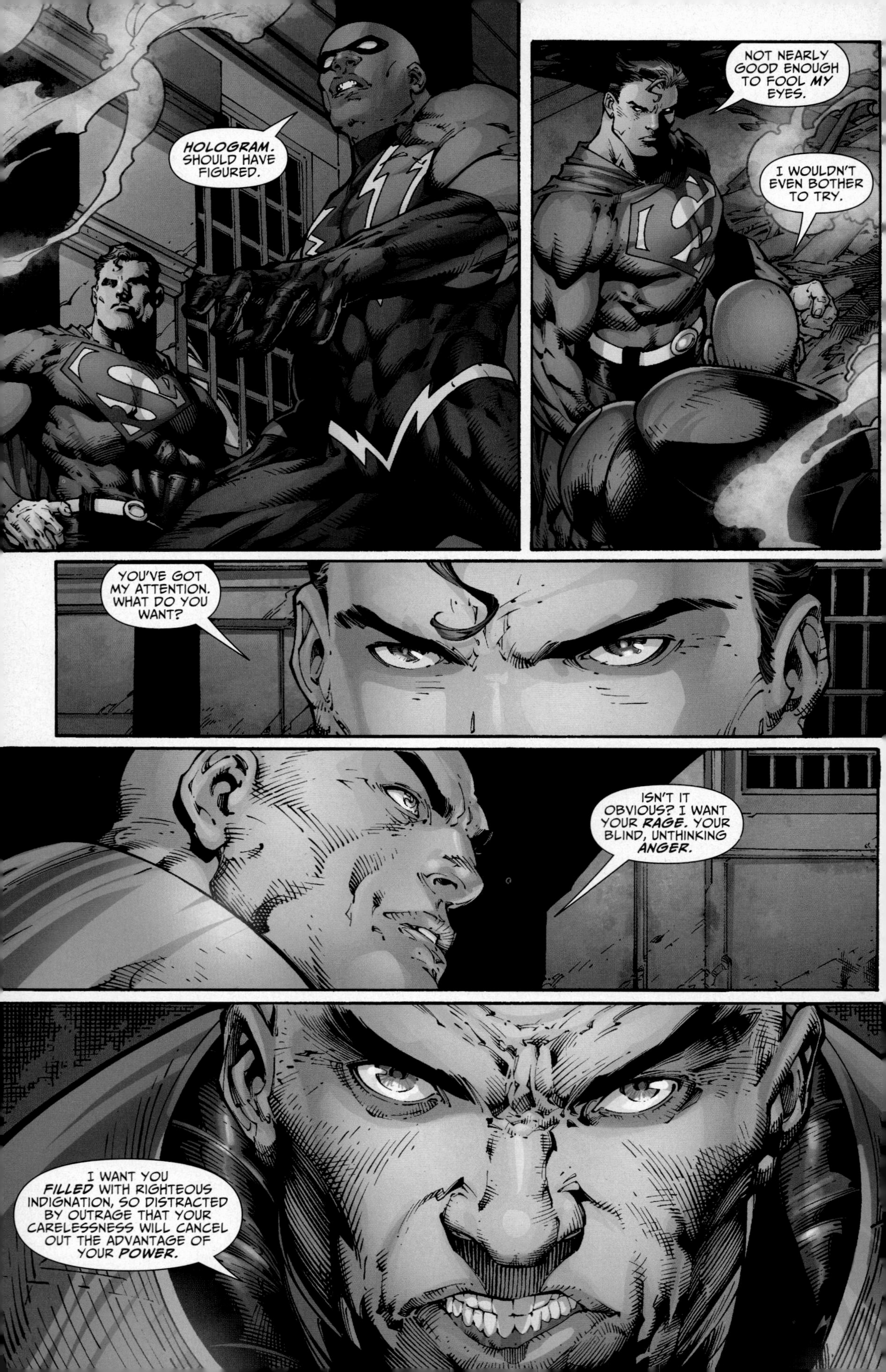
HOLOGRAM. SHOULD HAVE FIGURED.
NOT NEARLY GOOD ENOUGH TO FOOL MY EYES.
I WOULDN'T EVEN BOTHER TO TRY.
YOU'VE GOT MY ATTENTION. WHAT DO YOU WANT?
ISN'T IT OBVIOUS? I WANT YOUR RAGE. YOUR BLIND, UNTHINKING ANGER.
I WANT YOU FILLED WITH RIGHTEOUS INDIGNATION, SO DISTRACTED BY OUTRAGE THAT YOUR CARELESSNESS WILL CANCEL OUT THE ADVANTAGE OF YOUR POWER.

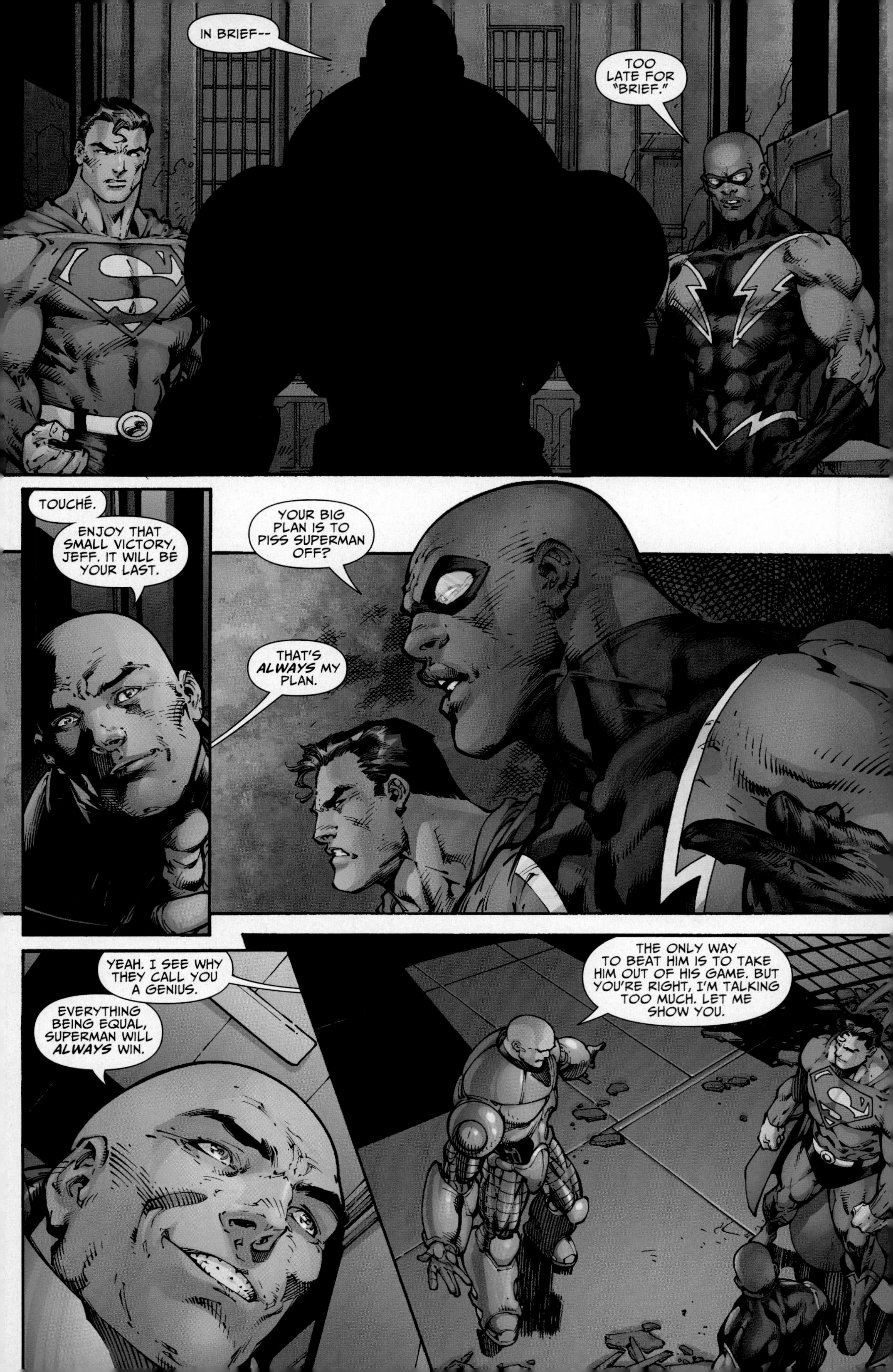
IN BRIEF--
TOO LATE FOR "BRIEF."
TOUCHÉ.
ENJOY THAT SMALL VICTORY, JEFF. IT WILL BE YOUR LAST.
YOUR BIG PLAN IS TO PISS SUPERMAN OFF?
THAT'S *ALWAYS* MY PLAN.
YEAH. I SEE WHY THEY CALL YOU A GENIUS.
EVERYTHING BEING EQUAL, SUPERMAN WILL *ALWAYS* WIN.
THE ONLY WAY TO BEAT HIM IS TO TAKE HIM OUT OF HIS GAME. BUT YOU'RE RIGHT, I'M TALKING TOO MUCH. LET ME SHOW YOU.

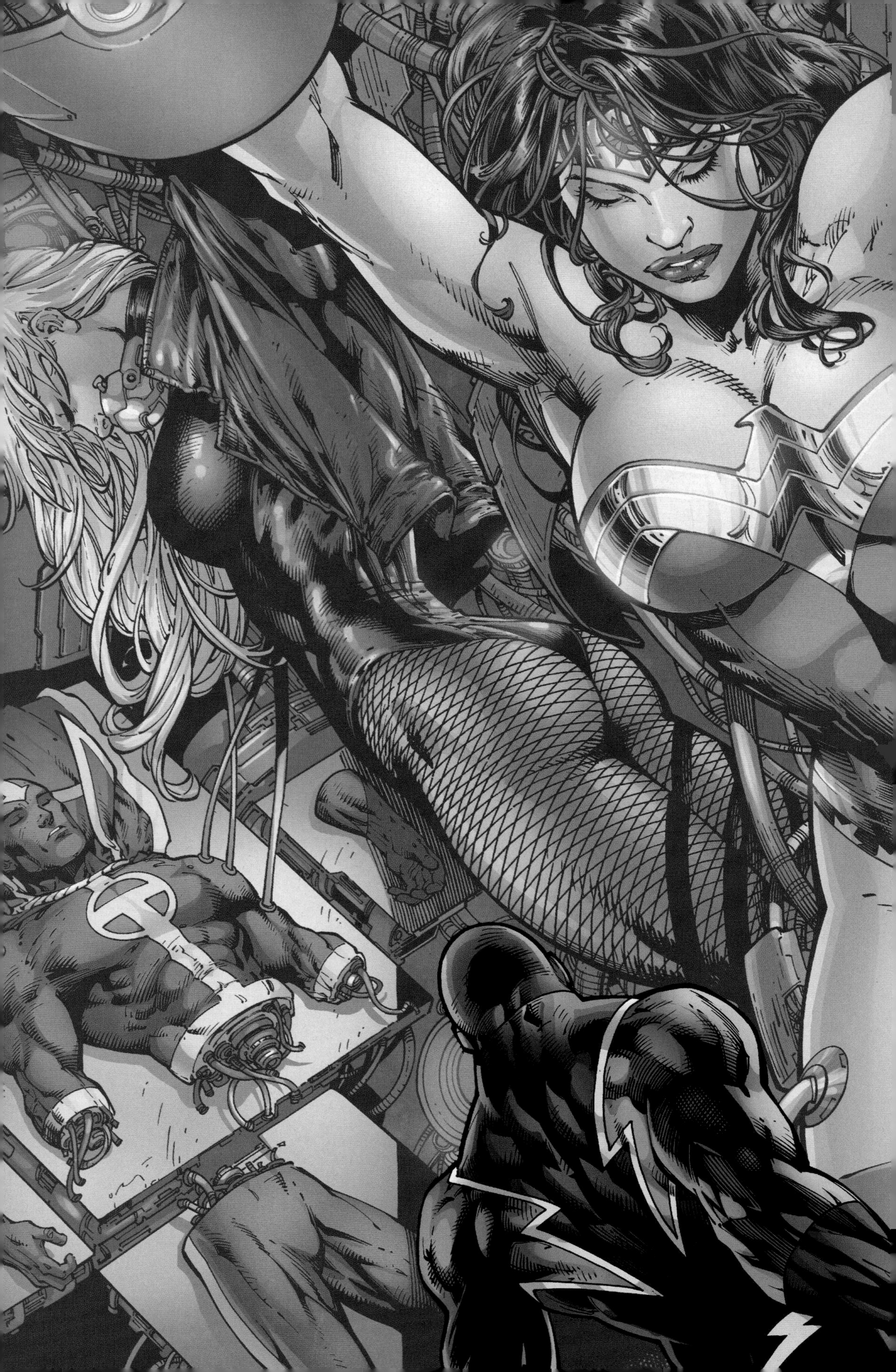

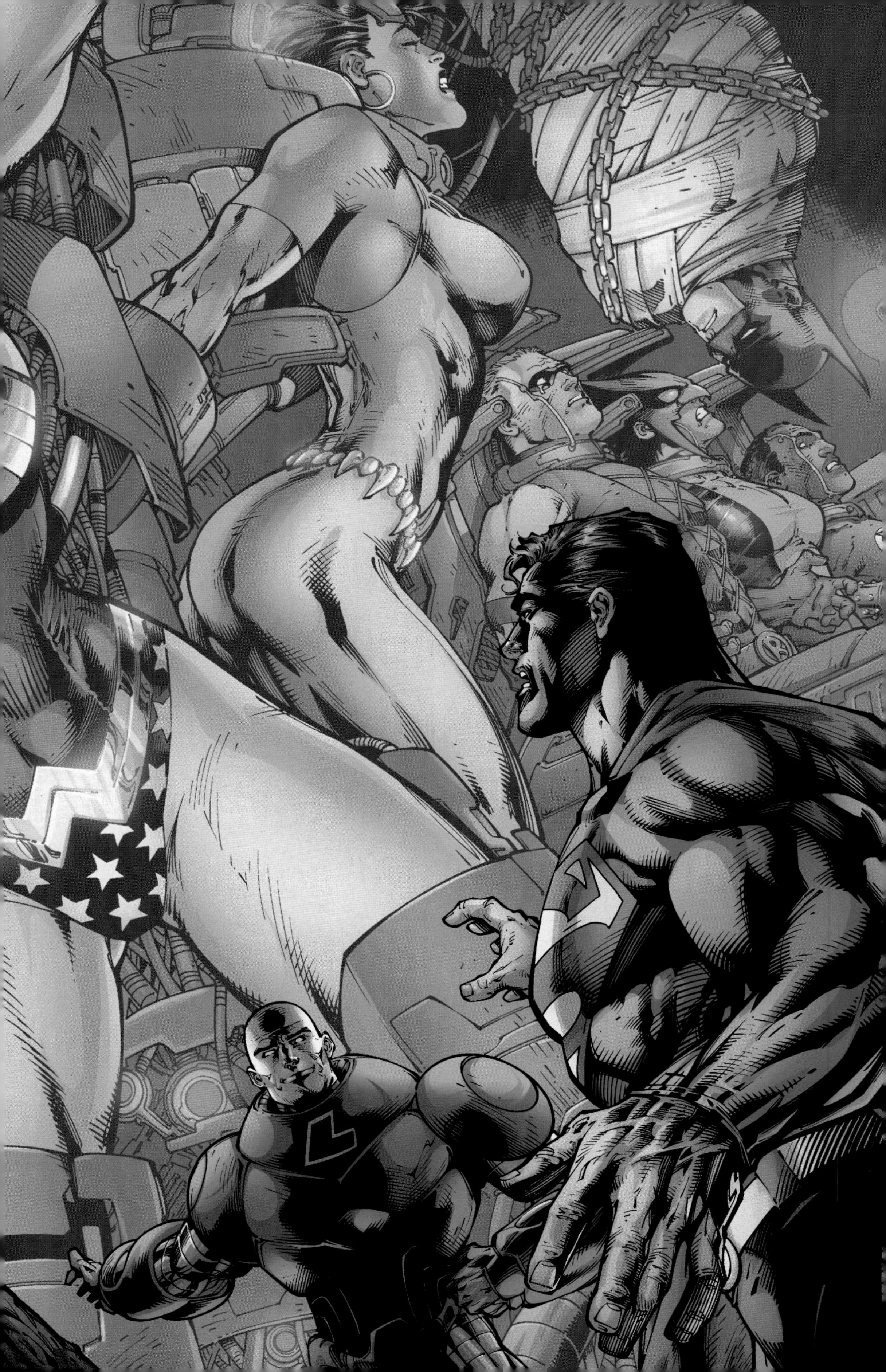

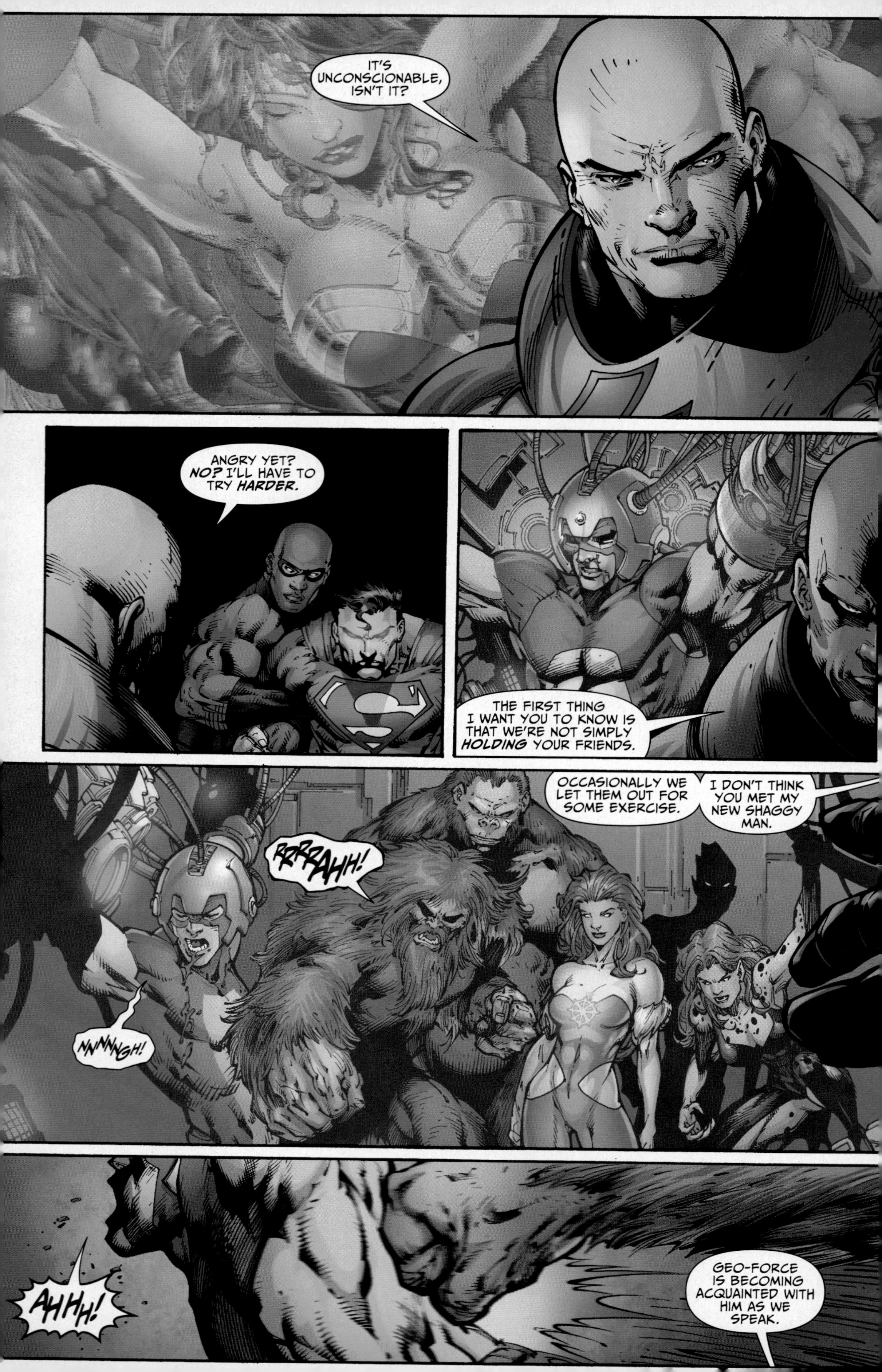
IT'S UNCONSCIONABLE, ISN'T IT?
ANGRY YET? NO? I'LL HAVE TO TRY HARDER.
THE FIRST THING I WANT YOU TO KNOW IS THAT WE'RE NOT SIMPLY HOLDING YOUR FRIENDS.
OCCASIONALLY WE LET THEM OUT FOR SOME EXERCISE.
I DON'T THINK YOU MET MY NEW SHAGGY MAN.
RRRRAHH!
NNNNNGH!
AHHH!
GEO-FORCE IS BECOMING ACQUAINTED WITH HIM AS WE SPEAK.

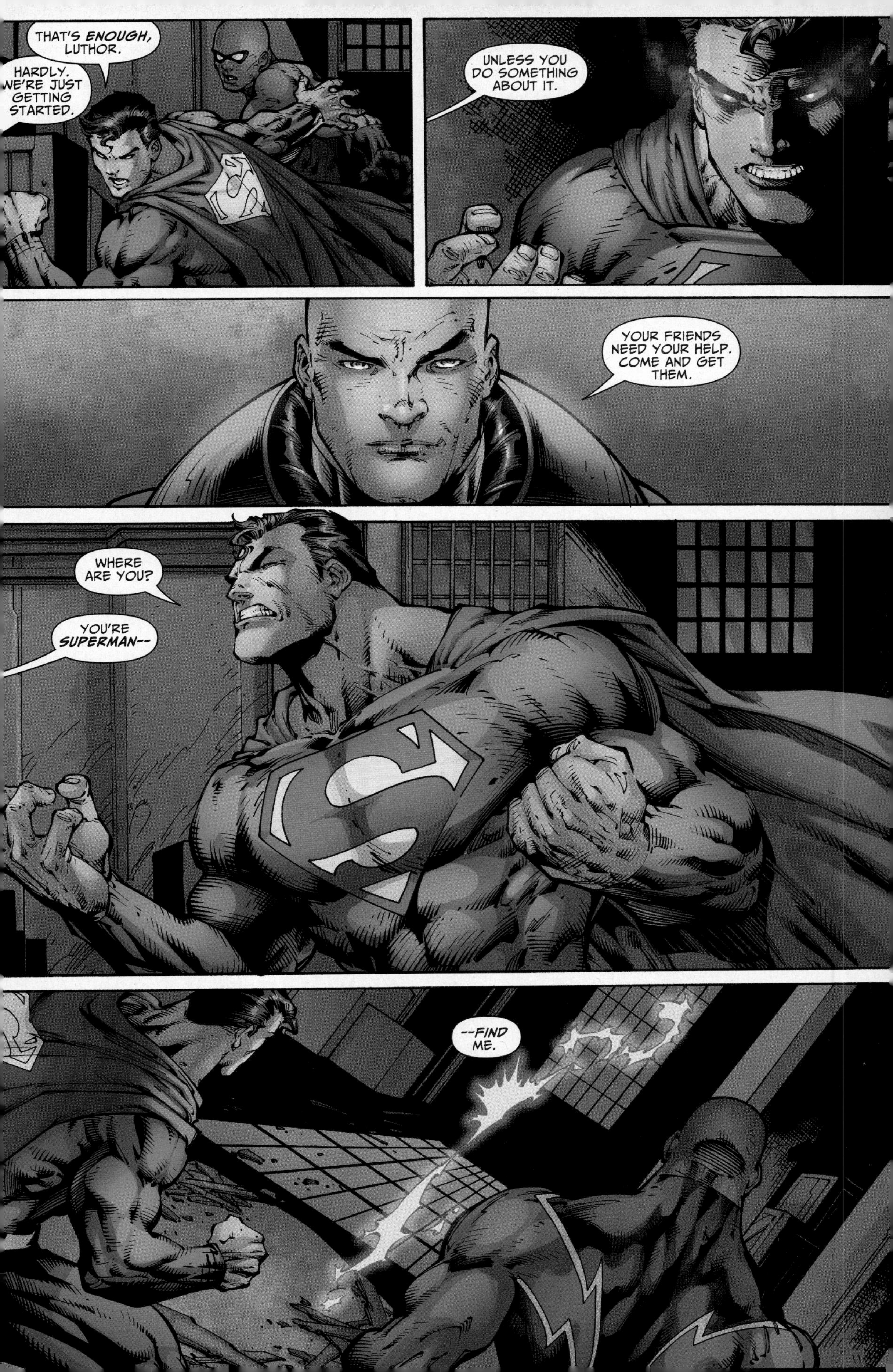
THAT'S ENOUGH, LUTHOR.
HARDLY. WE'RE JUST GETTING STARTED.
UNLESS YOU DO SOMETHING ABOUT IT.
YOUR FRIENDS NEED YOUR HELP. COME AND GET THEM.
WHERE ARE YOU?
YOU'RE SUPERMAN--
--FIND ME.

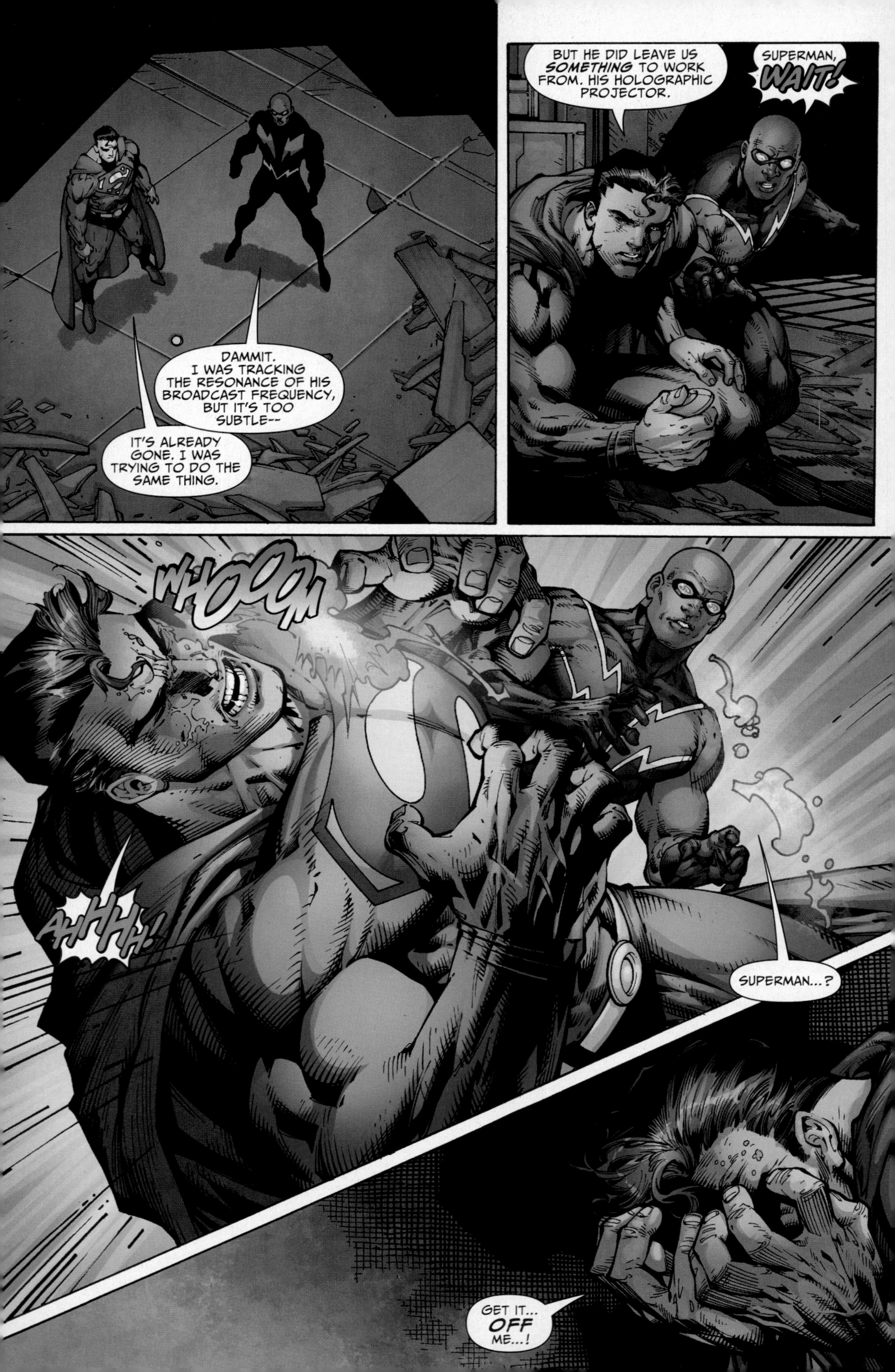
DAMMIT. I WAS TRACKING THE RESONANCE OF HIS BROADCAST FREQUENCY, BUT IT'S TOO SUBTLE--
IT'S ALREADY GONE. I WAS TRYING TO DO THE SAME THING.
BUT HE DID LEAVE US *SOMETHING* TO WORK FROM. HIS HOLOGRAPHIC PROJECTOR.
SUPERMAN, **WAIT!**
WHOOOM
AHHHH!
SUPERMAN...?
GET IT... **OFF** ME...!

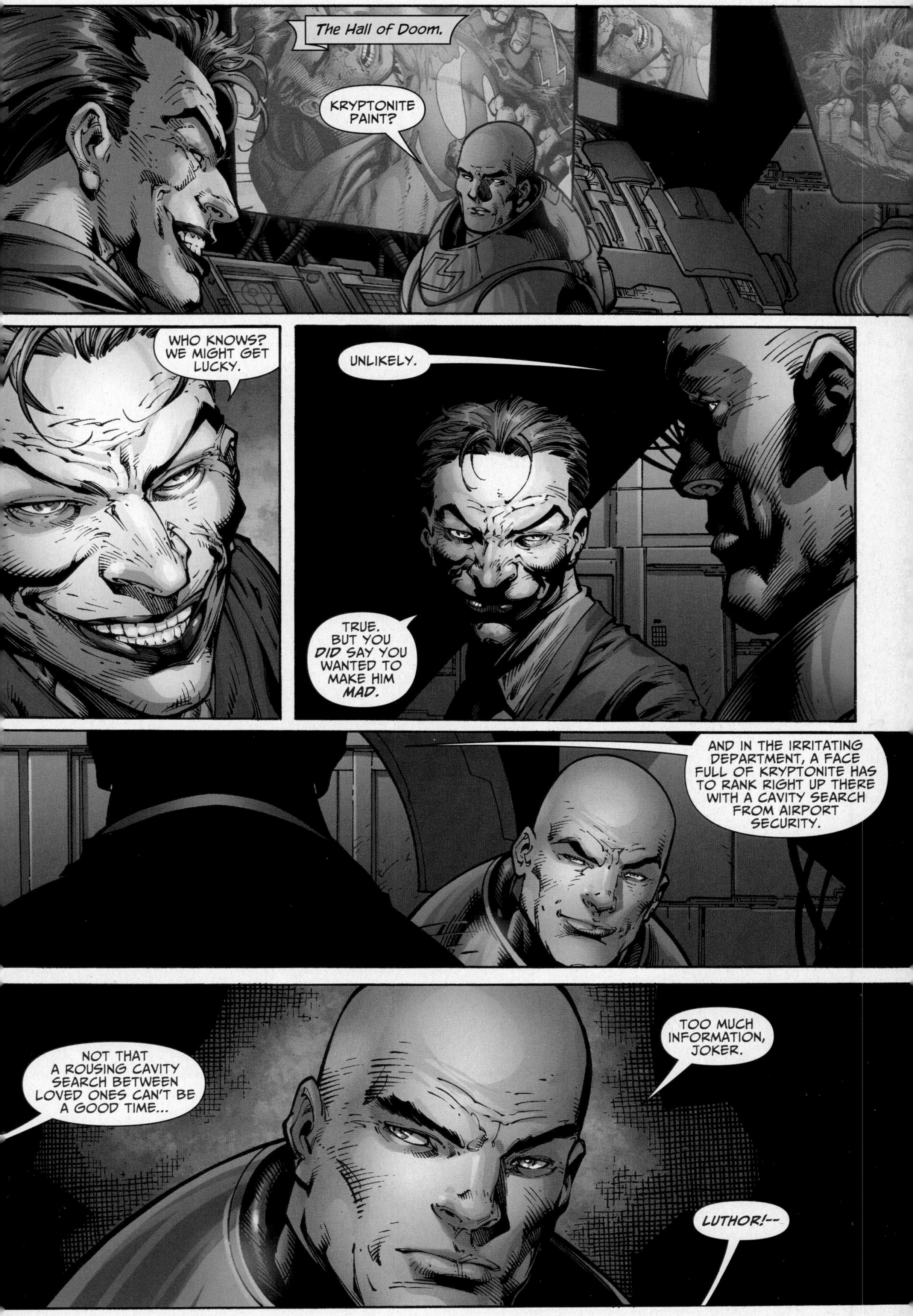
The Hall of Doom.
KRYPTONITE PAINT?
WHO KNOWS? WE MIGHT GET LUCKY.
UNLIKELY.
TRUE. BUT YOU *DID* SAY YOU WANTED TO MAKE HIM *MAD.*
AND IN THE IRRITATING DEPARTMENT, A FACE FULL OF KRYPTONITE HAS TO RANK RIGHT UP THERE WITH A CAVITY SEARCH FROM AIRPORT SECURITY.
NOT THAT A ROUSING CAVITY SEARCH BETWEEN LOVED ONES CAN'T BE A GOOD TIME...
TOO MUCH INFORMATION, JOKER.
LUTHOR!--

--I NEED SOME *HELP!* GRODD'S ABOUT TO *KILL* GEO-FORCE!

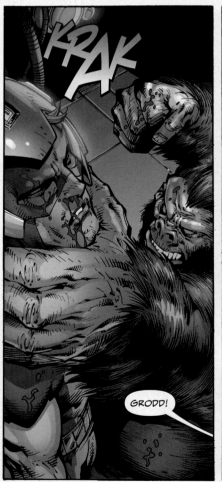

KRAK

GRODD!

THAT'S *ENOUGH.* WE HAVE AN AGREEMENT.

HE'S FUN TO HIT.

BE THAT AS IT MAY.

TORTURE IS FINE, BUT NO ONE IS TO BE KILLED UNTIL AFTER SUPERMAN IS CAPTURED.

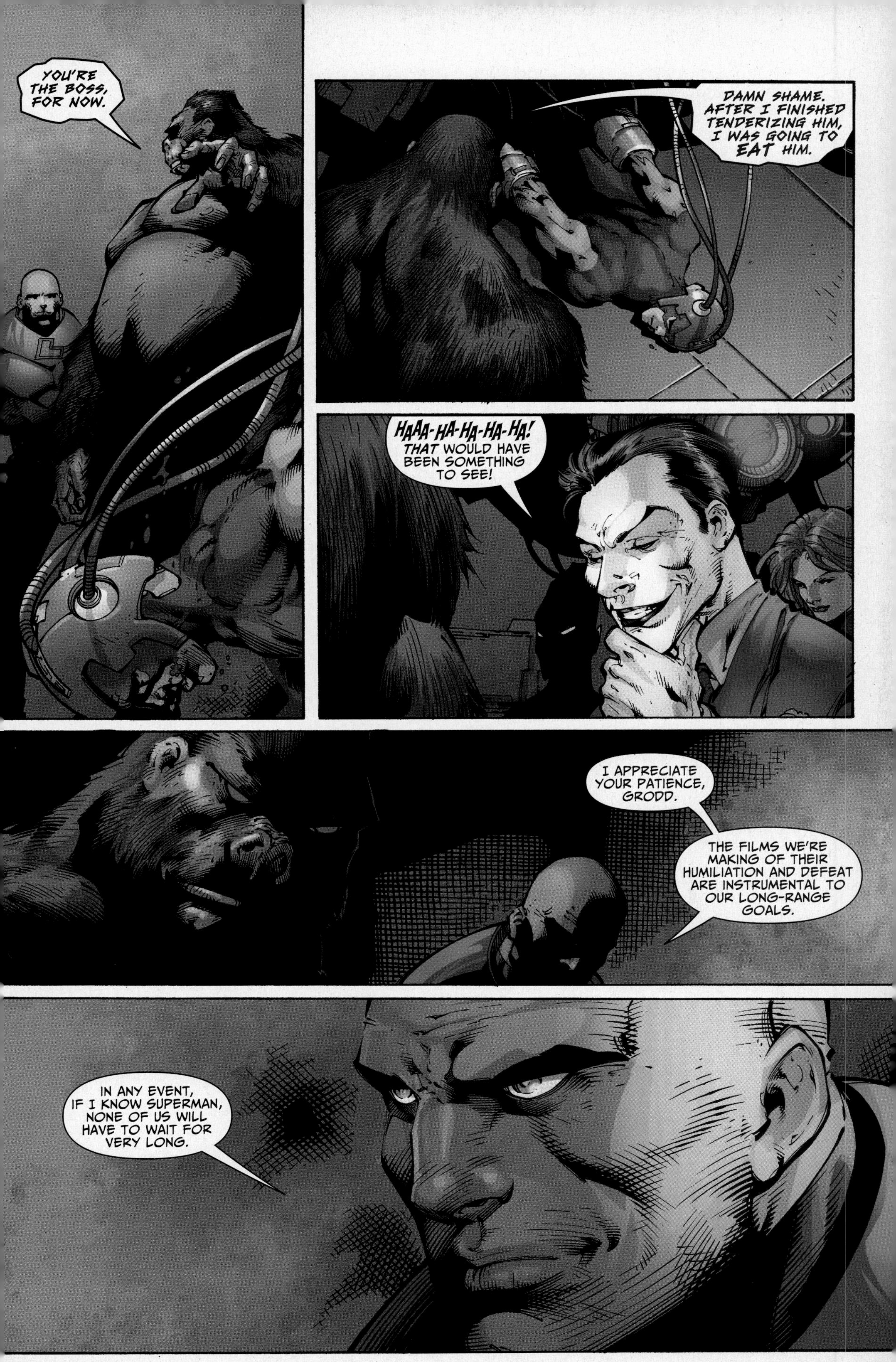
YOU'RE THE BOSS, FOR NOW.
DAMN SHAME. AFTER I FINISHED TENDERIZING HIM, I WAS GOING TO EAT HIM.
HAAA-HA-HA-HA-HA! THAT WOULD HAVE BEEN SOMETHING TO SEE!
I APPRECIATE YOUR PATIENCE, GRODD.
THE FILMS WE'RE MAKING OF THEIR HUMILIATION AND DEFEAT ARE INSTRUMENTAL TO OUR LONG-RANGE GOALS.
IN ANY EVENT, IF I KNOW SUPERMAN, NONE OF US WILL HAVE TO WAIT FOR VERY LONG.

JUSTICE LEAGUE of AMERICA

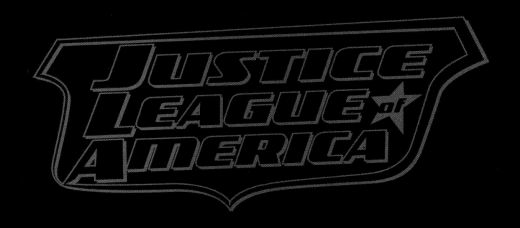

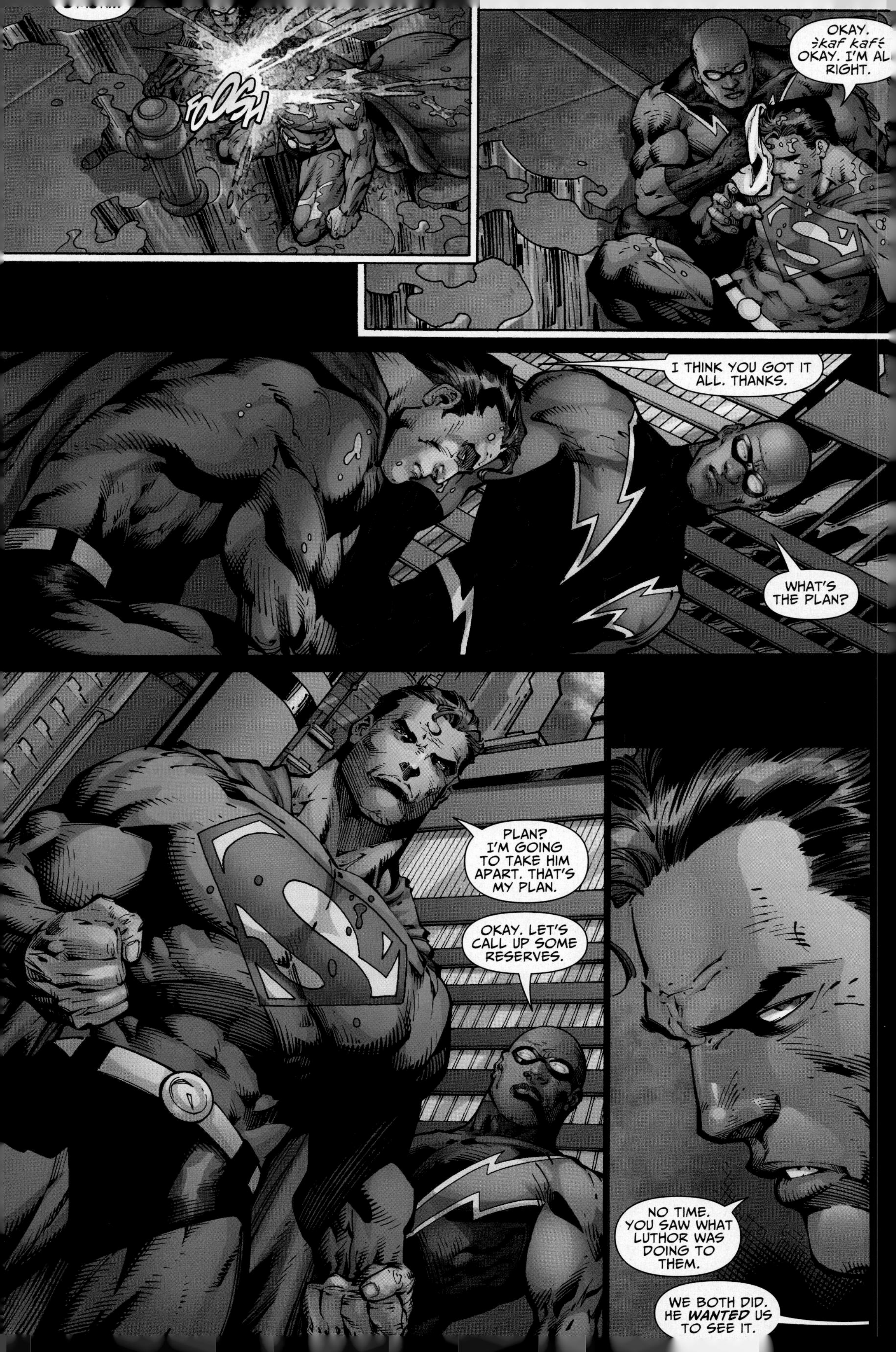
FOOSH
OKAY. ≈kaf kaf≈ OKAY. I'M AL RIGHT.
I THINK YOU GOT IT ALL. THANKS.
WHAT'S THE PLAN?
PLAN? I'M GOING TO TAKE HIM APART. THAT'S MY PLAN.
OKAY. LET'S CALL UP SOME RESERVES.
NO TIME. YOU SAW WHAT LUTHOR WAS DOING TO THEM.
WE BOTH DID. HE *WANTED* US TO SEE IT.

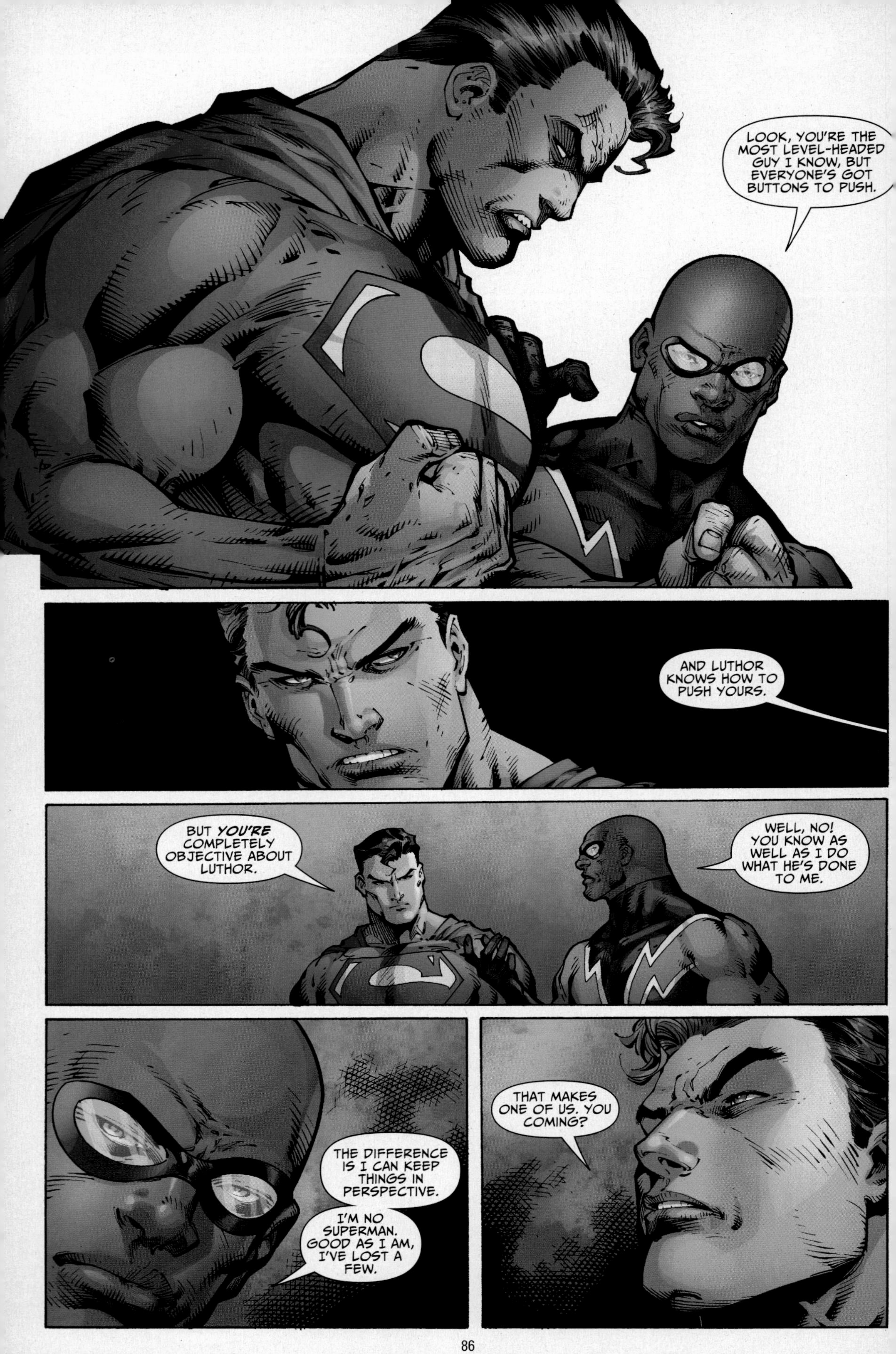
LOOK, YOU'RE THE MOST LEVEL-HEADED GUY I KNOW, BUT EVERYONE'S GOT BUTTONS TO PUSH.
AND LUTHOR KNOWS HOW TO PUSH YOURS.
BUT *YOU'RE* COMPLETELY OBJECTIVE ABOUT LUTHOR.
WELL, NO! YOU KNOW AS WELL AS I DO WHAT HE'S DONE TO ME.
THE DIFFERENCE IS I CAN KEEP THINGS IN PERSPECTIVE.
I'M NO SUPERMAN. GOOD AS I AM, I'VE LOST A FEW.
THAT MAKES ONE OF US. YOU COMING?

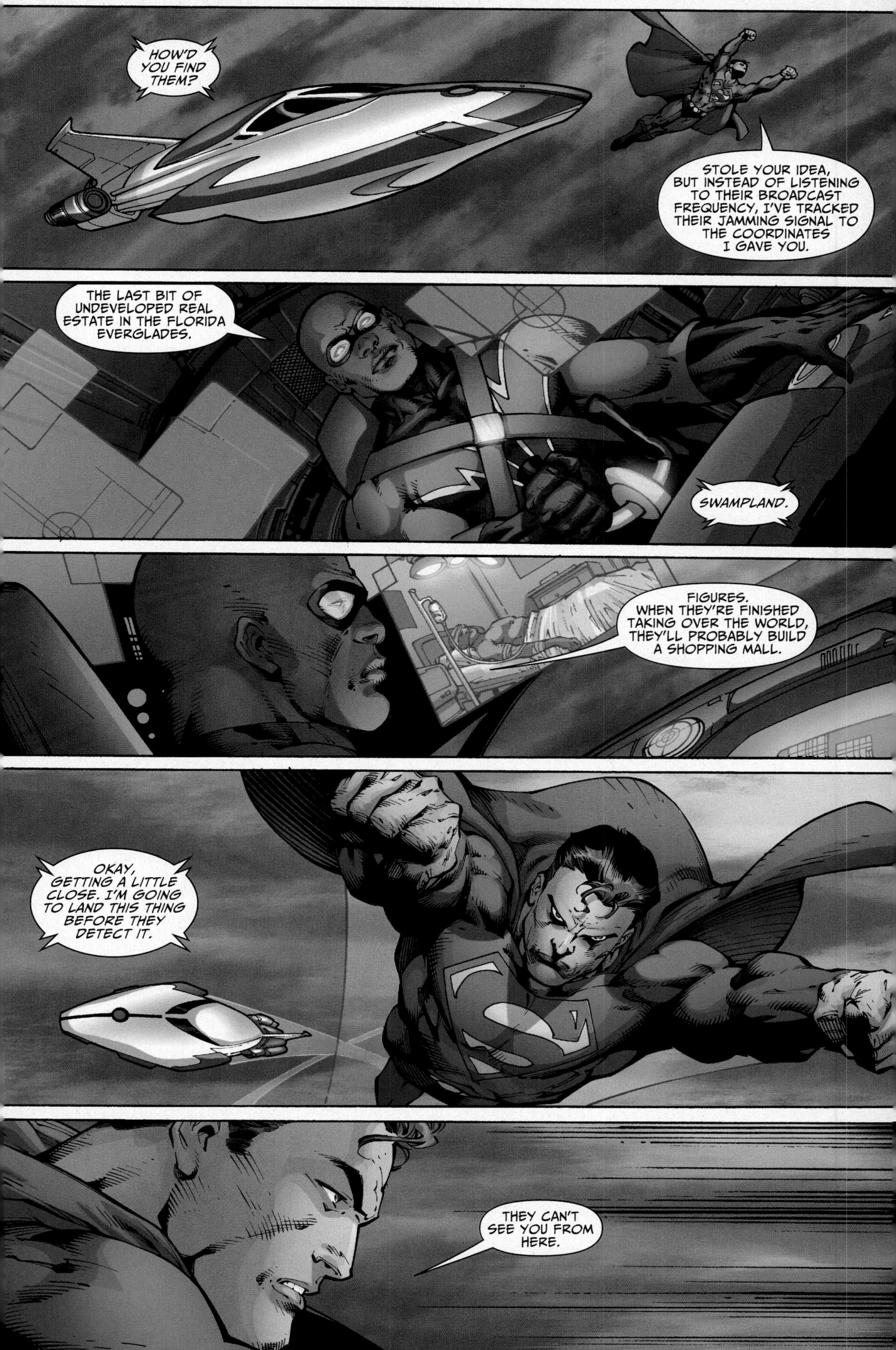
HOW'D YOU FIND THEM?
STOLE YOUR IDEA, BUT INSTEAD OF LISTENING TO THEIR BROADCAST FREQUENCY, I'VE TRACKED THEIR JAMMING SIGNAL TO THE COORDINATES I GAVE YOU.
THE LAST BIT OF UNDEVELOPED REAL ESTATE IN THE FLORIDA EVERGLADES.
SWAMPLAND.
FIGURES. WHEN THEY'RE FINISHED TAKING OVER THE WORLD, THEY'LL PROBABLY BUILD A SHOPPING MALL.
OKAY, GETTING A LITTLE CLOSE. I'M GOING TO LAND THIS THING BEFORE THEY DETECT IT.
THEY CAN'T SEE YOU FROM HERE.

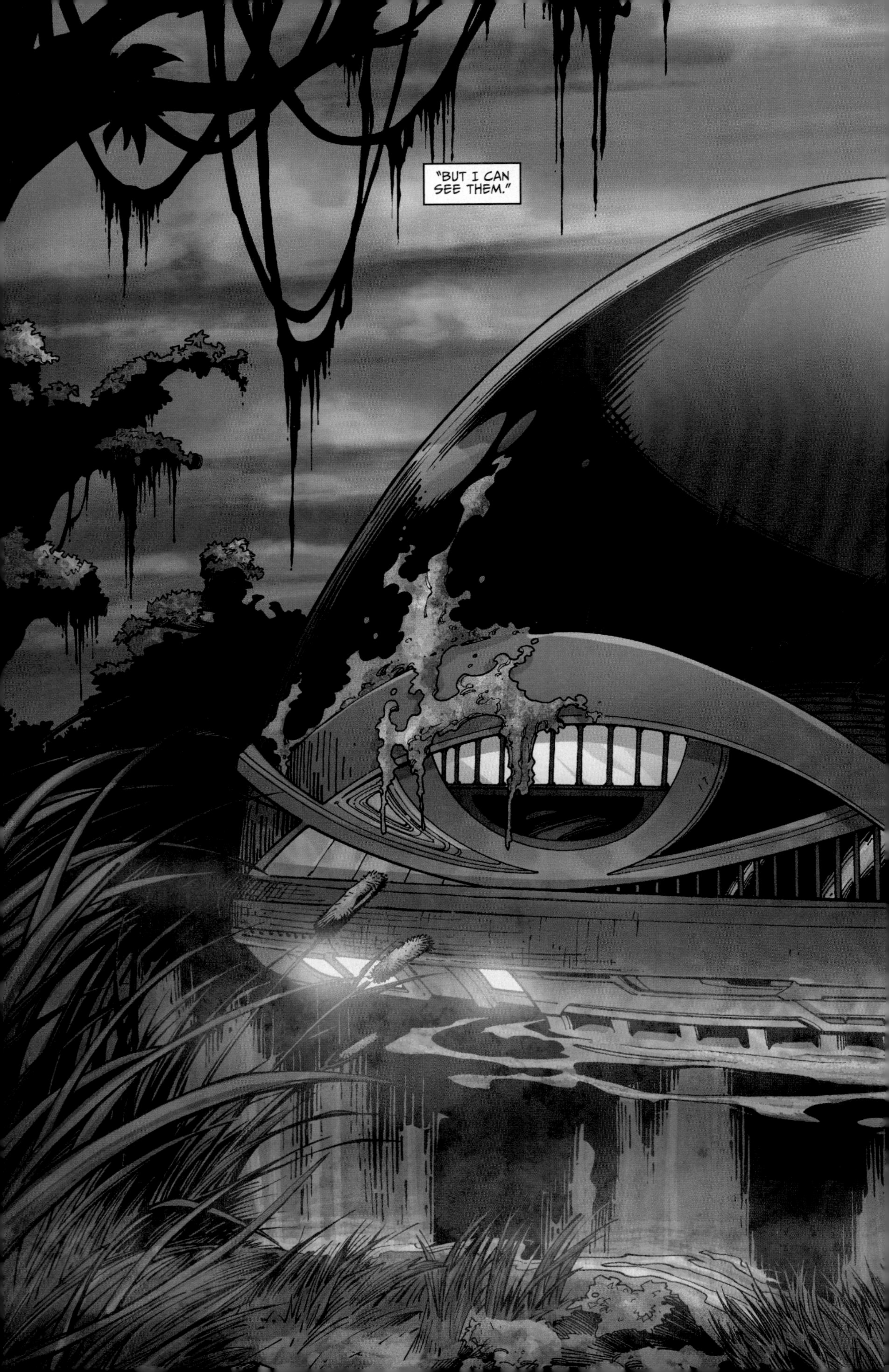
"BUT I CAN SEE THEM."

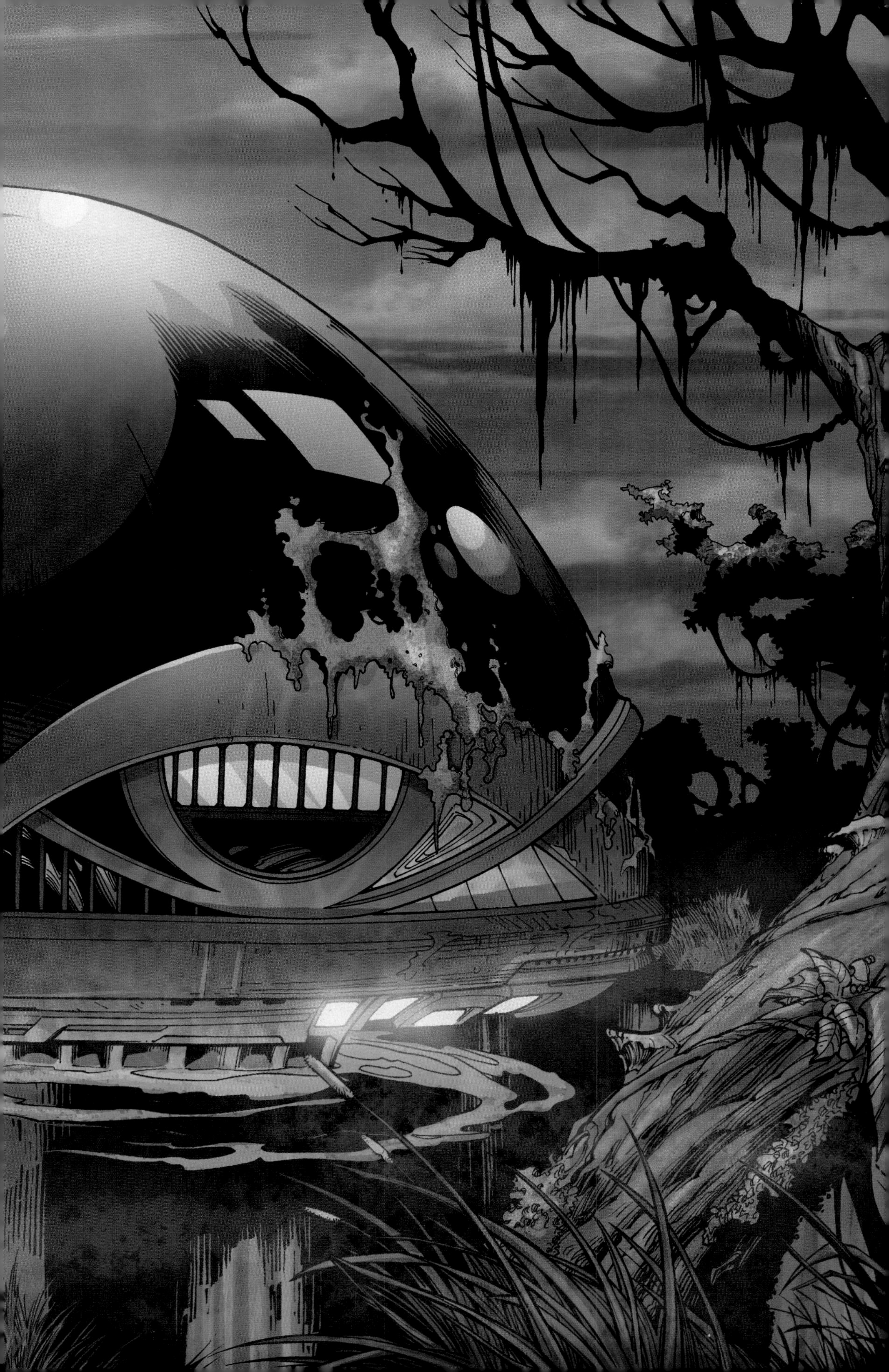

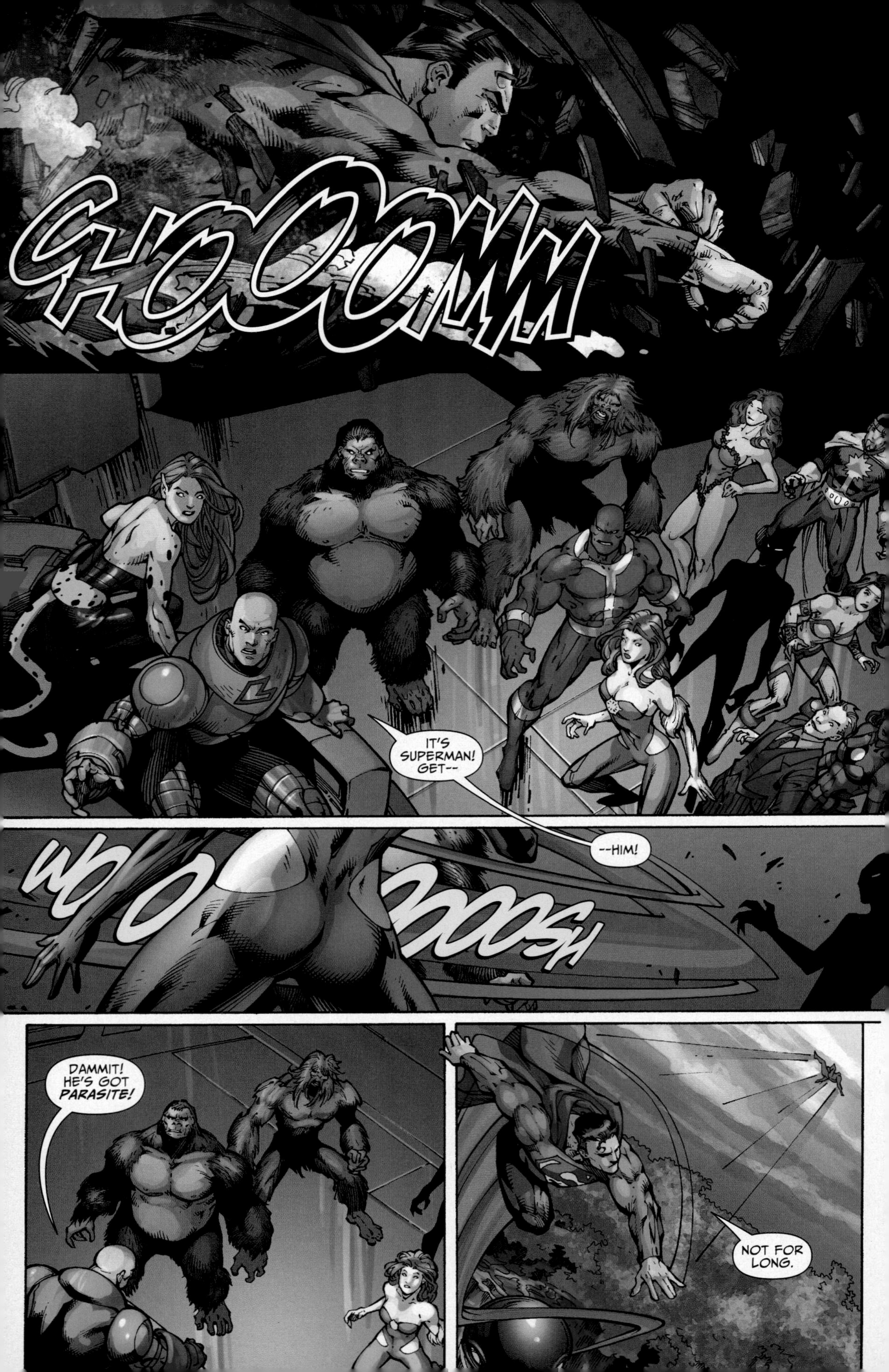
GHOOMM
IT'S SUPERMAN! GET--
--HIM!
WOOOOOSH
DAMMIT! HE'S GOT *PARASITE!*
NOT FOR LONG.

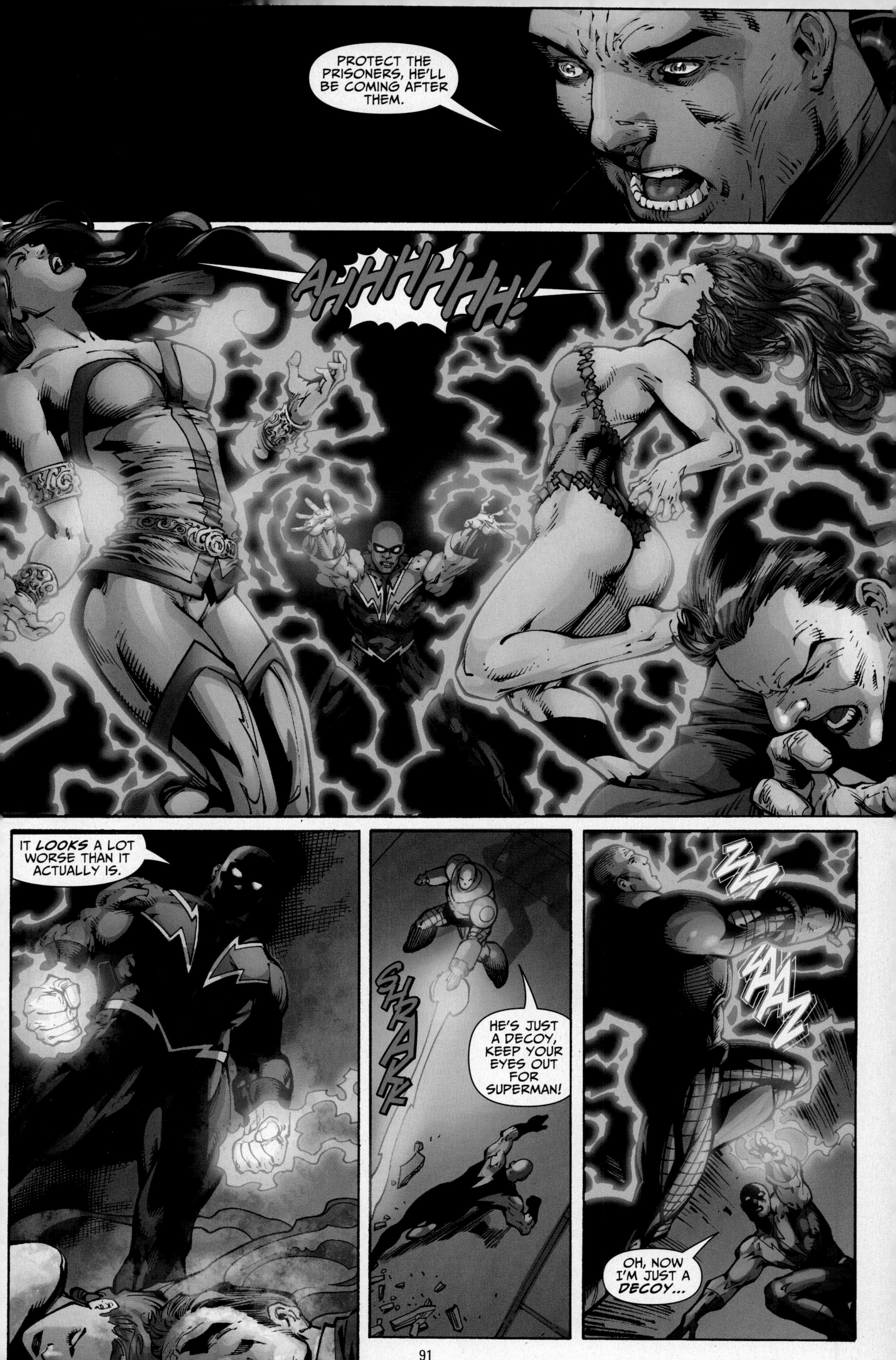
PROTECT THE PRISONERS, HE'LL BE COMING AFTER THEM.
AHHHHHH!
IT LOOKS A LOT WORSE THAN IT ACTUALLY IS.
SHRAKK
HE'S JUST A DECOY, KEEP YOUR EYES OUT FOR SUPERMAN!
ZZZ
KZAAM
OH, NOW I'M JUST A DECOY...

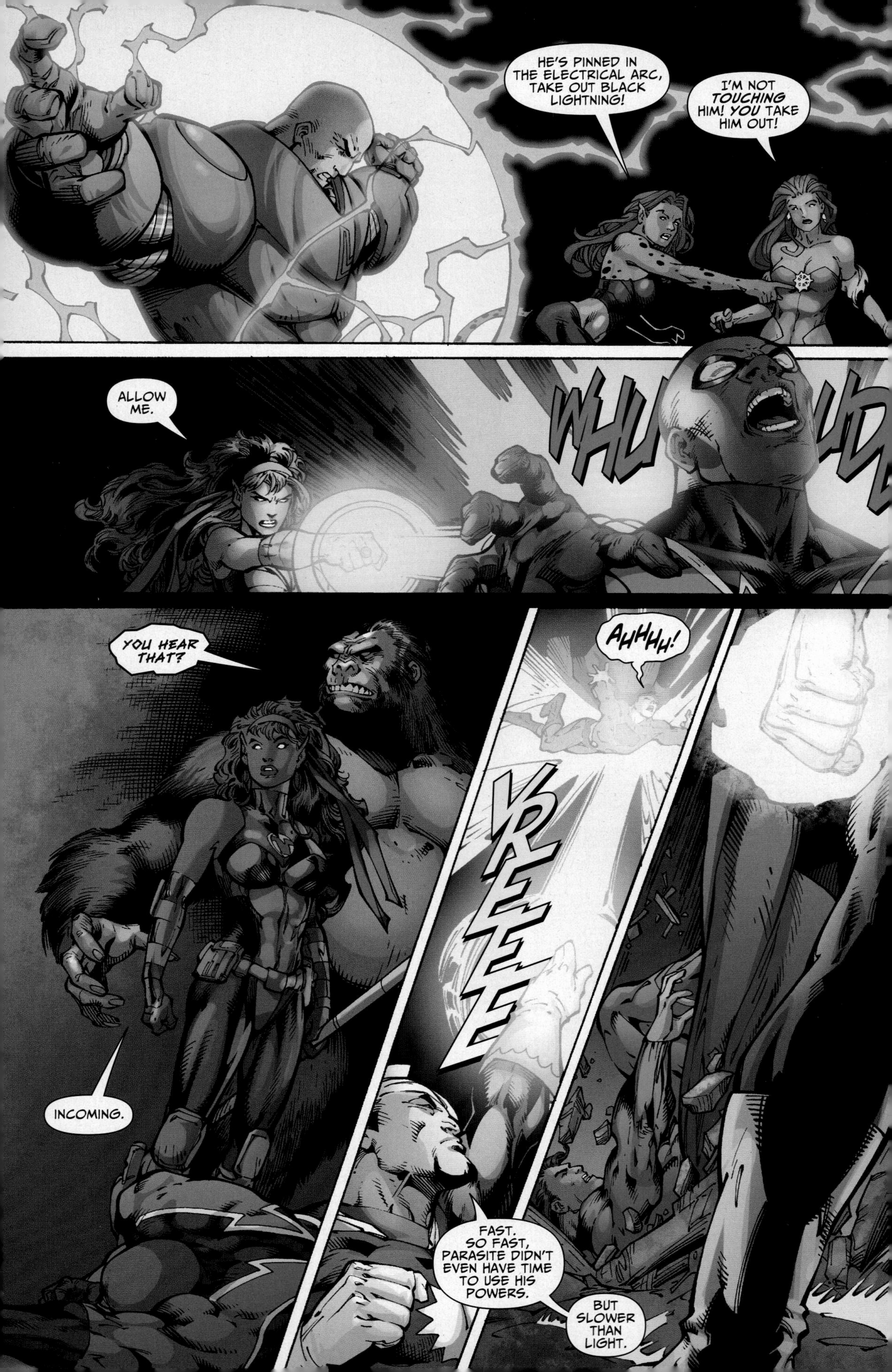

HE'S PINNED IN THE ELECTRICAL ARC, TAKE OUT BLACK LIGHTNING!
I'M NOT *TOUCHING* HIM! *YOU* TAKE HIM OUT!
ALLOW ME.
WHUDD
YOU HEAR THAT?
INCOMING.
AHHHH!
VREEEEE
FAST. SO FAST, PARASITE DIDN'T EVEN HAVE TIME TO USE HIS POWERS.
BUT SLOWER THAN LIGHT.

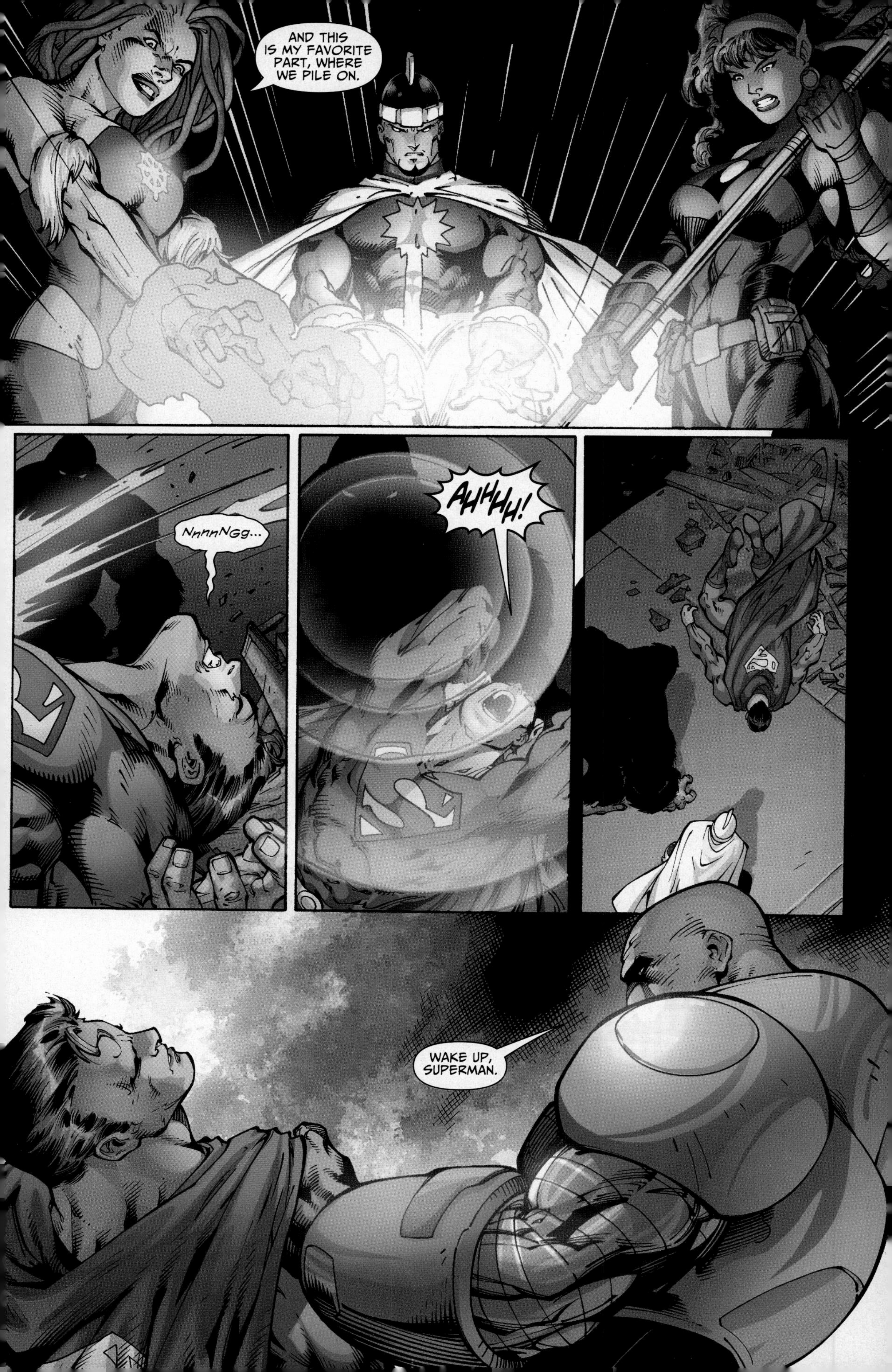
AND THIS IS MY FAVORITE PART, WHERE WE PILE ON.
NnnnNGg...
AHHHH!
WAKE UP, SUPERMAN.

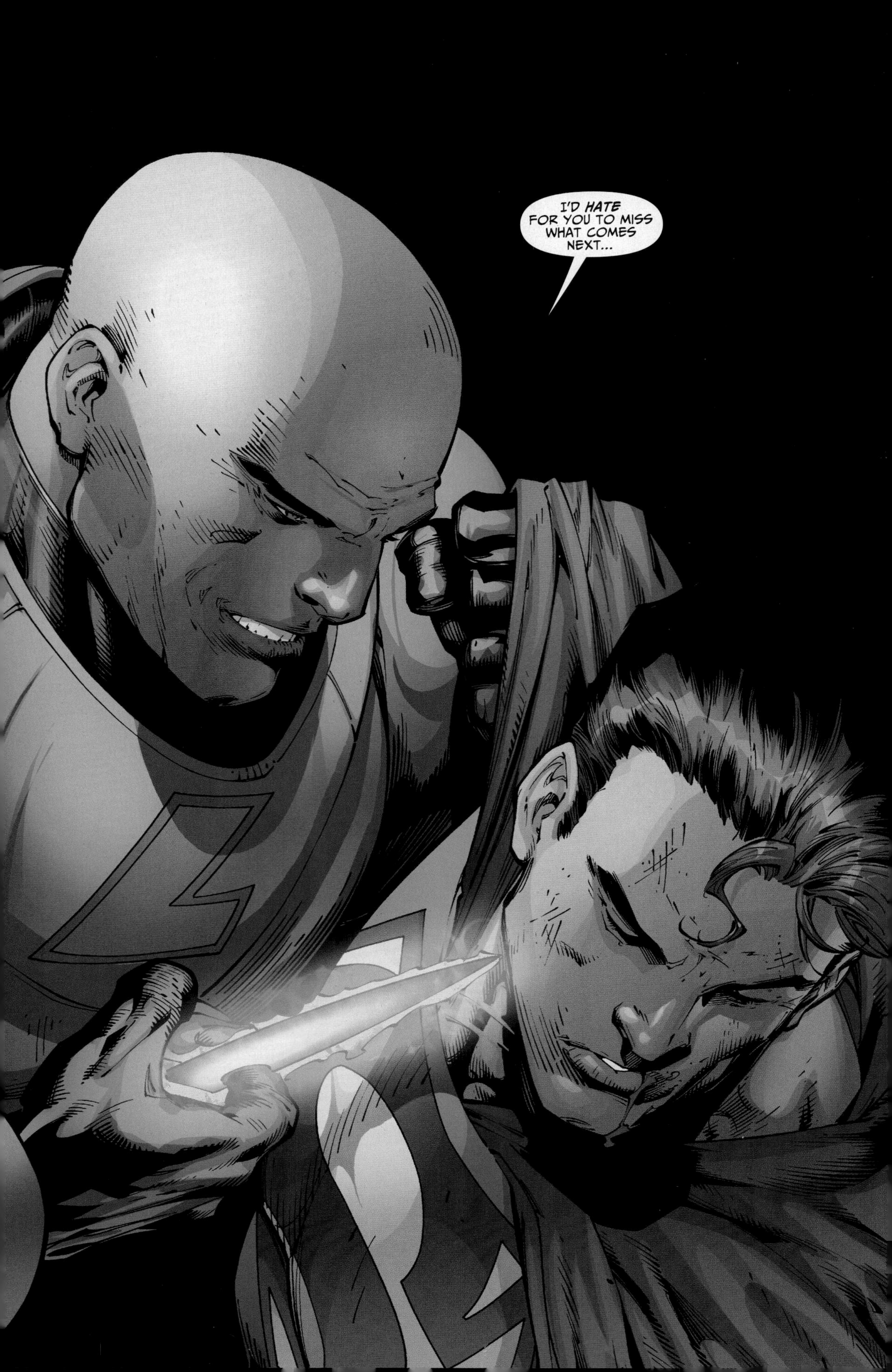
I'D HATE FOR YOU TO MISS WHAT COMES NEXT...

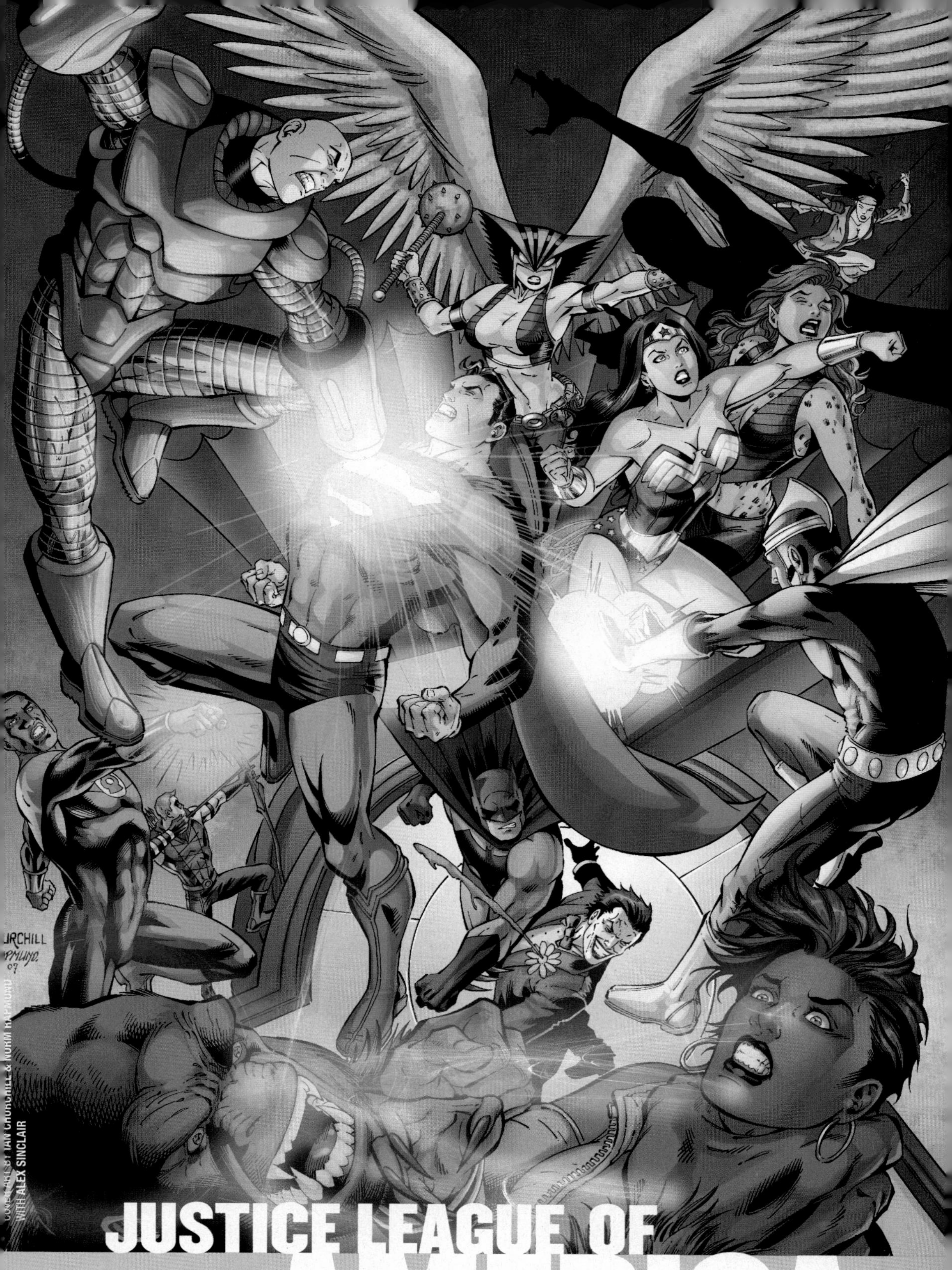

COVER ART BY IAN CHURCHILL & NORM RAPMUND WITH ALEX SINCLAIR

JUSTICE LEAGUE OF AMERICA

CHAPTER FOUR

"I have to admit. This *looks* pretty bad."

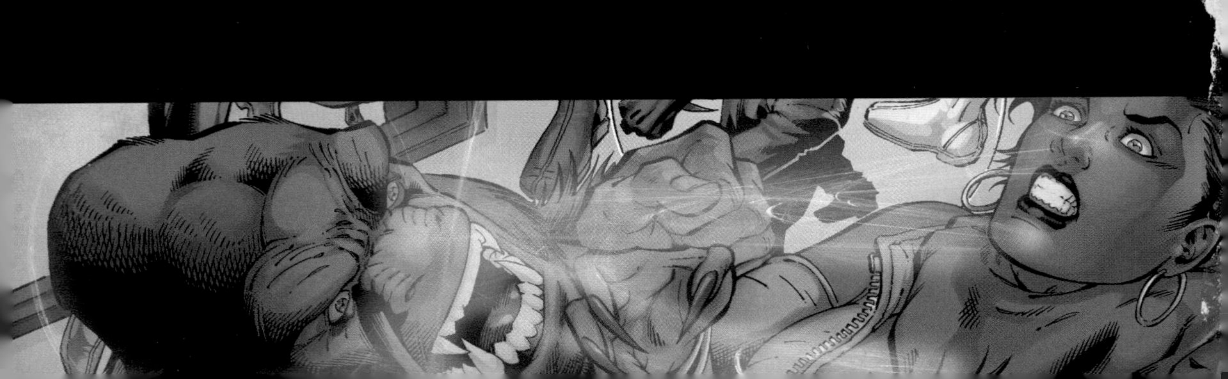

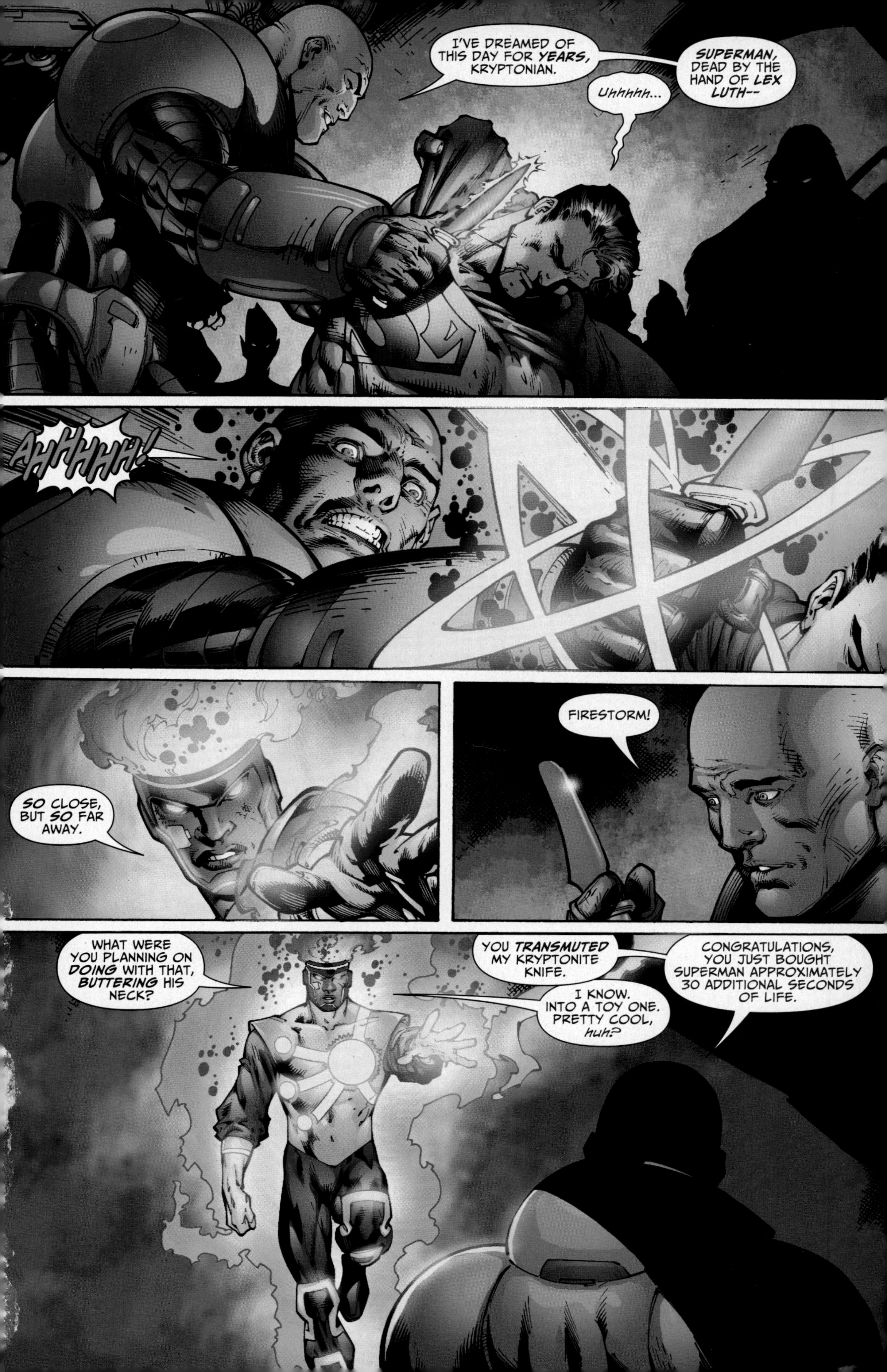

I'VE DREAMED OF THIS DAY FOR YEARS, KRYPTONIAN.
Uhhhhh...
SUPERMAN, DEAD BY THE HAND OF LEX LUTH--
AHHHHH!
SO CLOSE, BUT SO FAR AWAY.
FIRESTORM!
WHAT WERE YOU PLANNING ON DOING WITH THAT, BUTTERING HIS NECK?
YOU TRANSMUTED MY KRYPTONITE KNIFE.
I KNOW. INTO A TOY ONE. PRETTY COOL, huh?
CONGRATULATIONS, YOU JUST BOUGHT SUPERMAN APPROXIMATELY 30 ADDITIONAL SECONDS OF LIFE.

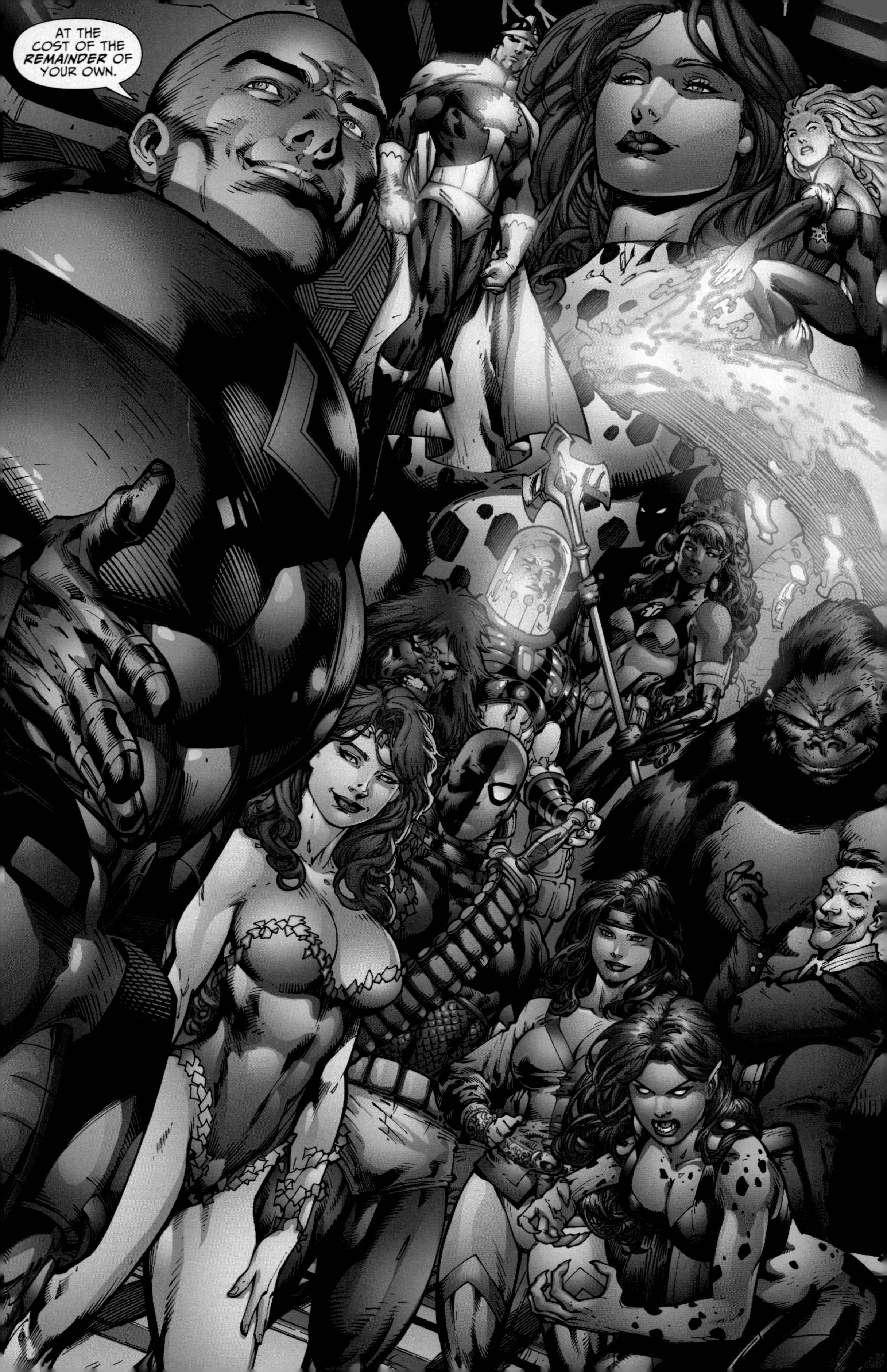
AT THE COST OF THE *REMAINDER* OF YOUR OWN.

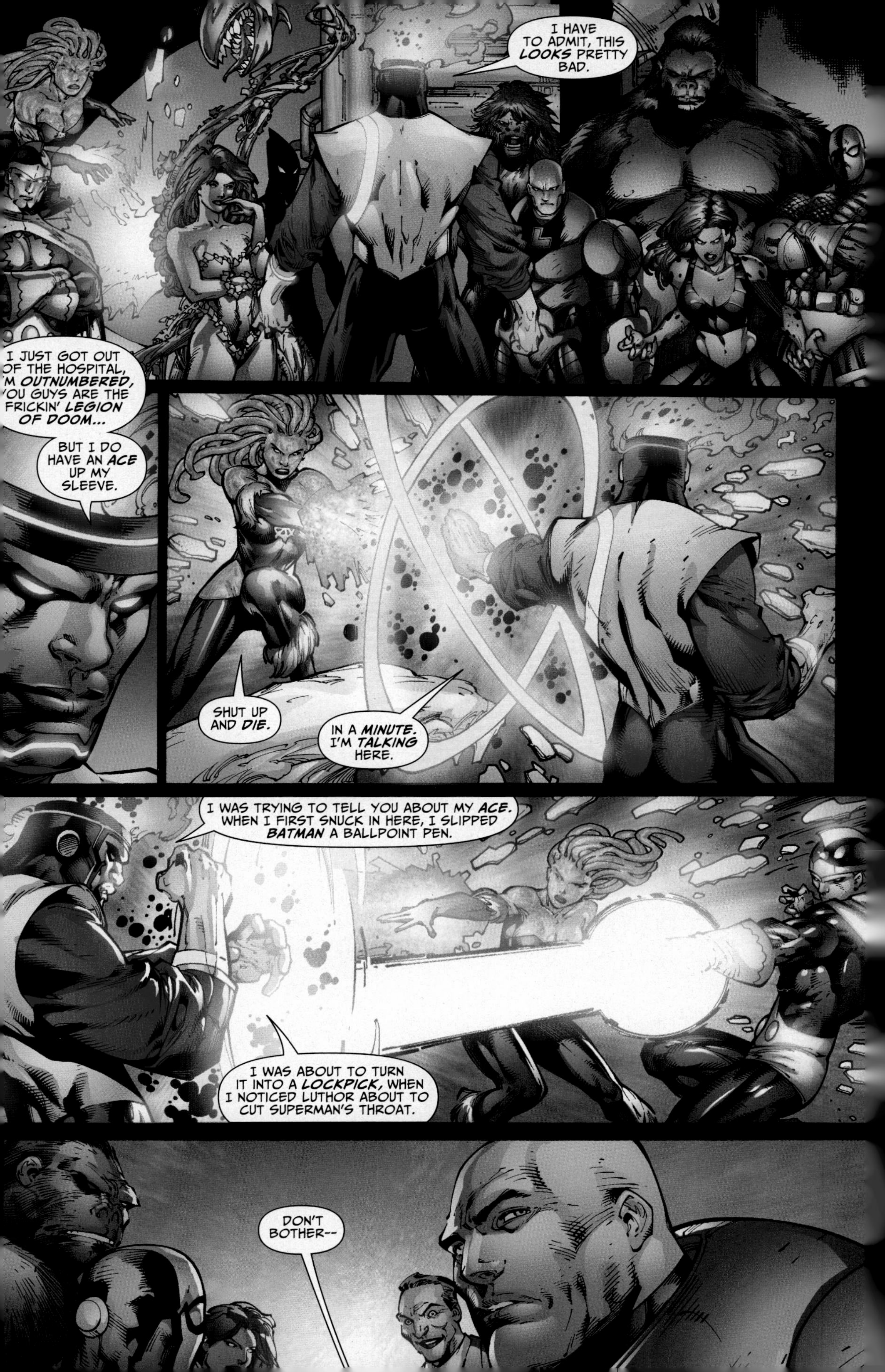
I HAVE TO ADMIT, THIS LOOKS PRETTY BAD.
I JUST GOT OUT OF THE HOSPITAL, I'M OUTNUMBERED, YOU GUYS ARE THE FRICKIN' LEGION OF DOOM...
BUT I DO HAVE AN ACE UP MY SLEEVE.
SHUT UP AND DIE.
IN A MINUTE. I'M TALKING HERE.
I WAS TRYING TO TELL YOU ABOUT MY ACE. WHEN I FIRST SNUCK IN HERE, I SLIPPED BATMAN A BALLPOINT PEN.
I WAS ABOUT TO TURN IT INTO A LOCKPICK, WHEN I NOTICED LUTHOR ABOUT TO CUT SUPERMAN'S THROAT.
DON'T BOTHER--

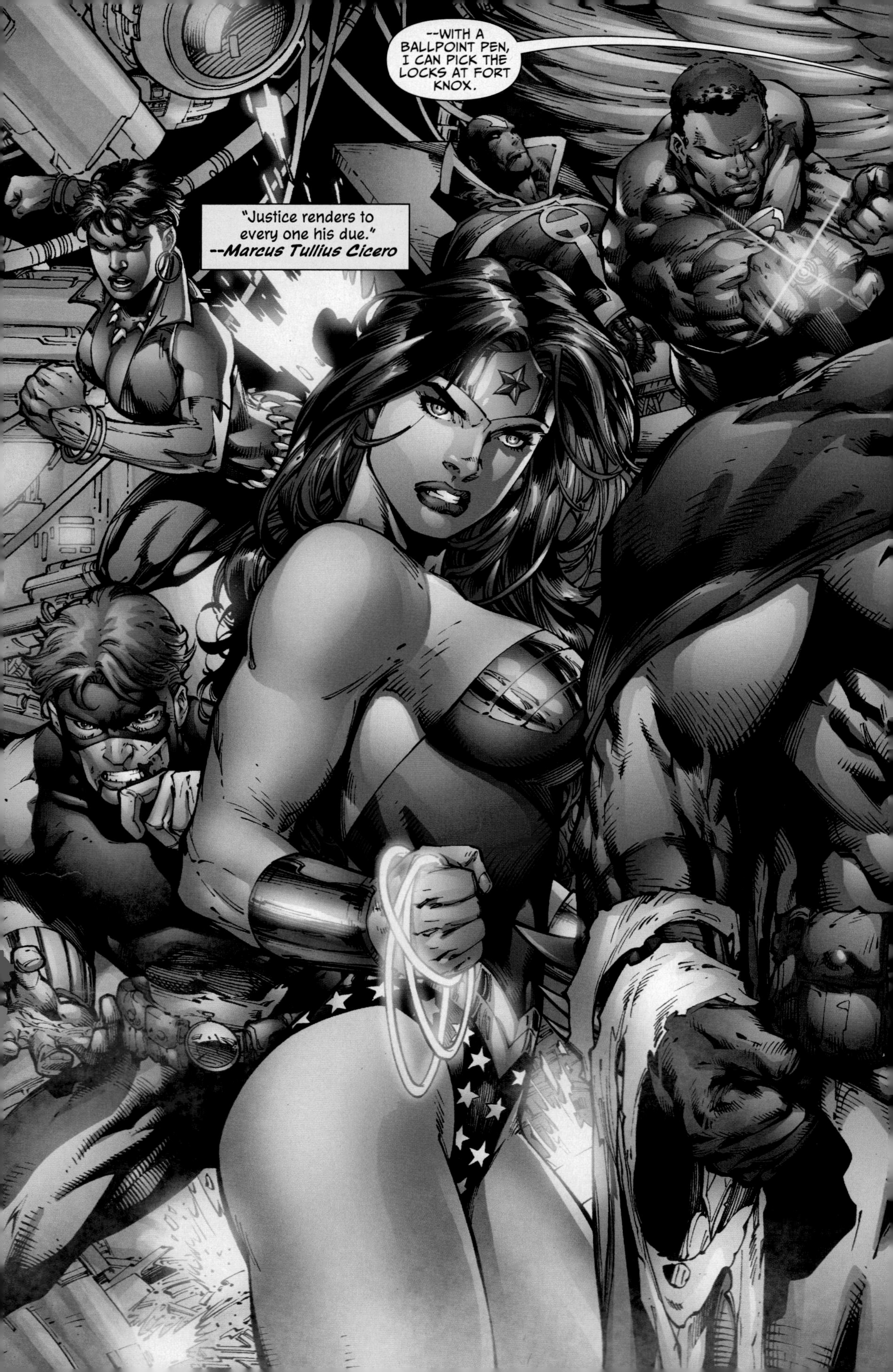
--WITH A BALLPOINT PEN, I CAN PICK THE LOCKS AT FORT KNOX.
"Justice renders to every one his due."
--Marcus Tullius Cicero

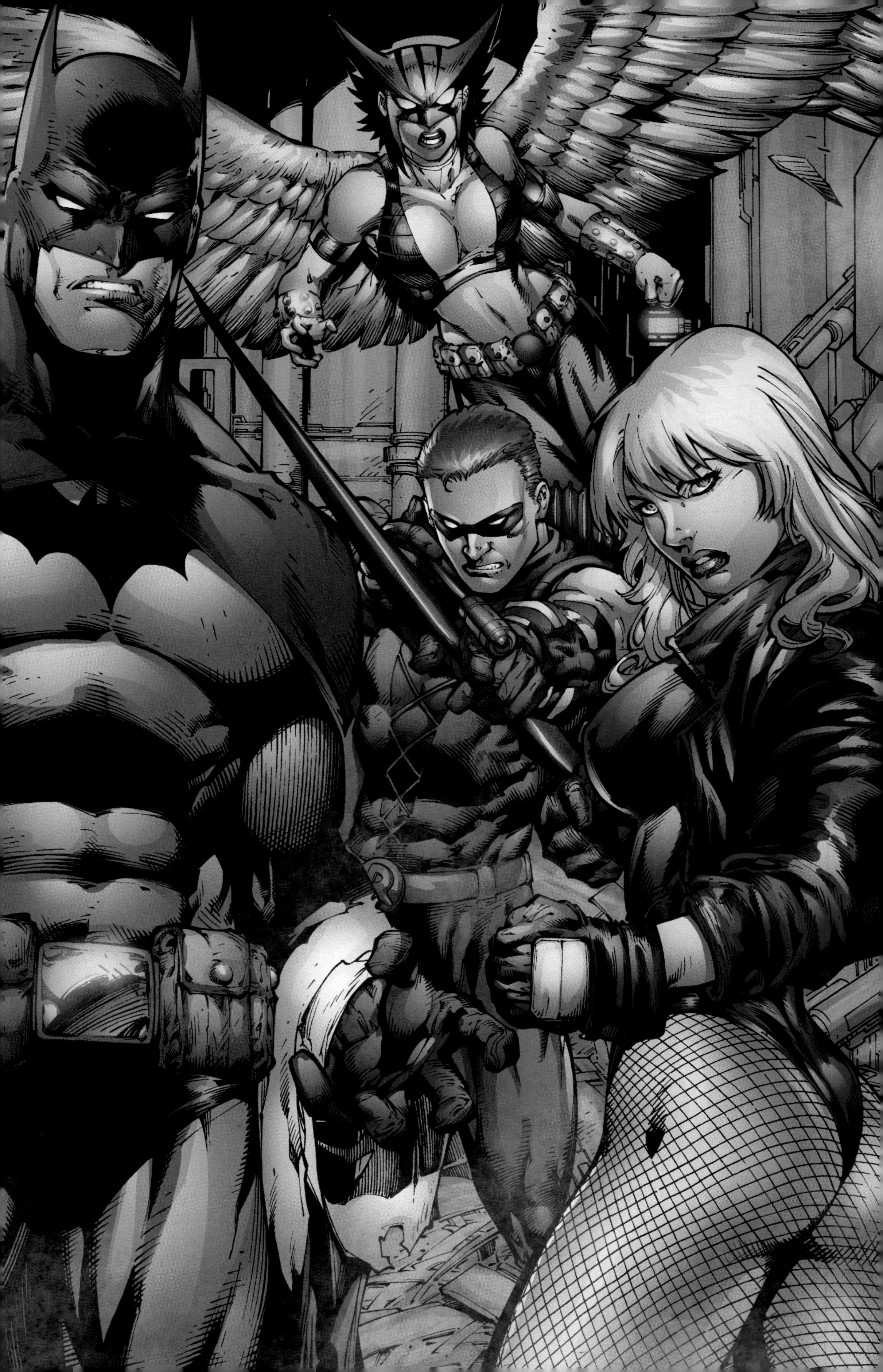

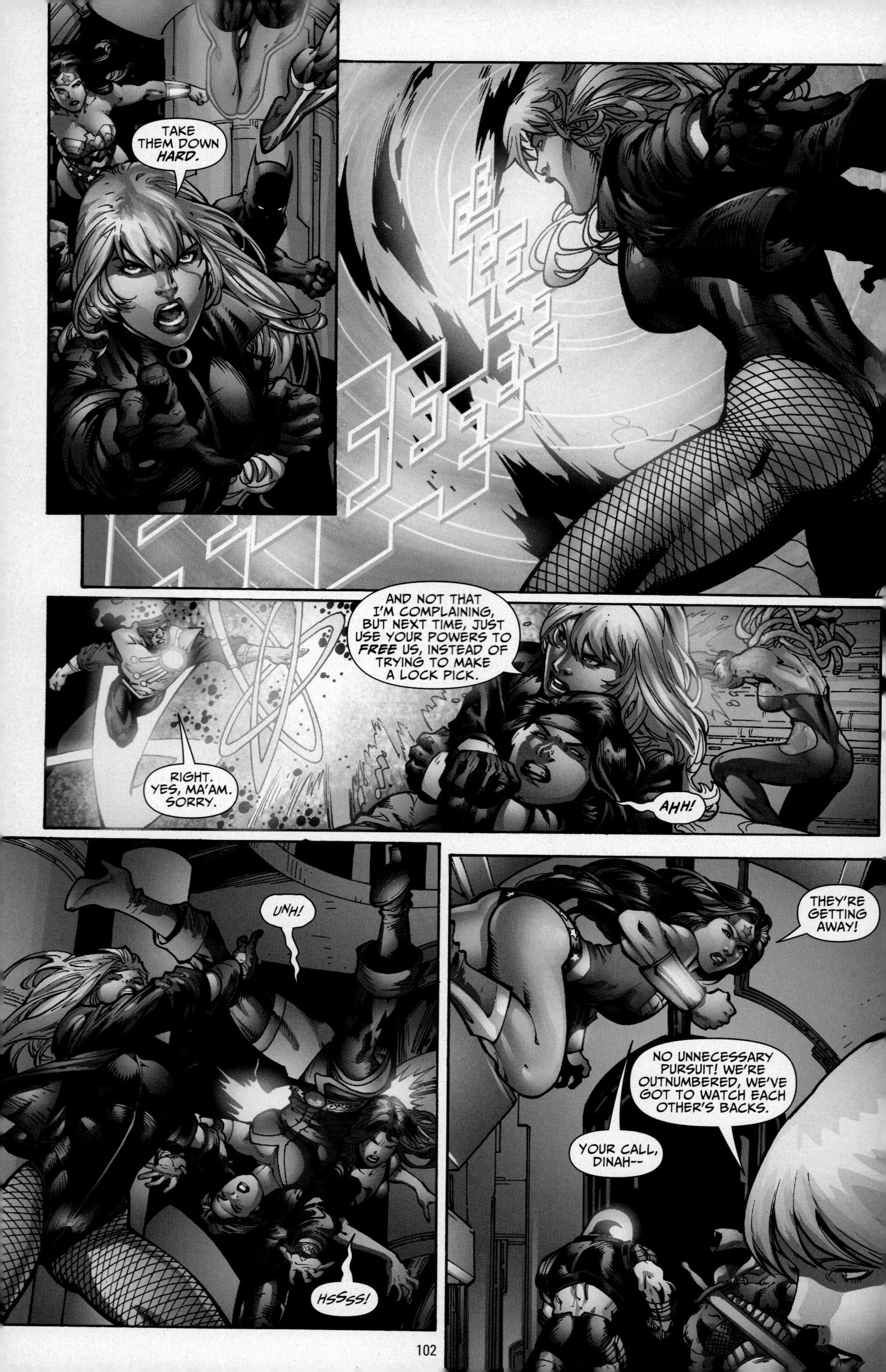
TAKE THEM DOWN HARD.
AND NOT THAT I'M COMPLAINING, BUT NEXT TIME, JUST USE YOUR POWERS TO FREE US, INSTEAD OF TRYING TO MAKE A LOCK PICK.
RIGHT. YES, MA'AM. SORRY.
AHH!
UNH!
HSSSS!
THEY'RE GETTING AWAY!
NO UNNECESSARY PURSUIT! WE'RE OUTNUMBERED, WE'VE GOT TO WATCH EACH OTHER'S BACKS.
YOUR CALL, DINAH--

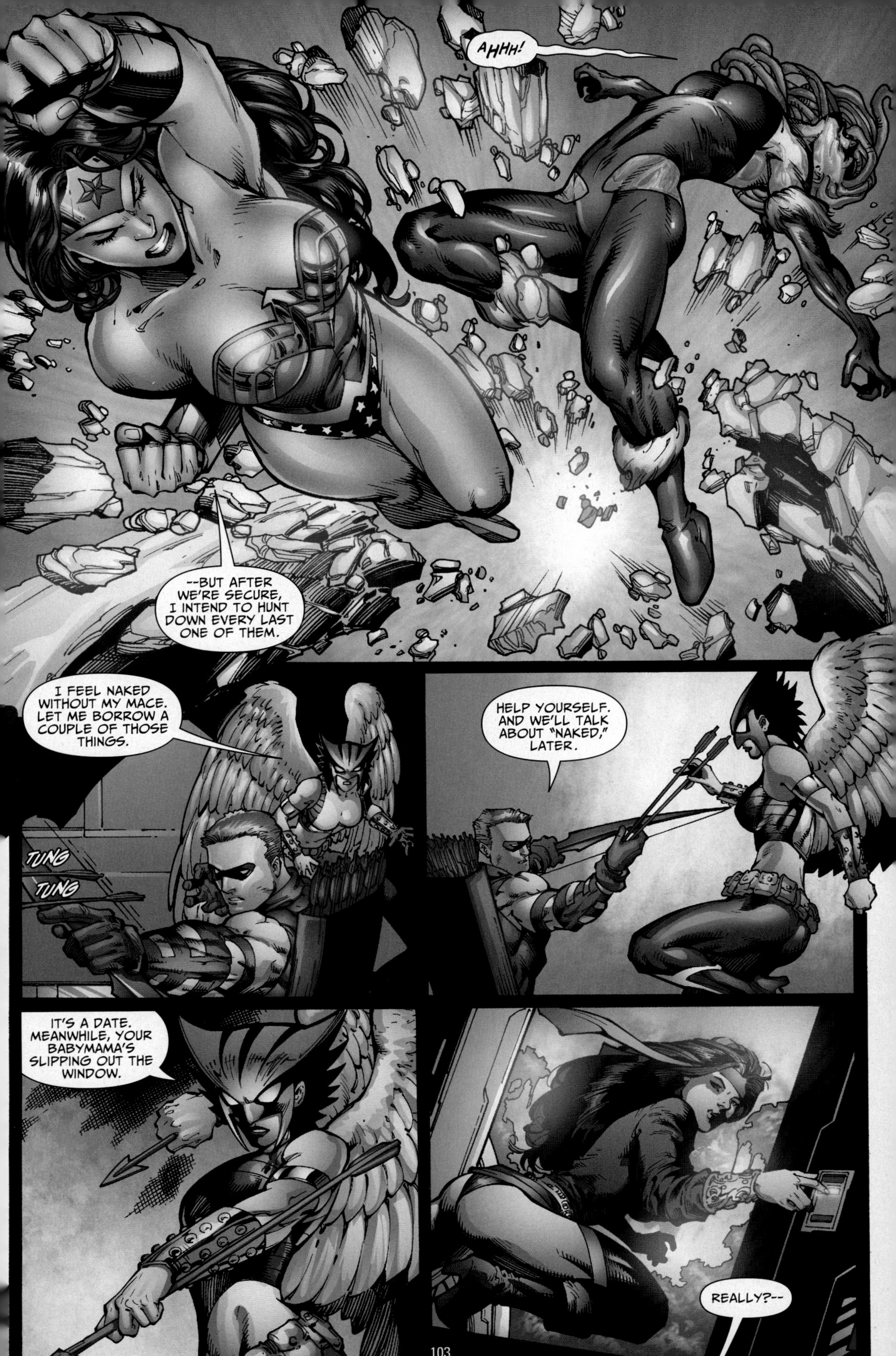
AHHH!
--BUT AFTER WE'RE SECURE, I INTEND TO HUNT DOWN EVERY LAST ONE OF THEM.
I FEEL NAKED WITHOUT MY MACE. LET ME BORROW A COUPLE OF THOSE THINGS.
TUNG
TUNG
HELP YOURSELF. AND WE'LL TALK ABOUT "NAKED," LATER.
IT'S A DATE. MEANWHILE, YOUR BABYMAMA'S SLIPPING OUT THE WINDOW.
REALLY?--

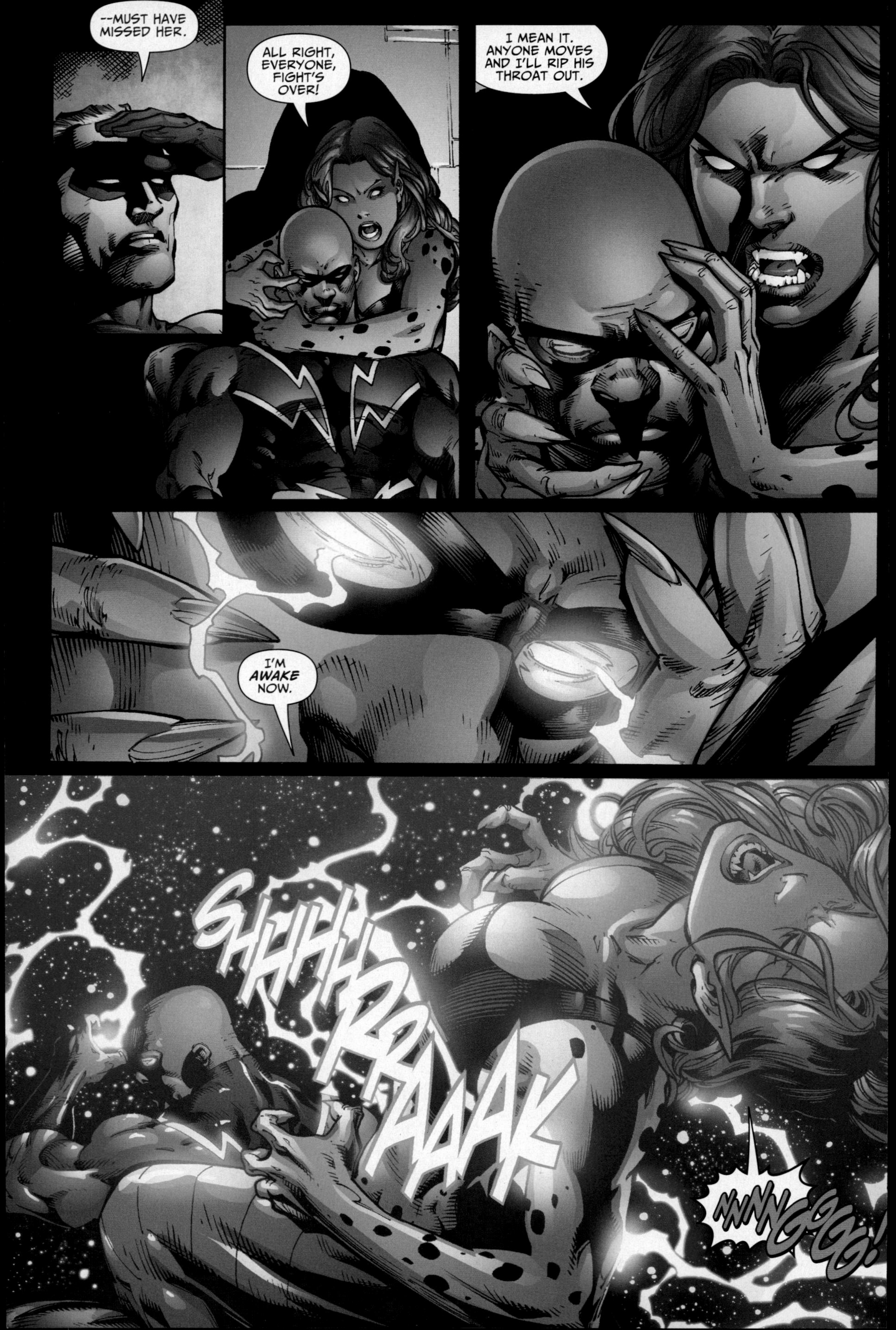
--MUST HAVE MISSED HER.
ALL RIGHT, EVERYONE, FIGHT'S OVER!
I MEAN IT. ANYONE MOVES AND I'LL RIP HIS THROAT OUT.
I'M AWAKE NOW.
SHHHRRAAAK
NNNNGGGG!

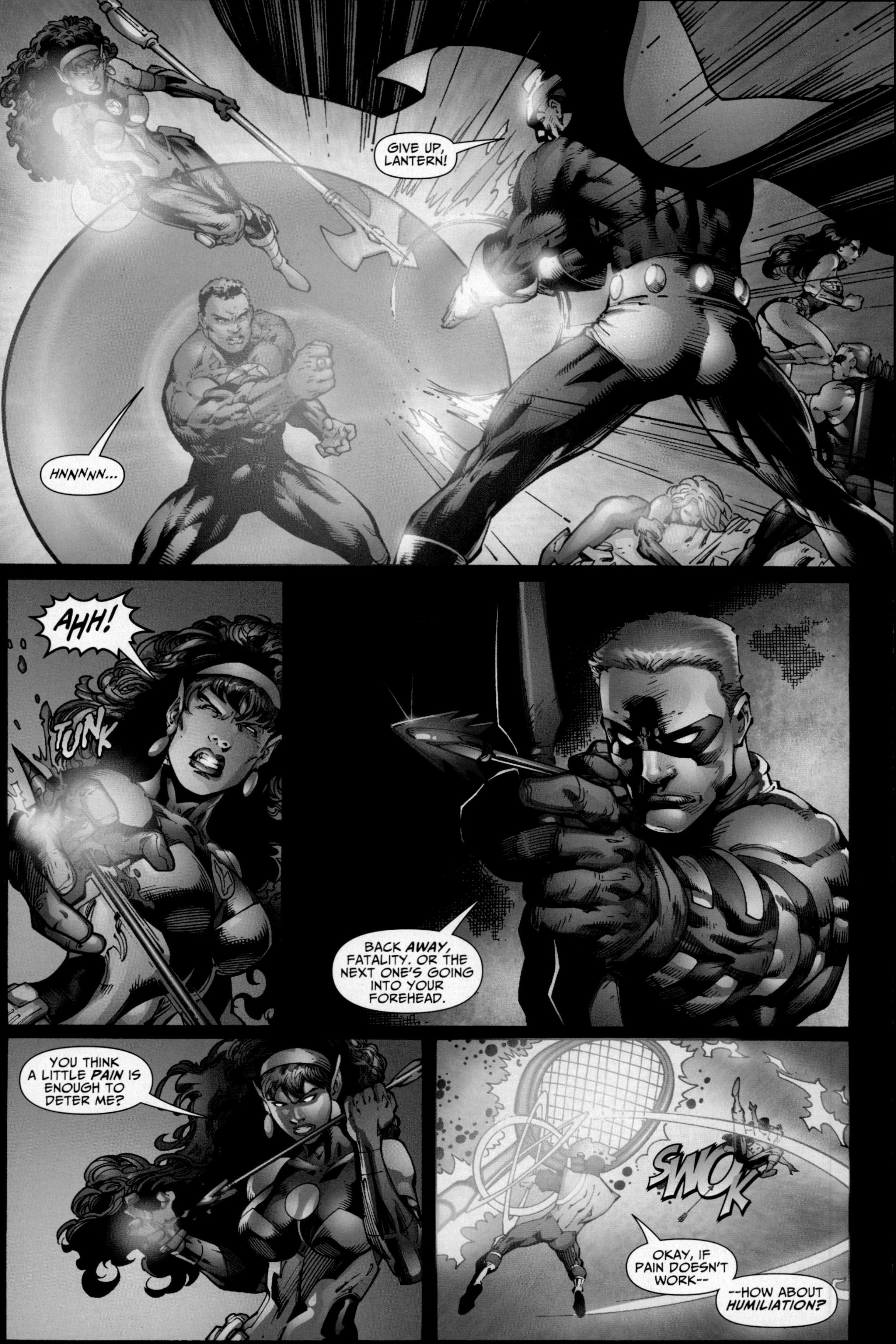
GIVE UP, LANTERN!
HNNNNN...
AHH!
TUNK
BACK AWAY, FATALITY. OR THE NEXT ONE'S GOING INTO YOUR FOREHEAD.
YOU THINK A LITTLE PAIN IS ENOUGH TO DETER ME?
SWOK
OKAY, IF PAIN DOESN'T WORK--
--HOW ABOUT HUMILIATION?

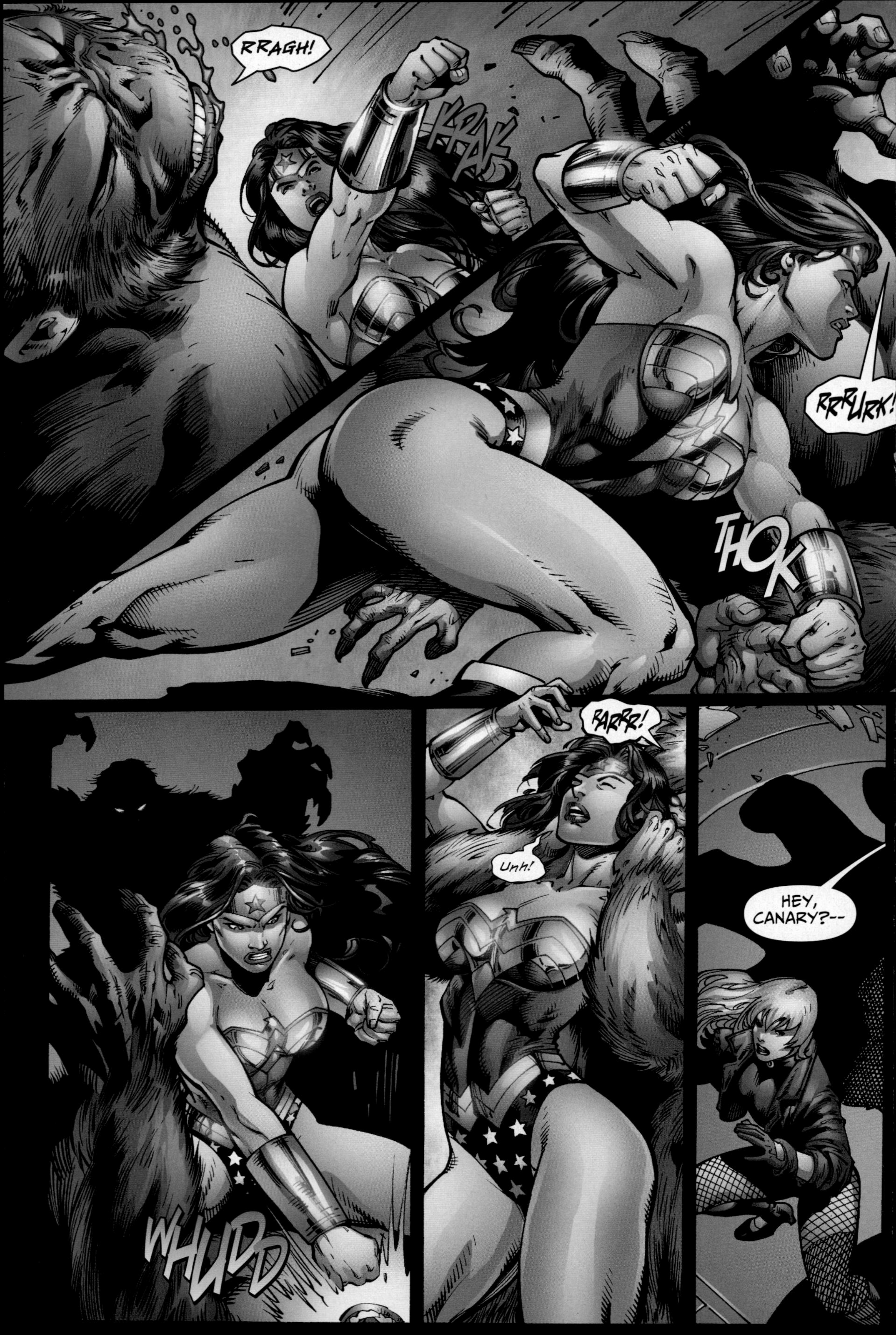
RRAGH!
KRAK
RRRURK!
THOK
WHUDD
RARRR!
Unh!
HEY, CANARY?--

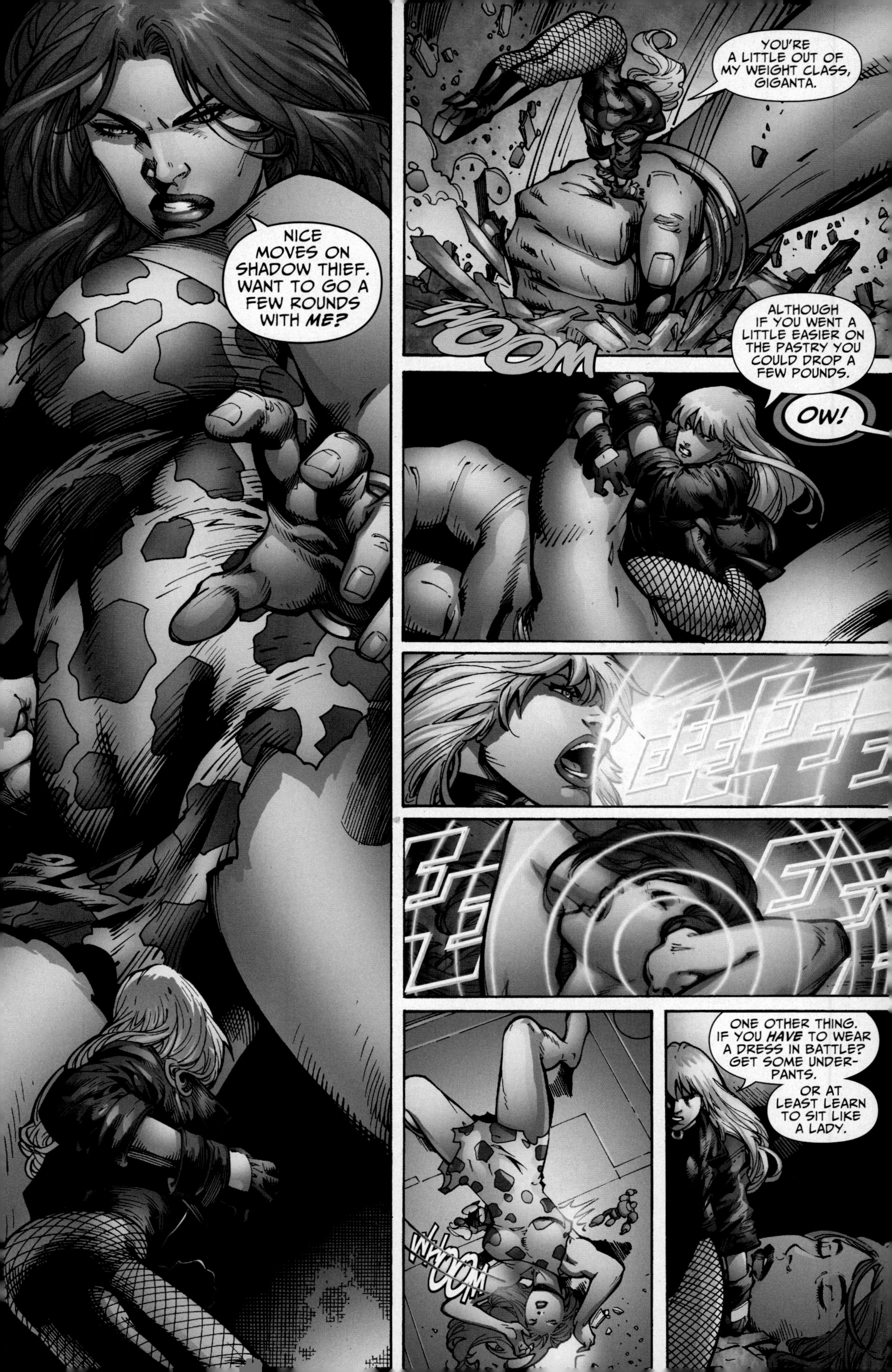
NICE MOVES ON SHADOW THIEF. WANT TO GO A FEW ROUNDS WITH *ME?*
YOU'RE A LITTLE OUT OF MY WEIGHT CLASS, GIGANTA.
WHOOOM
ALTHOUGH IF YOU WENT A LITTLE EASIER ON THE PASTRY YOU COULD DROP A FEW POUNDS.
OW!
ONE OTHER THING. IF YOU *HAVE* TO WEAR A DRESS IN BATTLE? GET SOME UNDER-PANTS.
OR AT LEAST LEARN TO SIT LIKE A LADY.
WHOOM!

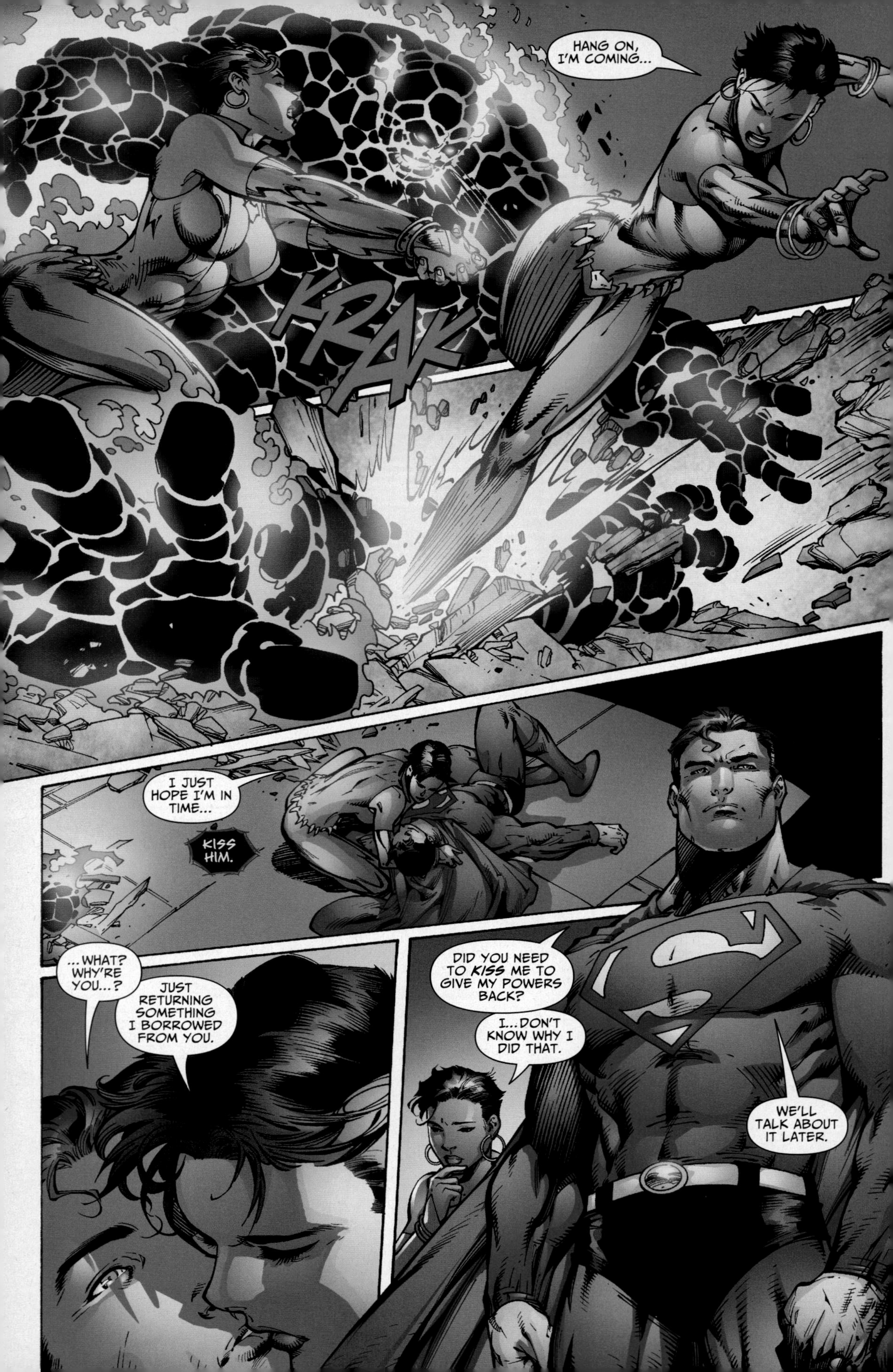
HANG ON, I'M COMING...
KRAK
I JUST HOPE I'M IN TIME...
KISS HIM.
...WHAT? WHY'RE YOU...?
JUST RETURNING SOMETHING I BORROWED FROM YOU.
DID YOU NEED TO *KISS* ME TO GIVE MY POWERS BACK?
I...DON'T KNOW WHY I DID THAT.
WE'LL TALK ABOUT IT LATER.

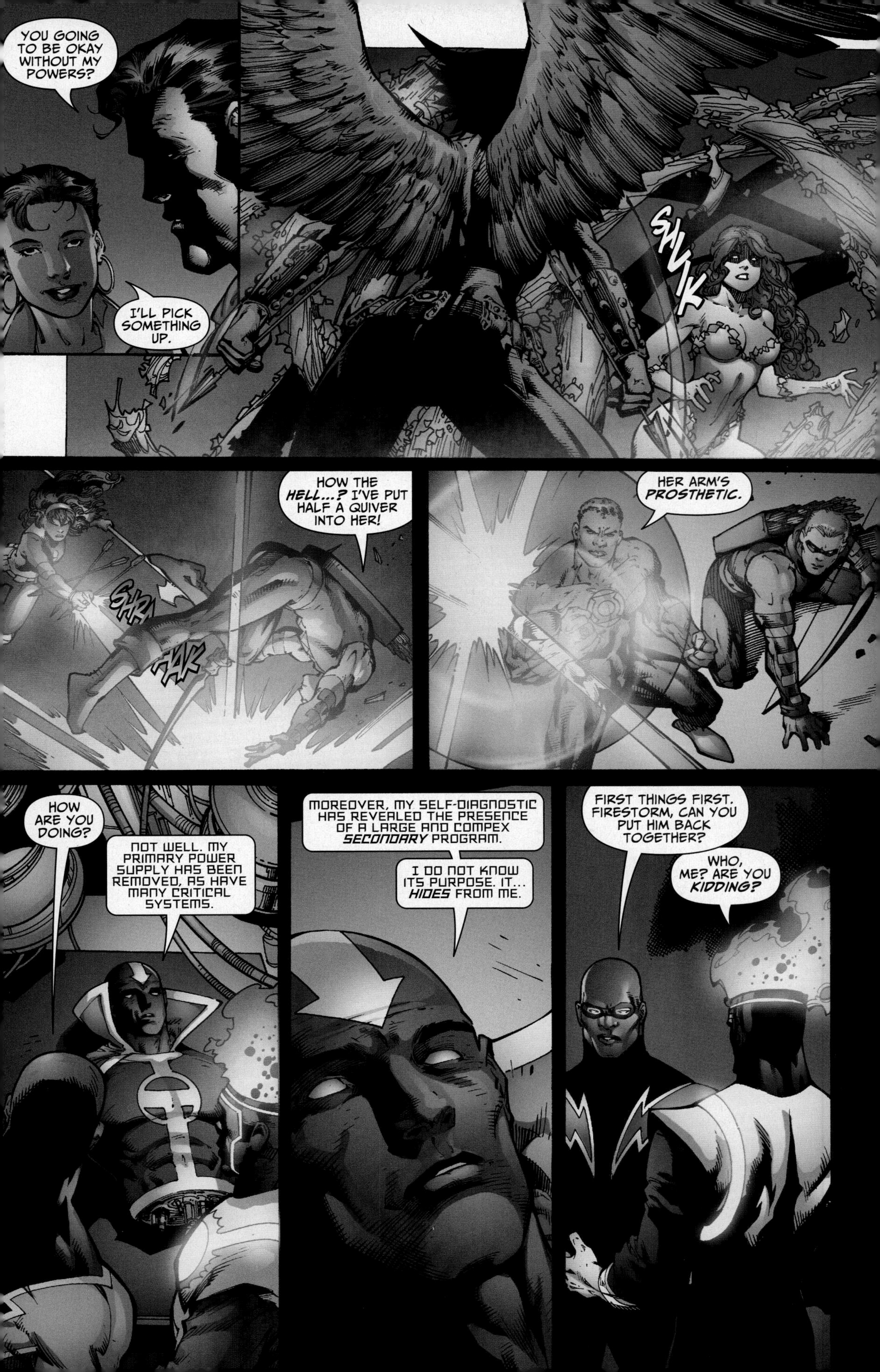
YOU GOING TO BE OKAY WITHOUT MY POWERS?
I'LL PICK SOMETHING UP.
SHUNK
HOW THE HELL...? I'VE PUT HALF A QUIVER INTO HER!
SHRAK
HER ARM'S PROSTHETIC.
HOW ARE YOU DOING?
NOT WELL. MY PRIMARY POWER SUPPLY HAS BEEN REMOVED, AS HAVE MANY CRITICAL SYSTEMS.
MOREOVER, MY SELF-DIAGNOSTIC HAS REVEALED THE PRESENCE OF A LARGE AND COMPEX SECONDARY PROGRAM.
I DO NOT KNOW ITS PURPOSE. IT... HIDES FROM ME.
FIRST THINGS FIRST. FIRESTORM, CAN YOU PUT HIM BACK TOGETHER?
WHO, ME? ARE YOU KIDDING?

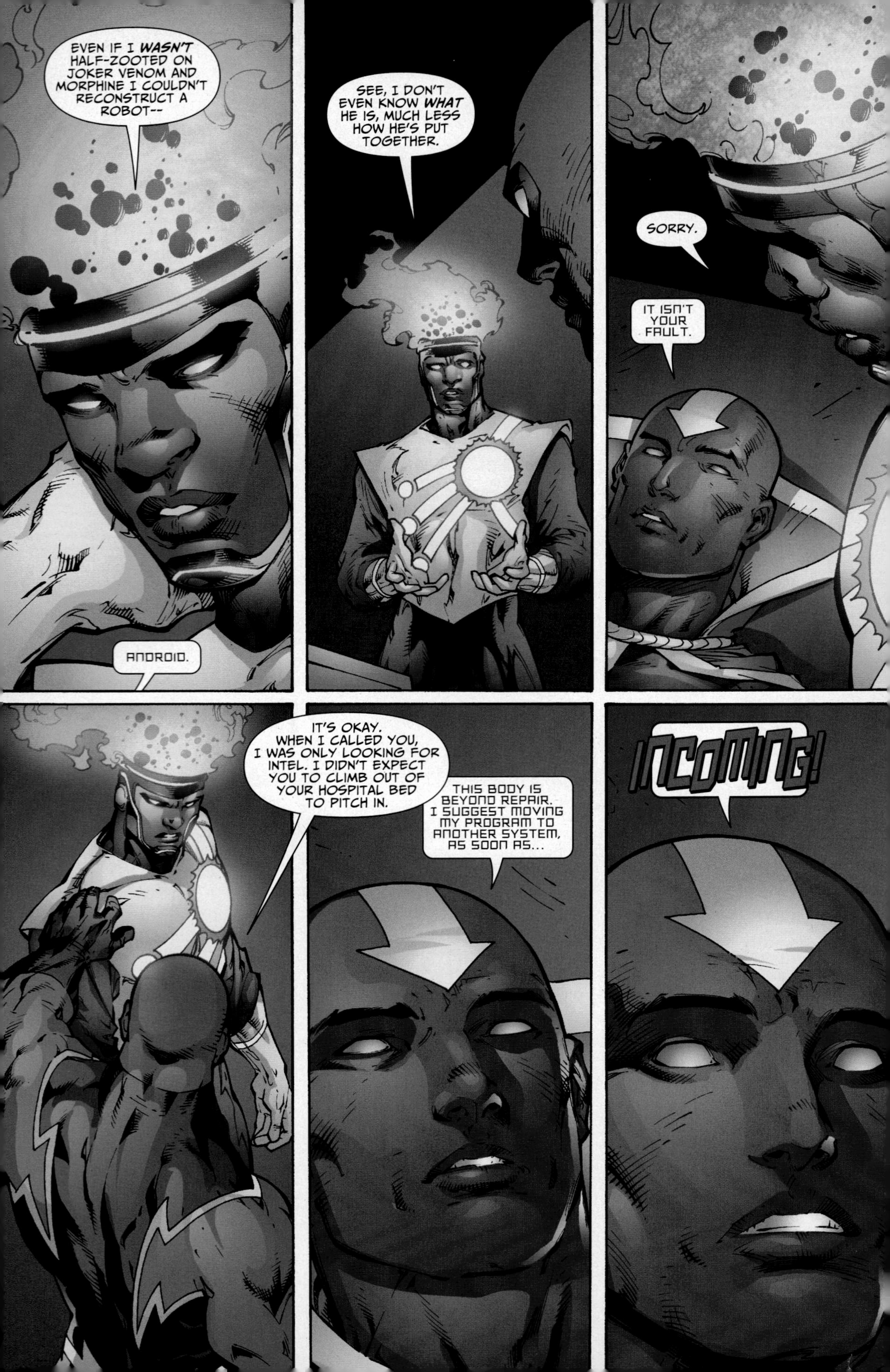
EVEN IF I WASN'T HALF-ZOOTED ON JOKER VENOM AND MORPHINE I COULDN'T RECONSTRUCT A ROBOT--
ANDROID.
SEE, I DON'T EVEN KNOW WHAT HE IS, MUCH LESS HOW HE'S PUT TOGETHER.
SORRY.
IT ISN'T YOUR FAULT.
IT'S OKAY. WHEN I CALLED YOU, I WAS ONLY LOOKING FOR INTEL. I DIDN'T EXPECT YOU TO CLIMB OUT OF YOUR HOSPITAL BED TO PITCH IN.
THIS BODY IS BEYOND REPAIR. I SUGGEST MOVING MY PROGRAM TO ANOTHER SYSTEM, AS SOON AS...
INCOMING!

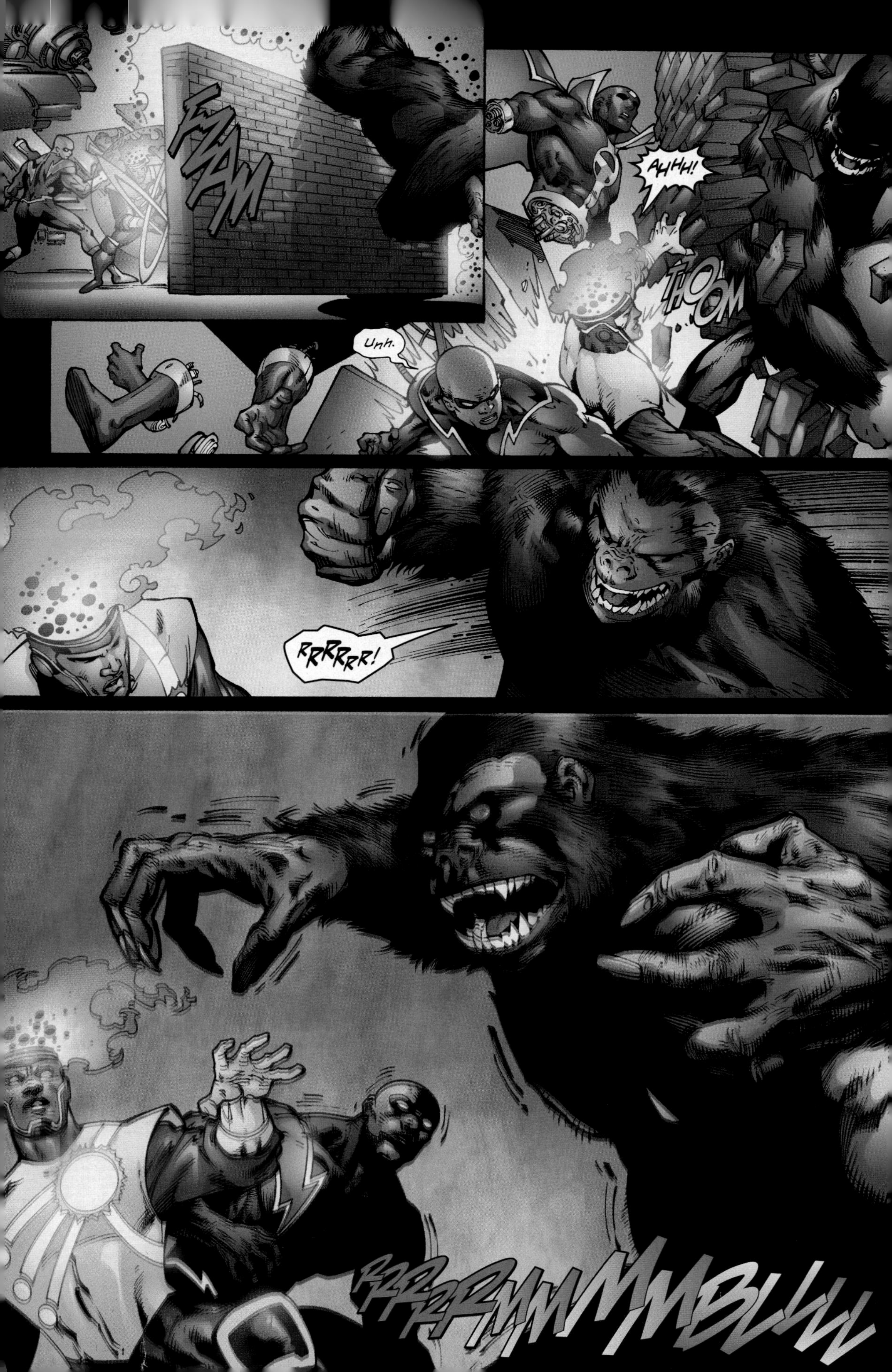
FWAM
AHHH!
THOOM
Unh.
RRRRRR!
RRRRRRMMMMMBLLL

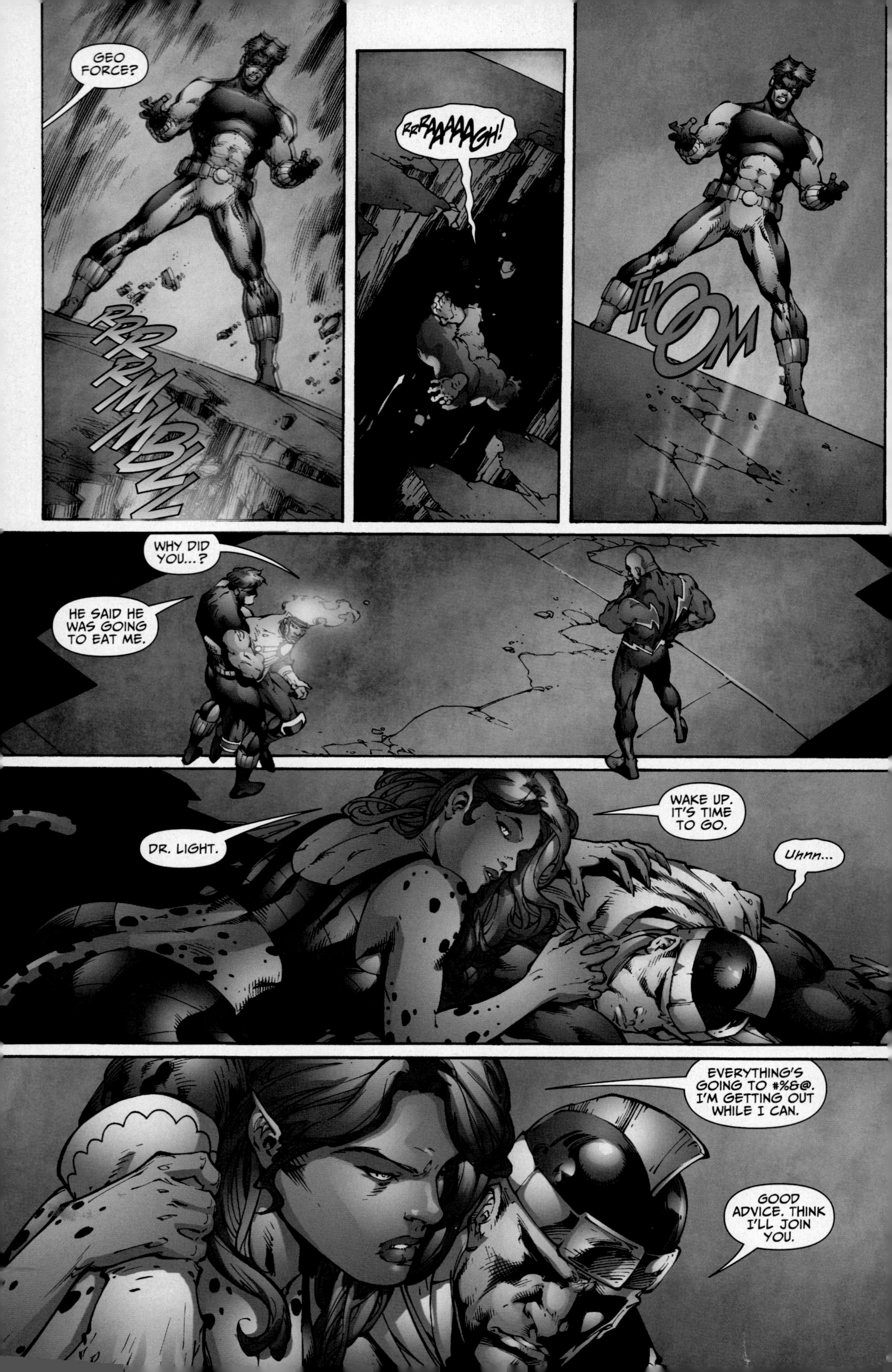
GEO FORCE?
RRRRMMBLLL
RRRAAAAAGH!
THOOM
WHY DID YOU...?
HE SAID HE WAS GOING TO EAT ME.
DR. LIGHT.
WAKE UP. IT'S TIME TO GO.
Uhnn...
EVERYTHING'S GOING TO #%&@. I'M GETTING OUT WHILE I CAN.
GOOD ADVICE. THINK I'LL JOIN YOU.

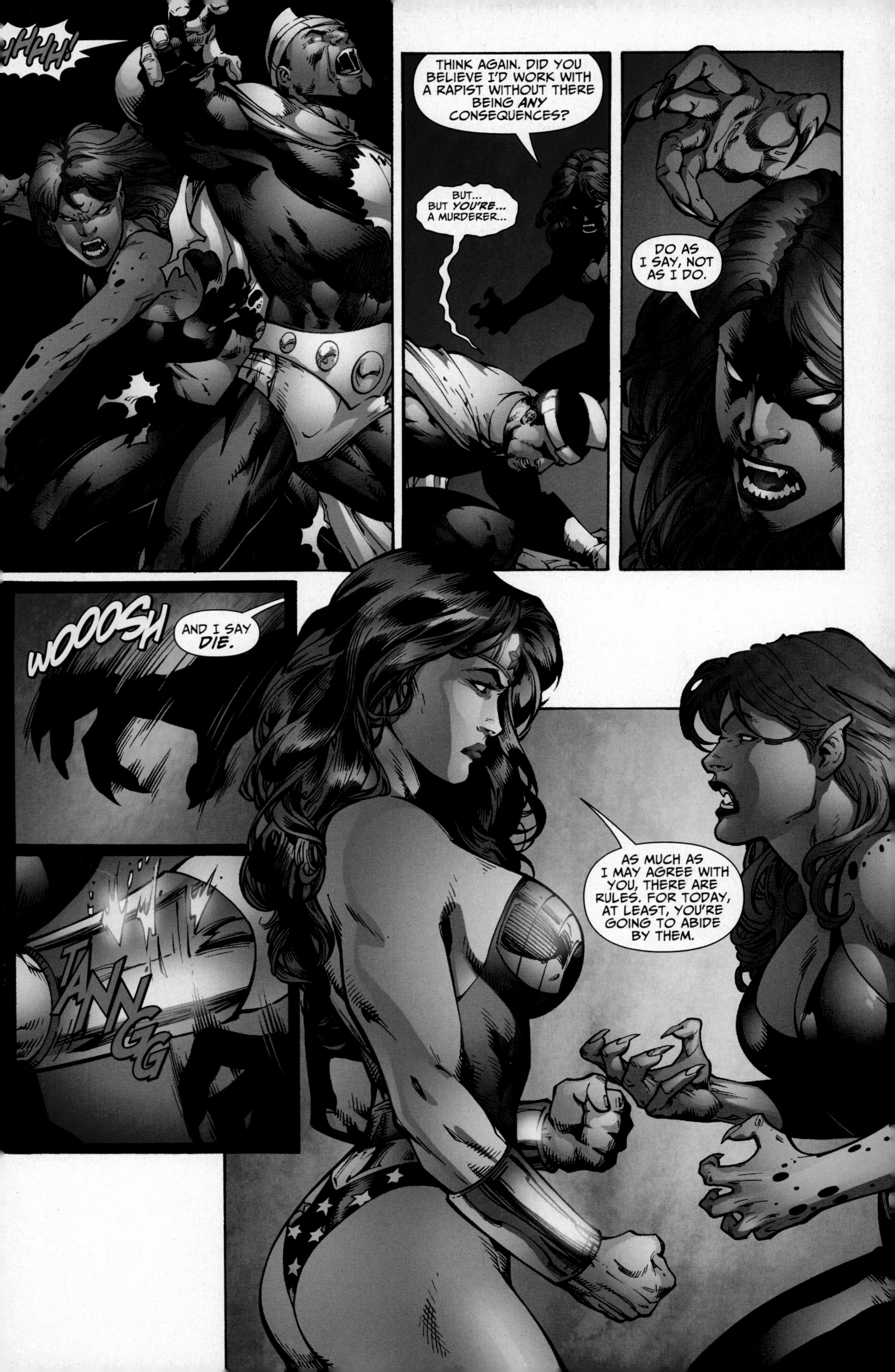

...HHHH!
THINK AGAIN. DID YOU BELIEVE I'D WORK WITH A RAPIST WITHOUT THERE BEING ANY CONSEQUENCES?
BUT... BUT YOU'RE... A MURDERER...
DO AS I SAY, NOT AS I DO.
WOOOSH
AND I SAY DIE.
TANNGG
AS MUCH AS I MAY AGREE WITH YOU, THERE ARE RULES. FOR TODAY, AT LEAST, YOU'RE GOING TO ABIDE BY THEM.

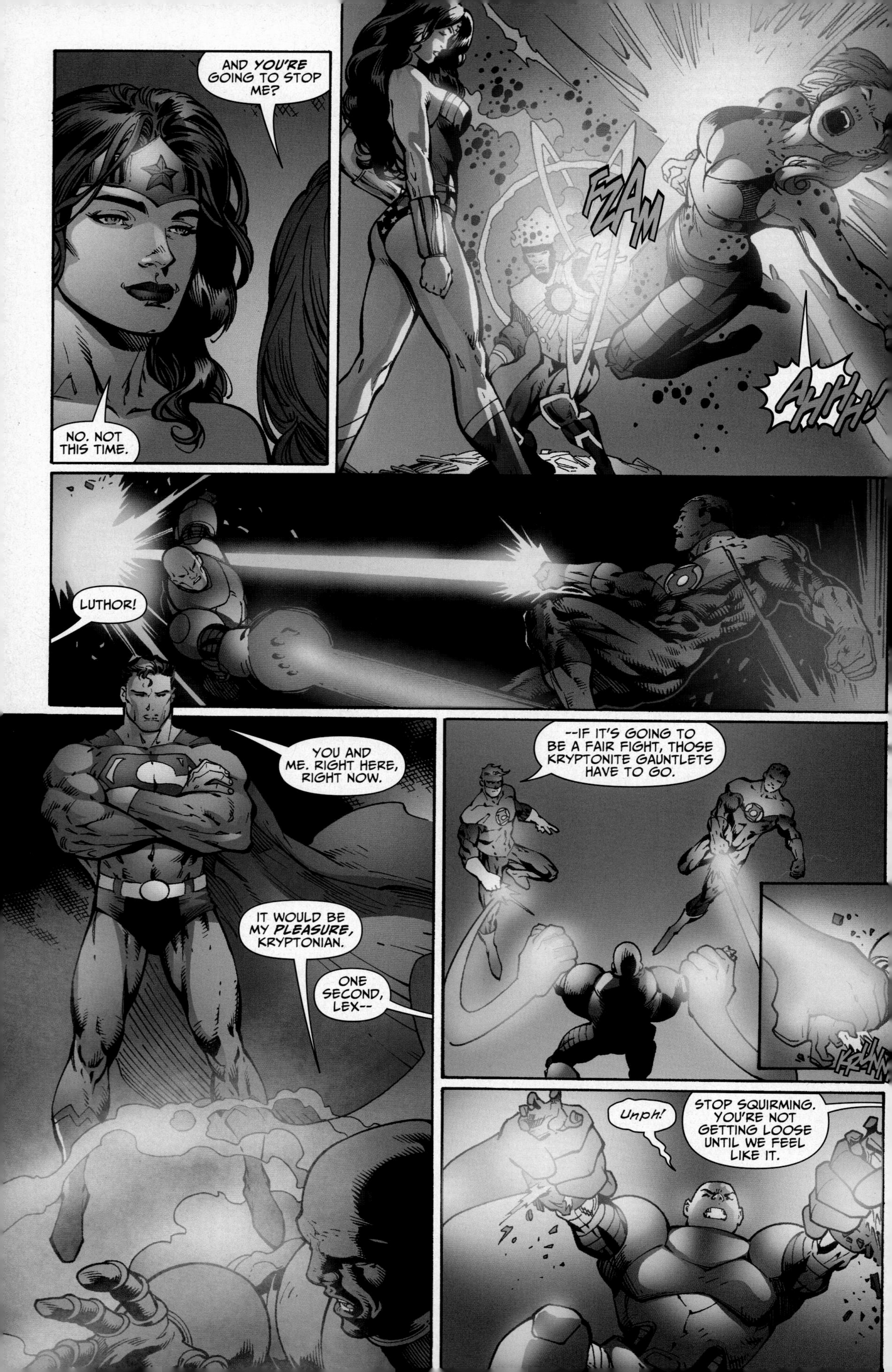
AND YOU'RE GOING TO STOP ME?
NO. NOT THIS TIME.
FZAM
AHHH!
LUTHOR!
YOU AND ME. RIGHT HERE, RIGHT NOW.
IT WOULD BE MY PLEASURE, KRYPTONIAN.
ONE SECOND, LEX--
--IF IT'S GOING TO BE A FAIR FIGHT, THOSE KRYPTONITE GAUNTLETS HAVE TO GO.
Unph!
STOP SQUIRMING. YOU'RE NOT GETTING LOOSE UNTIL WE FEEL LIKE IT.

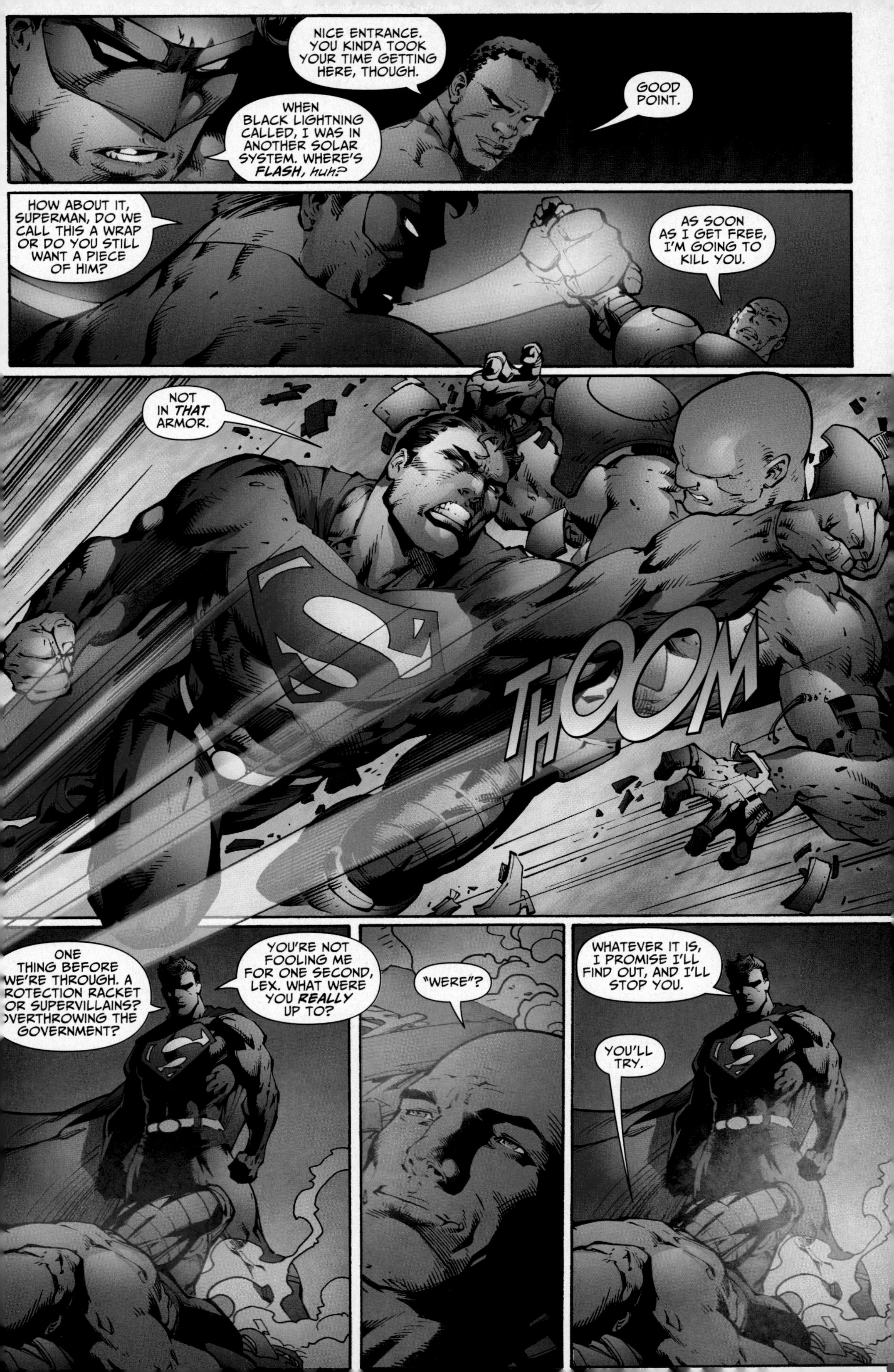
NICE ENTRANCE. YOU KINDA TOOK YOUR TIME GETTING HERE, THOUGH.
WHEN BLACK LIGHTNING CALLED, I WAS IN ANOTHER SOLAR SYSTEM. WHERE'S *FLASH*, *huh?*
GOOD POINT.
HOW ABOUT IT, SUPERMAN, DO WE CALL THIS A WRAP OR DO YOU STILL WANT A PIECE OF HIM?
AS SOON AS I GET FREE, I'M GOING TO KILL YOU.
NOT IN *THAT* ARMOR.
THOOM
ONE THING BEFORE WE'RE THROUGH. A ROTECTION RACKET OR SUPERVILLAINS? VERTHROWING THE GOVERNMENT?
YOU'RE NOT FOOLING ME FOR ONE SECOND, LEX. WHAT WERE YOU *REALLY* UP TO?
"WERE"?
WHATEVER IT IS, I PROMISE I'LL FIND OUT, AND I'LL STOP YOU.
YOU'LL TRY.

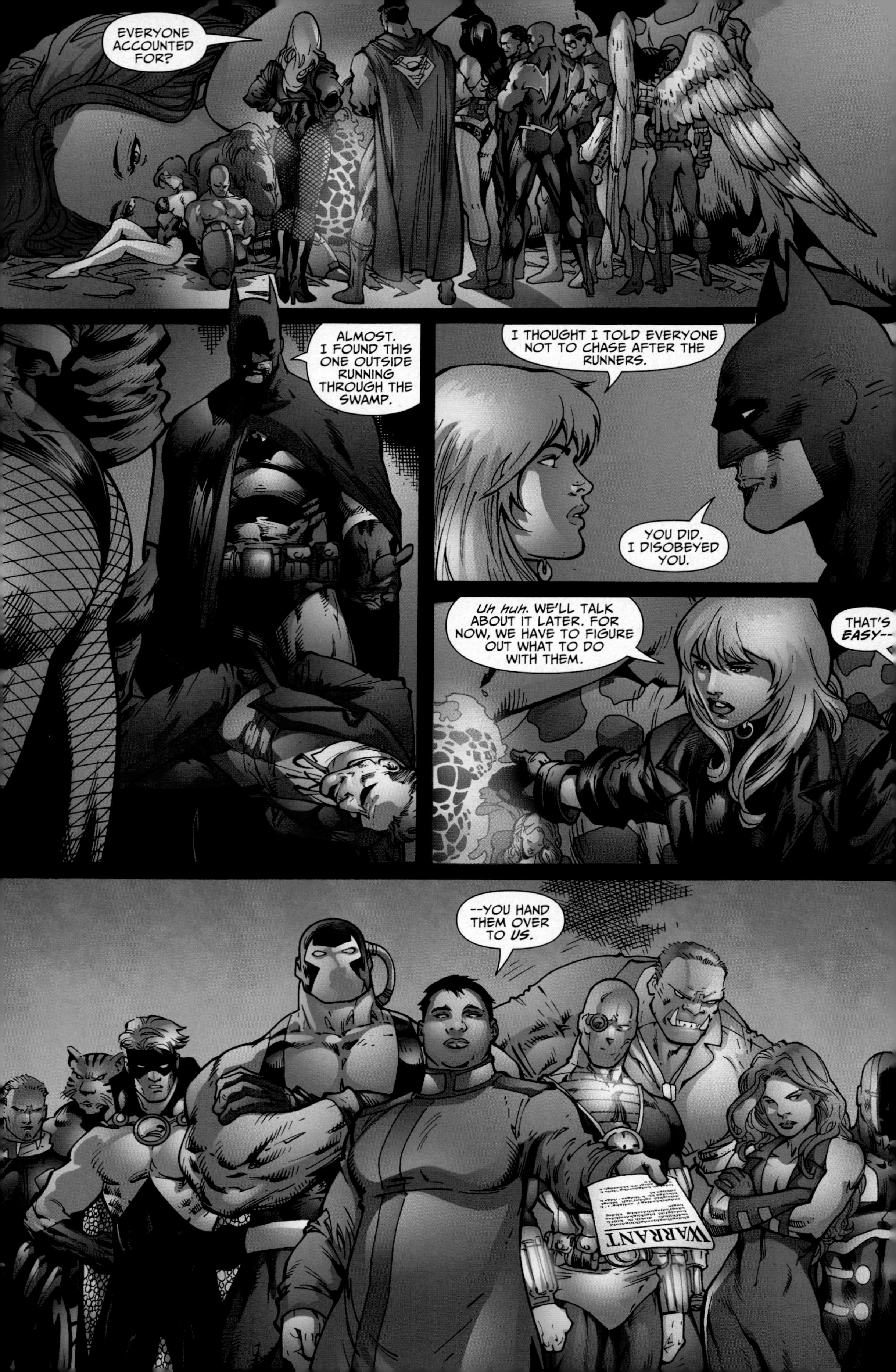
EVERYONE ACCOUNTED FOR?
ALMOST. I FOUND THIS ONE OUTSIDE RUNNING THROUGH THE SWAMP.
I THOUGHT I TOLD EVERYONE NOT TO CHASE AFTER THE RUNNERS.
YOU DID. I DISOBEYED YOU.
Uh huh. WE'LL TALK ABOUT IT LATER. FOR NOW, WE HAVE TO FIGURE OUT WHAT TO DO WITH THEM.
THAT'S *EASY*--
--YOU HAND THEM OVER TO *US.*
WARRANT

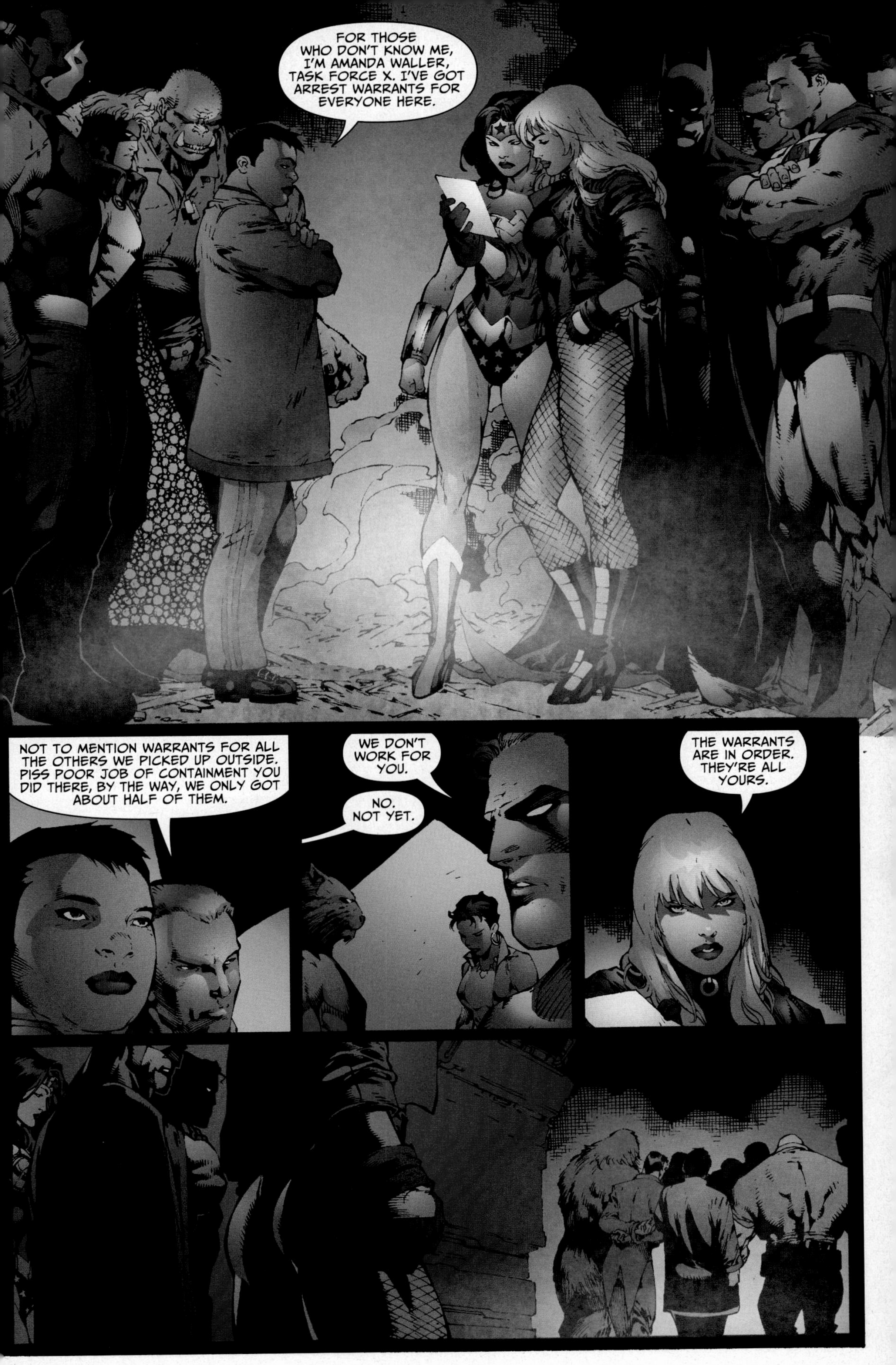
FOR THOSE WHO DON'T KNOW ME, I'M AMANDA WALLER, TASK FORCE X. I'VE GOT ARREST WARRANTS FOR EVERYONE HERE.
NOT TO MENTION WARRANTS FOR ALL THE OTHERS WE PICKED UP OUTSIDE. PISS POOR JOB OF CONTAINMENT YOU DID THERE, BY THE WAY, WE ONLY GOT ABOUT HALF OF THEM.
WE DON'T WORK FOR YOU.
NO. NOT YET.
THE WARRANTS ARE IN ORDER. THEY'RE ALL YOURS.

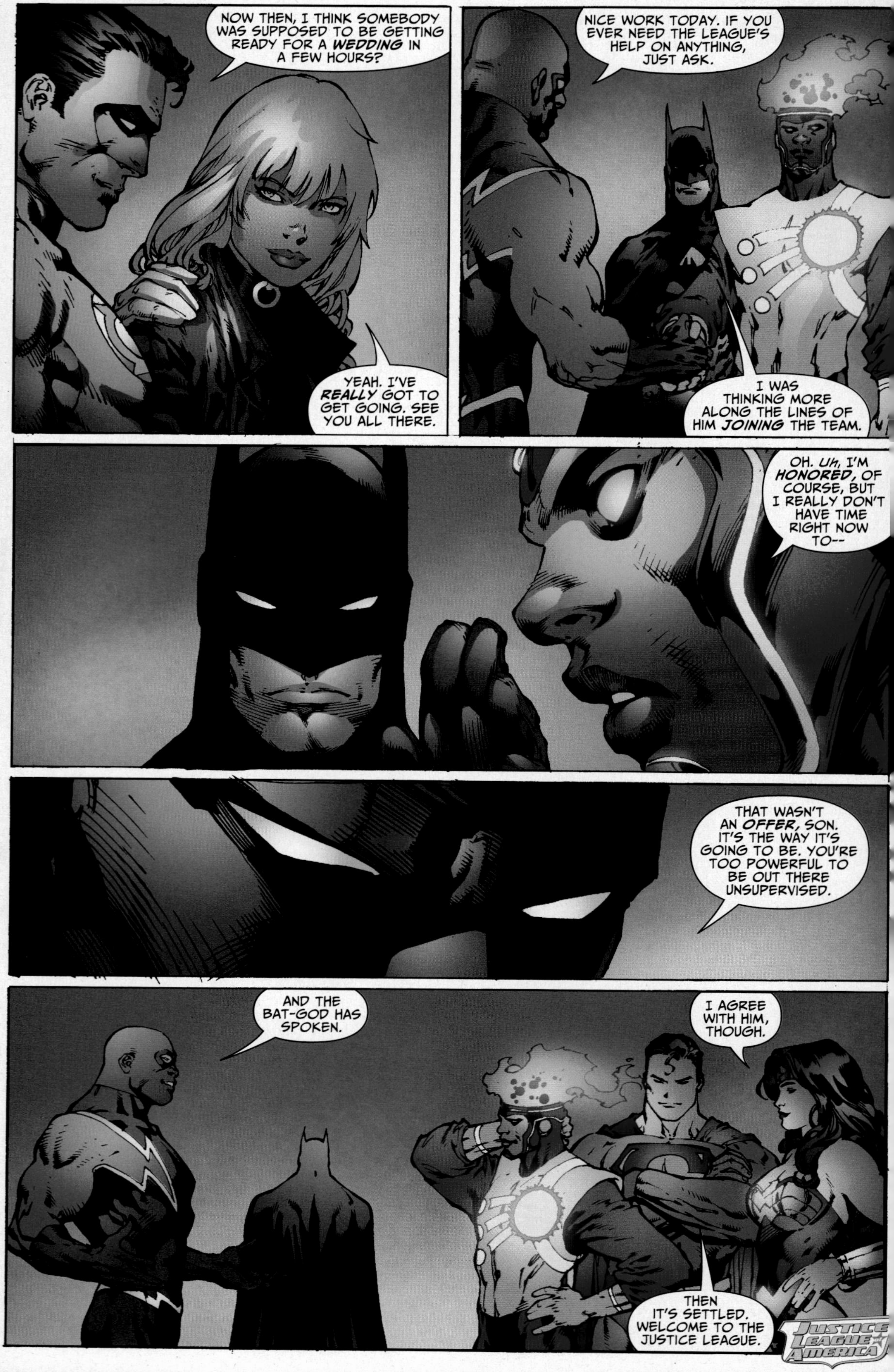
NOW THEN, I THINK SOMEBODY WAS SUPPOSED TO BE GETTING READY FOR A WEDDING IN A FEW HOURS?
YEAH. I'VE REALLY GOT TO GET GOING. SEE YOU ALL THERE.
NICE WORK TODAY. IF YOU EVER NEED THE LEAGUE'S HELP ON ANYTHING, JUST ASK.
I WAS THINKING MORE ALONG THE LINES OF HIM JOINING THE TEAM.
OH. Uh, I'M HONORED, OF COURSE, BUT I REALLY DON'T HAVE TIME RIGHT NOW TO--
THAT WASN'T AN OFFER, SON. IT'S THE WAY IT'S GOING TO BE. YOU'RE TOO POWERFUL TO BE OUT THERE UNSUPERVISED.
AND THE BAT-GOD HAS SPOKEN.
I AGREE WITH HIM, THOUGH.
THEN IT'S SETTLED. WELCOME TO THE JUSTICE LEAGUE.
JUSTICE LEAGUE OF AMERICA

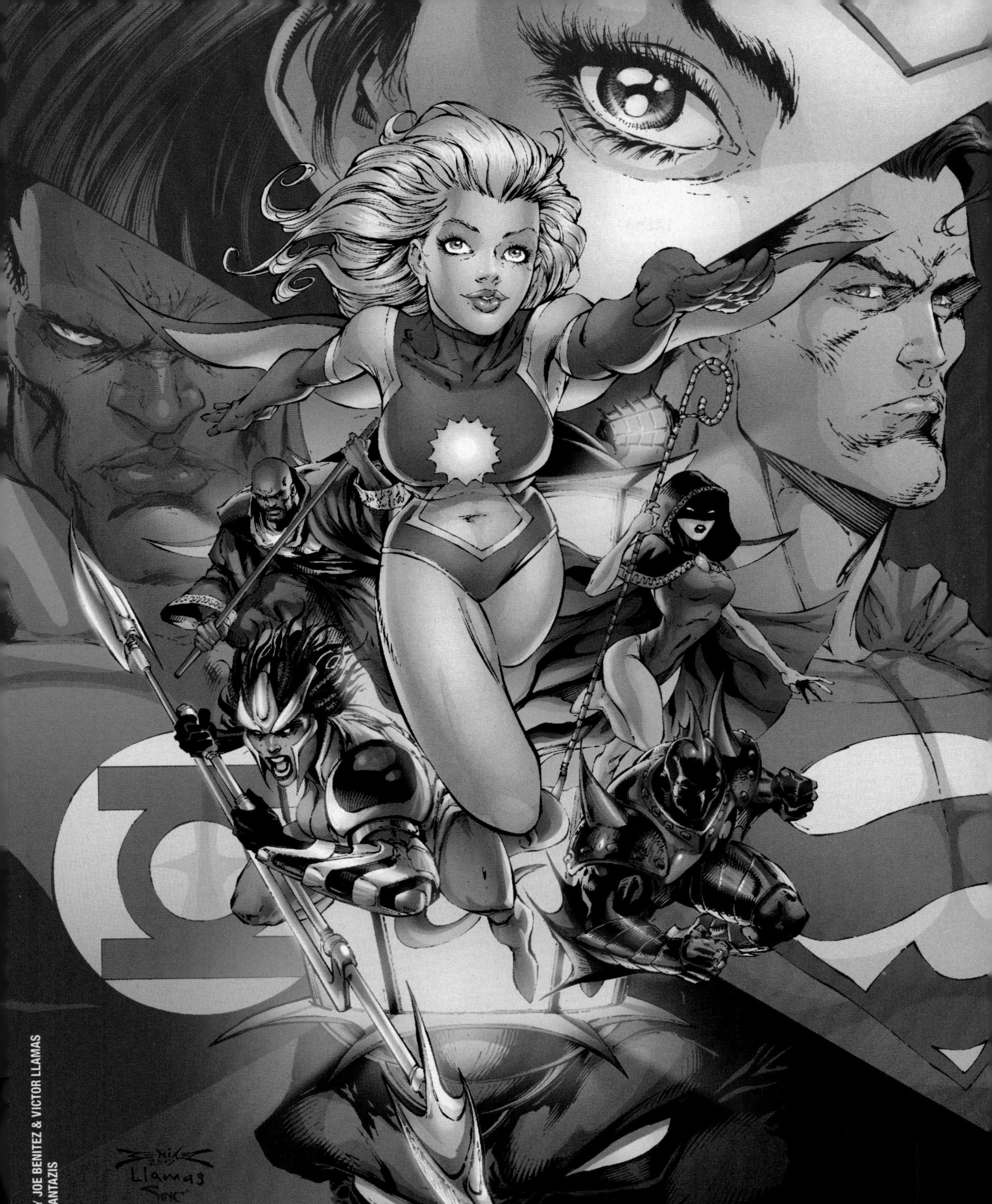

COVER ART BY **JOE BENITEZ & VICTOR LLAMAS**
WITH **PETE PANTAZIS**

JUSTICE LEAGUE OF AMERICA
BONUS STORIES

THE FOLLOWING STORY IS A PREQUEL TO
TANGENT: SUPERMAN'S REIGN

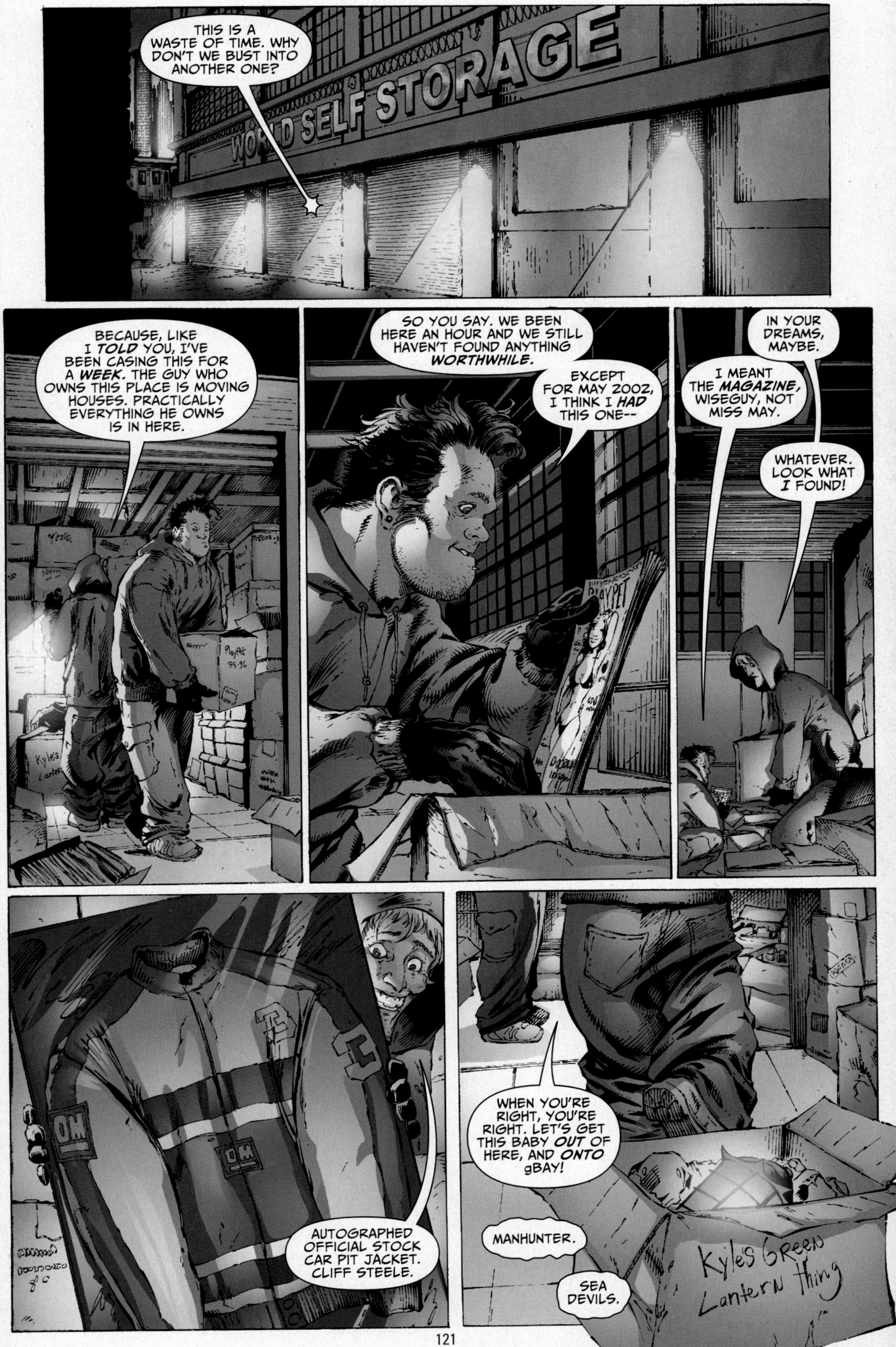

WORLD SELF STORAGE
THIS IS A WASTE OF TIME. WHY DON'T WE BUST INTO ANOTHER ONE?
BECAUSE, LIKE I TOLD YOU, I'VE BEEN CASING THIS FOR A WEEK. THE GUY WHO OWNS THIS PLACE IS MOVING HOUSES. PRACTICALLY EVERYTHING HE OWNS IS IN HERE.
PlayPet 95-96
SO YOU SAY. WE BEEN HERE AN HOUR AND WE STILL HAVEN'T FOUND ANYTHING WORTHWHILE.
EXCEPT FOR MAY 2002, I THINK I HAD THIS ONE--
PLAYPET
IN YOUR DREAMS, MAYBE.
I MEANT THE MAGAZINE, WISEGUY, NOT MISS MAY.
WHATEVER. LOOK WHAT I FOUND!
AUTOGRAPHED OFFICIAL STOCK CAR PIT JACKET. CLIFF STEELE.
WHEN YOU'RE RIGHT, YOU'RE RIGHT. LET'S GET THIS BABY OUT OF HERE, AND ONTO gBAY!
MANHUNTER.
SEA DEVILS.
Kyle's Green Lantern thing

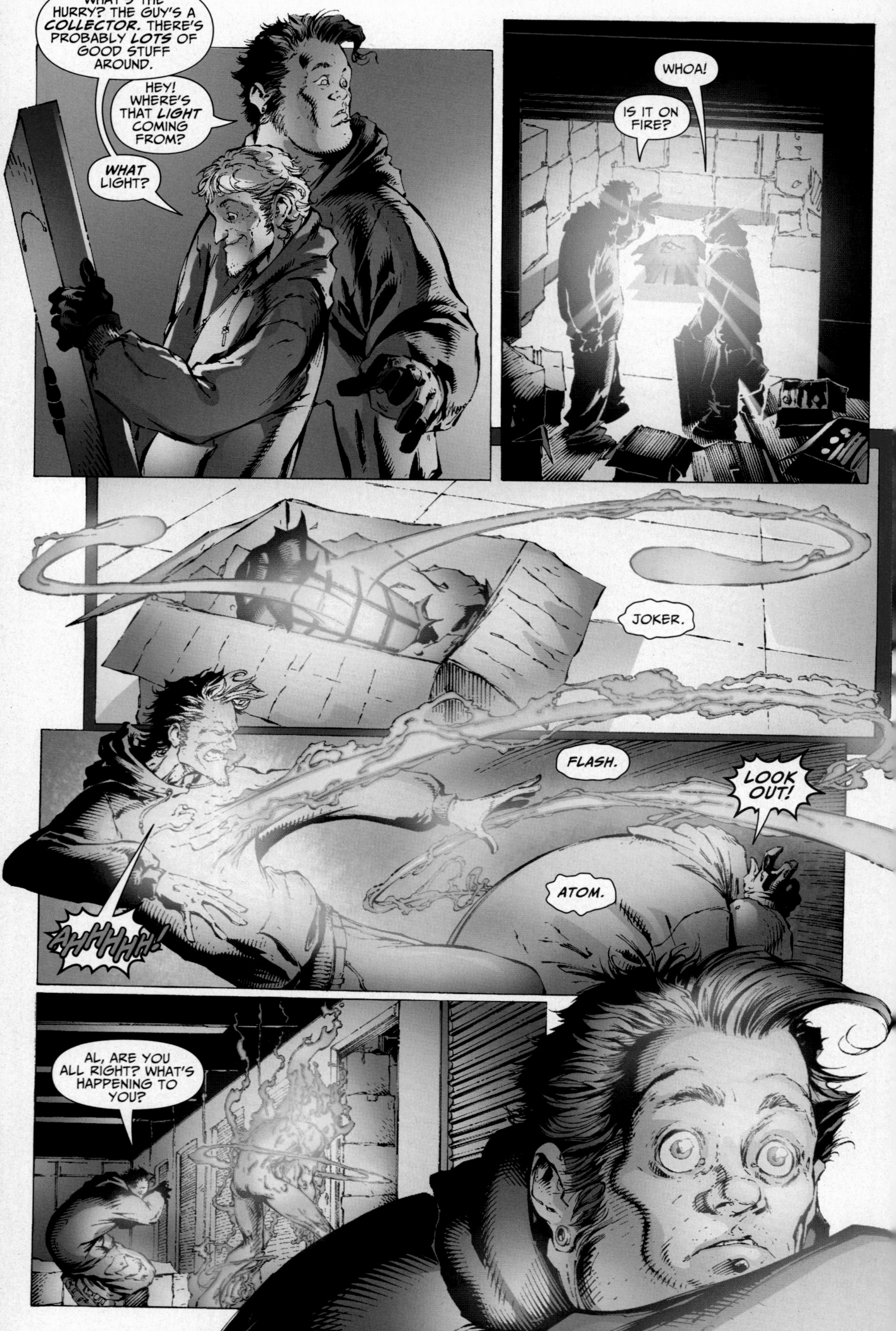
WHAT'S THE HURRY? THE GUY'S A COLLECTOR. THERE'S PROBABLY LOTS OF GOOD STUFF AROUND.
HEY! WHERE'S THAT LIGHT COMING FROM?
WHAT LIGHT?
WHOA!
IS IT ON FIRE?
JOKER.
FLASH.
LOOK OUT!
ATOM.
AHHHHHH!
AL, ARE YOU ALL RIGHT? WHAT'S HAPPENING TO YOU?

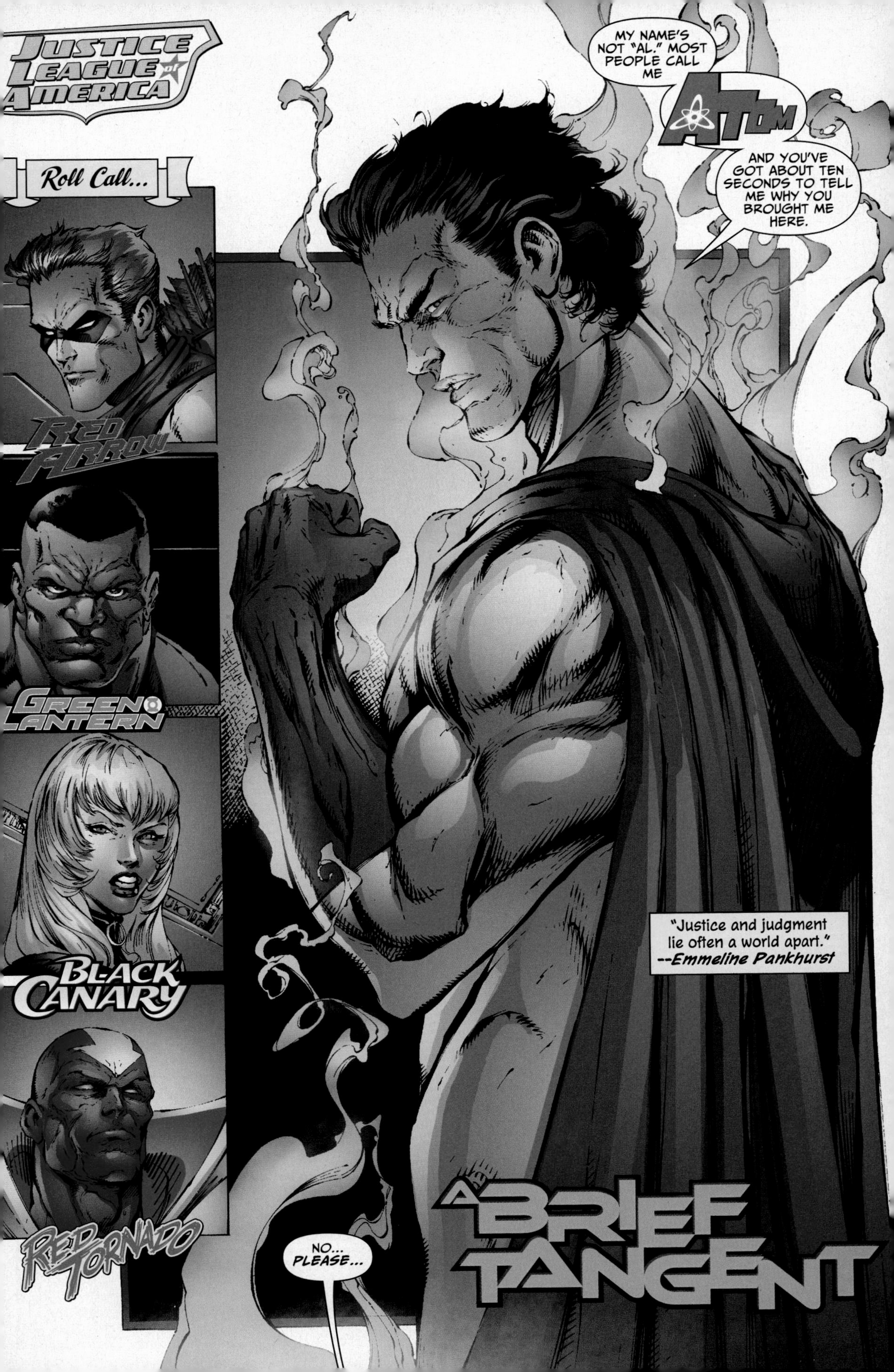
JUSTICE LEAGUE of AMERICA
Roll Call...
RED ARROW
GREEN LANTERN
BLACK CANARY
RED TORNADO
MY NAME'S NOT "AL." MOST PEOPLE CALL ME
ATOM
AND YOU'VE GOT ABOUT TEN SECONDS TO TELL ME WHY YOU BROUGHT ME HERE.
"Justice and judgment lie often a world apart." --Emmeline Pankhurst
NO... PLEASE...
A BRIEF TANGENT

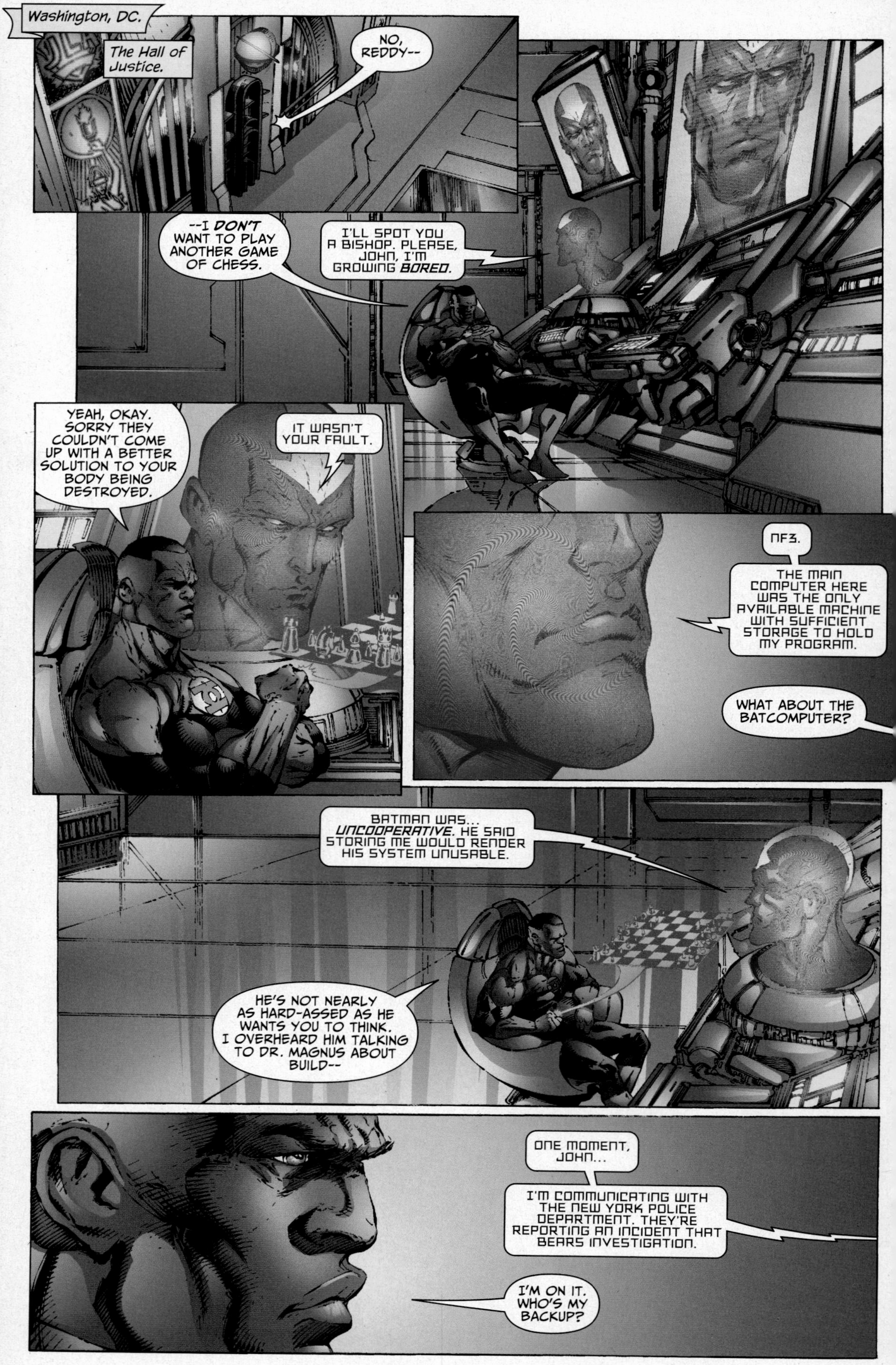

Washington, DC.
The Hall of Justice.
NO, REDDY--
--I DON'T WANT TO PLAY ANOTHER GAME OF CHESS.
I'LL SPOT YOU A BISHOP. PLEASE, JOHN, I'M GROWING BORED.
YEAH, OKAY. SORRY THEY COULDN'T COME UP WITH A BETTER SOLUTION TO YOUR BODY BEING DESTROYED.
IT WASN'T YOUR FAULT.
NF3.
THE MAIN COMPUTER HERE WAS THE ONLY AVAILABLE MACHINE WITH SUFFICIENT STORAGE TO HOLD MY PROGRAM.
WHAT ABOUT THE BATCOMPUTER?
BATMAN WAS... UNCOOPERATIVE. HE SAID STORING ME WOULD RENDER HIS SYSTEM UNUSABLE.
HE'S NOT NEARLY AS HARD-ASSED AS HE WANTS YOU TO THINK. I OVERHEARD HIM TALKING TO DR. MAGNUS ABOUT BUILD--
ONE MOMENT, JOHN...
I'M COMMUNICATING WITH THE NEW YORK POLICE DEPARTMENT. THEY'RE REPORTING AN INCIDENT THAT BEARS INVESTIGATION.
I'M ON IT. WHO'S MY BACKUP?

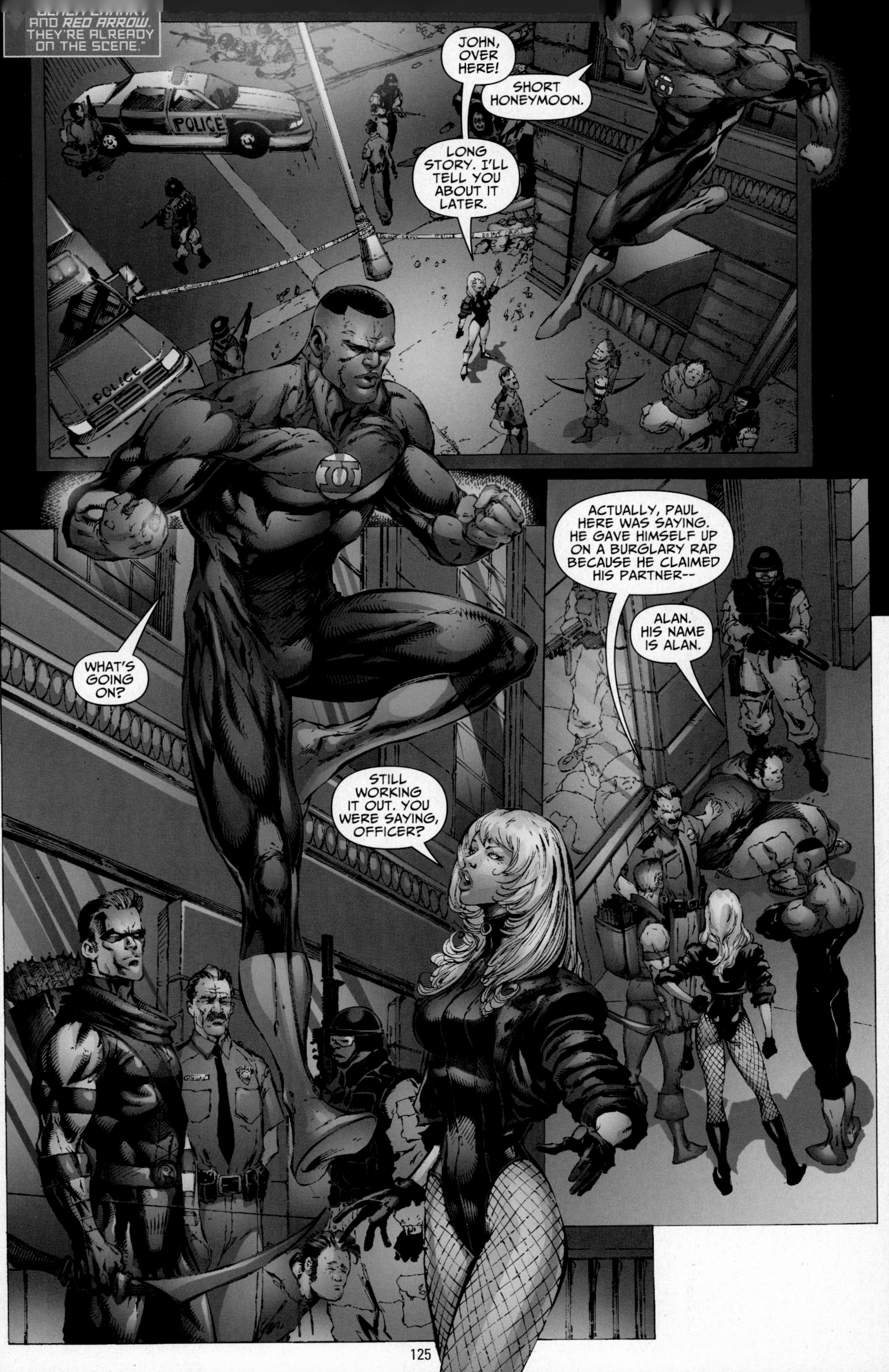
AND *RED ARROW.* THEY'RE ALREADY ON THE SCENE."
JOHN, OVER HERE!
SHORT HONEYMOON.
LONG STORY. I'LL TELL YOU ABOUT IT LATER.
WHAT'S GOING ON?
STILL WORKING IT OUT. YOU WERE SAYING, OFFICER?
ACTUALLY, PAUL HERE WAS SAYING. HE GAVE HIMSELF UP ON A BURGLARY RAP BECAUSE HE CLAIMED HIS PARTNER--
ALAN. HIS NAME IS ALAN.

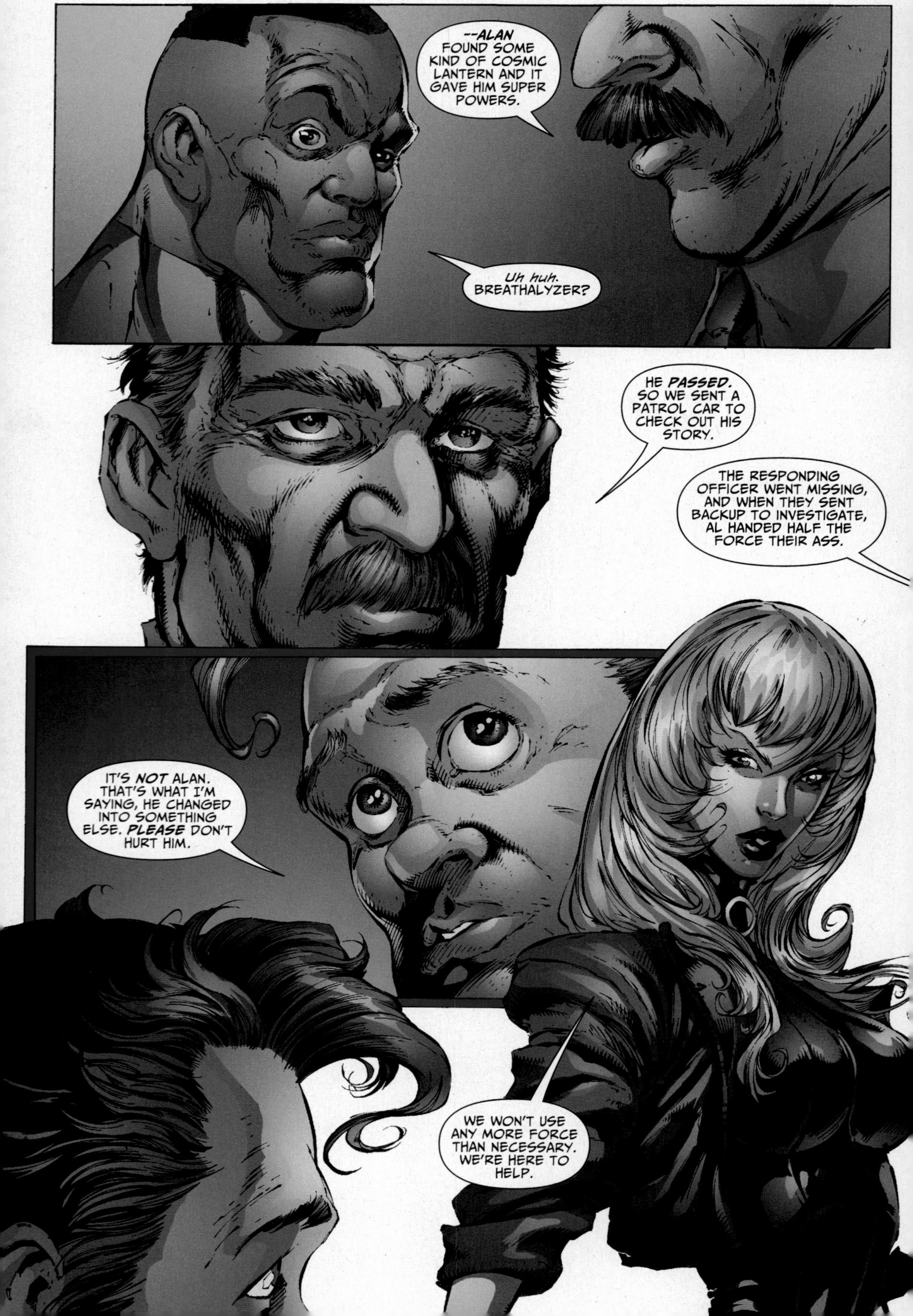
--ALAN FOUND SOME KIND OF COSMIC LANTERN AND IT GAVE HIM SUPER POWERS.
Uh huh. BREATHALYZER?
HE PASSED. SO WE SENT A PATROL CAR TO CHECK OUT HIS STORY.
THE RESPONDING OFFICER WENT MISSING, AND WHEN THEY SENT BACKUP TO INVESTIGATE, AL HANDED HALF THE FORCE THEIR ASS.
IT'S NOT ALAN. THAT'S WHAT I'M SAYING, HE CHANGED INTO SOMETHING ELSE. PLEASE DON'T HURT HIM.
WE WON'T USE ANY MORE FORCE THAN NECESSARY. WE'RE HERE TO HELP.

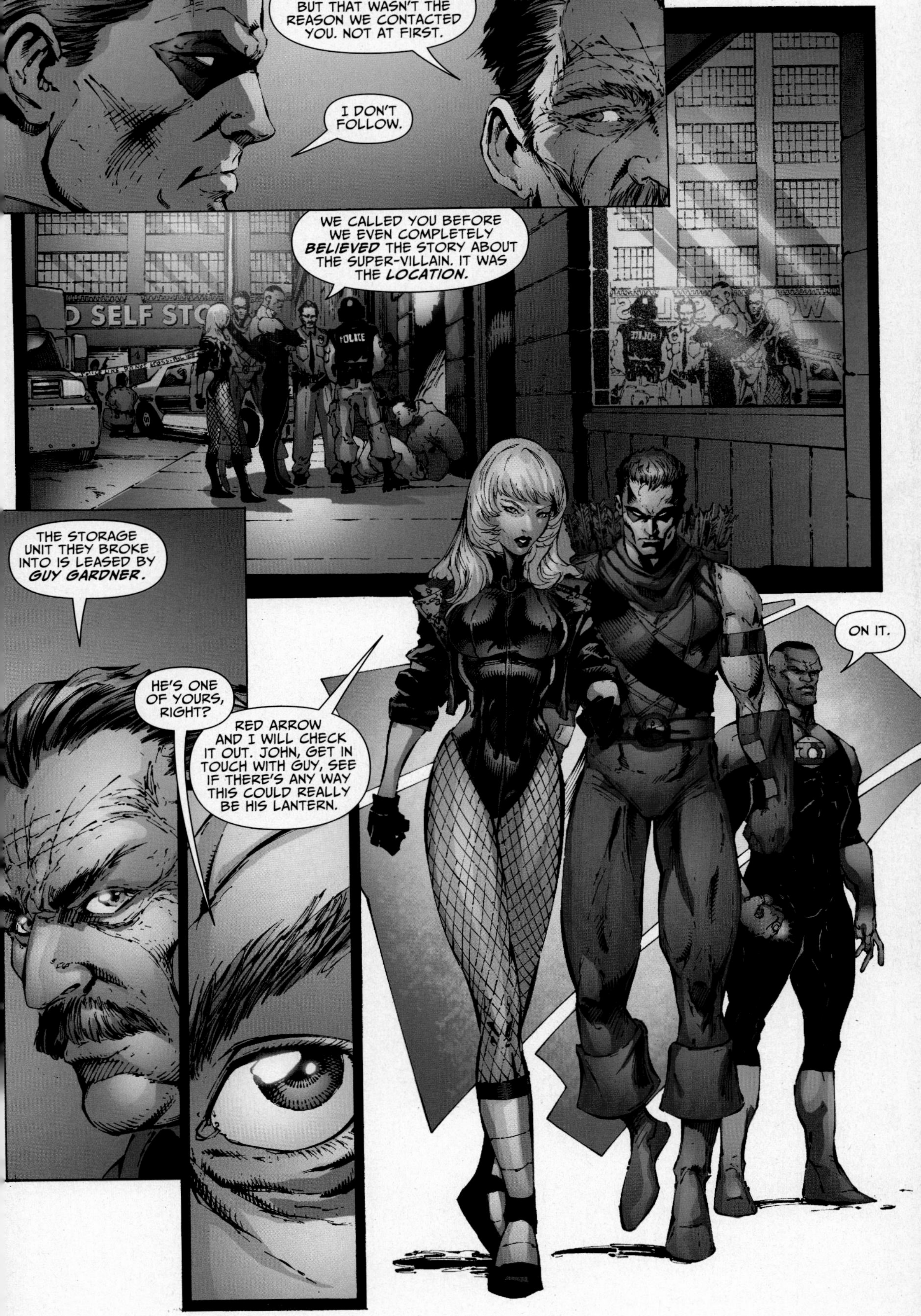

AND WE APPRECIATE IT, BUT THAT WASN'T THE REASON WE CONTACTED YOU. NOT AT FIRST.
I DON'T FOLLOW.
WE CALLED YOU BEFORE WE EVEN COMPLETELY *BELIEVED* THE STORY ABOUT THE SUPER-VILLAIN. IT WAS THE *LOCATION.*
D SELF STO
POLICE
THE STORAGE UNIT THEY BROKE INTO IS LEASED BY *GUY GARDNER.*
HE'S ONE OF YOURS, RIGHT?
RED ARROW AND I WILL CHECK IT OUT. JOHN, GET IN TOUCH WITH GUY, SEE IF THERE'S ANY WAY THIS COULD REALLY BE HIS LANTERN.
ON IT.

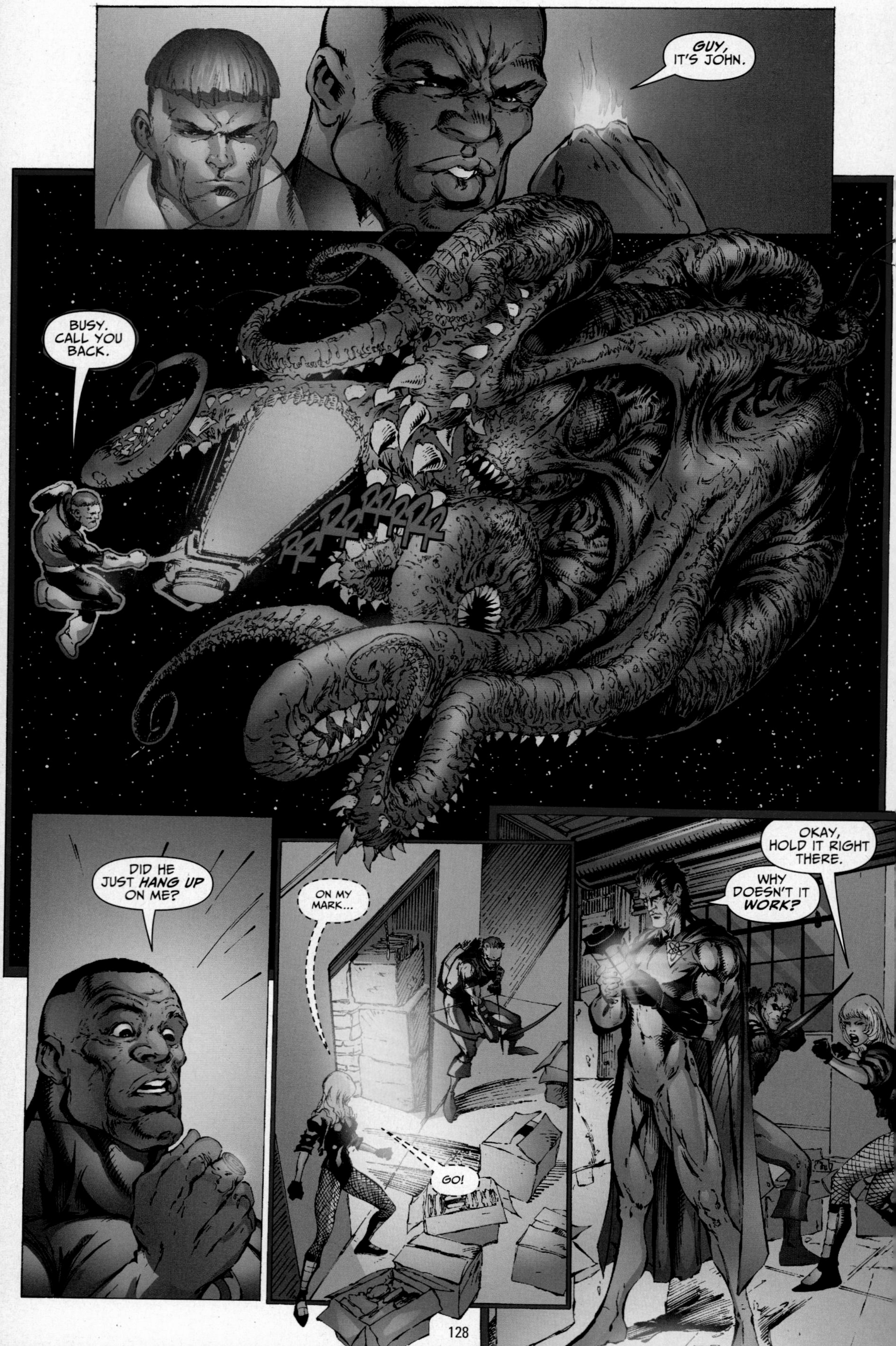
GUY, IT'S JOHN.
BUSY. CALL YOU BACK.
RRRRRRRRRRR
DID HE JUST HANG UP ON ME?
ON MY MARK...
GO!
OKAY, HOLD IT RIGHT THERE.
WHY DOESN'T IT WORK?

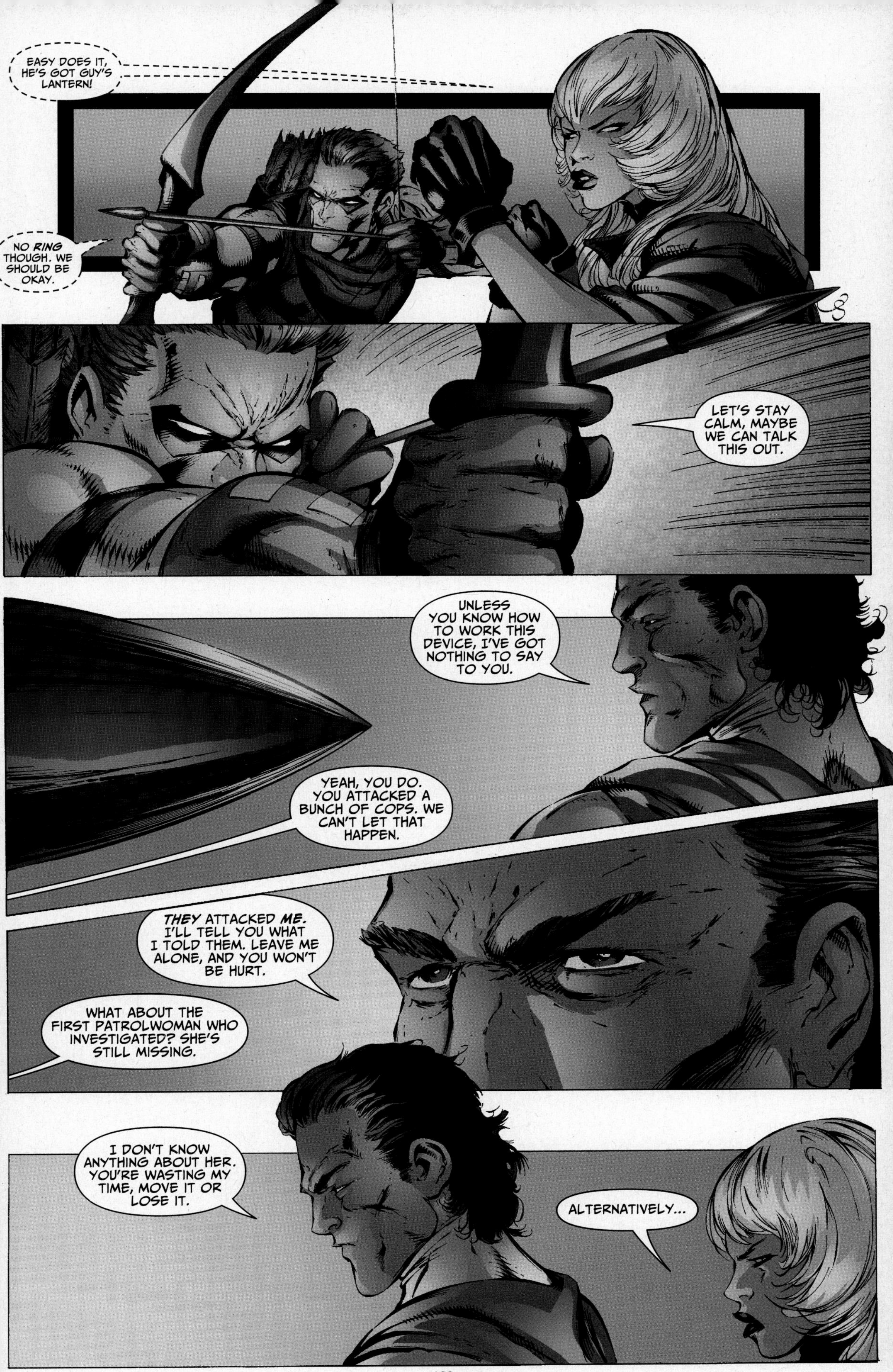
EASY DOES IT, HE'S GOT GUY'S LANTERN!
NO RING THOUGH. WE SHOULD BE OKAY.
LET'S STAY CALM, MAYBE WE CAN TALK THIS OUT.
UNLESS YOU KNOW HOW TO WORK THIS DEVICE, I'VE GOT NOTHING TO SAY TO YOU.
YEAH, YOU DO. YOU ATTACKED A BUNCH OF COPS. WE CAN'T LET THAT HAPPEN.
THEY ATTACKED ME. I'LL TELL YOU WHAT I TOLD THEM. LEAVE ME ALONE, AND YOU WON'T BE HURT.
WHAT ABOUT THE FIRST PATROLWOMAN WHO INVESTIGATED? SHE'S STILL MISSING.
I DON'T KNOW ANYTHING ABOUT HER. YOU'RE WASTING MY TIME, MOVE IT OR LOSE IT.
ALTERNATIVELY...

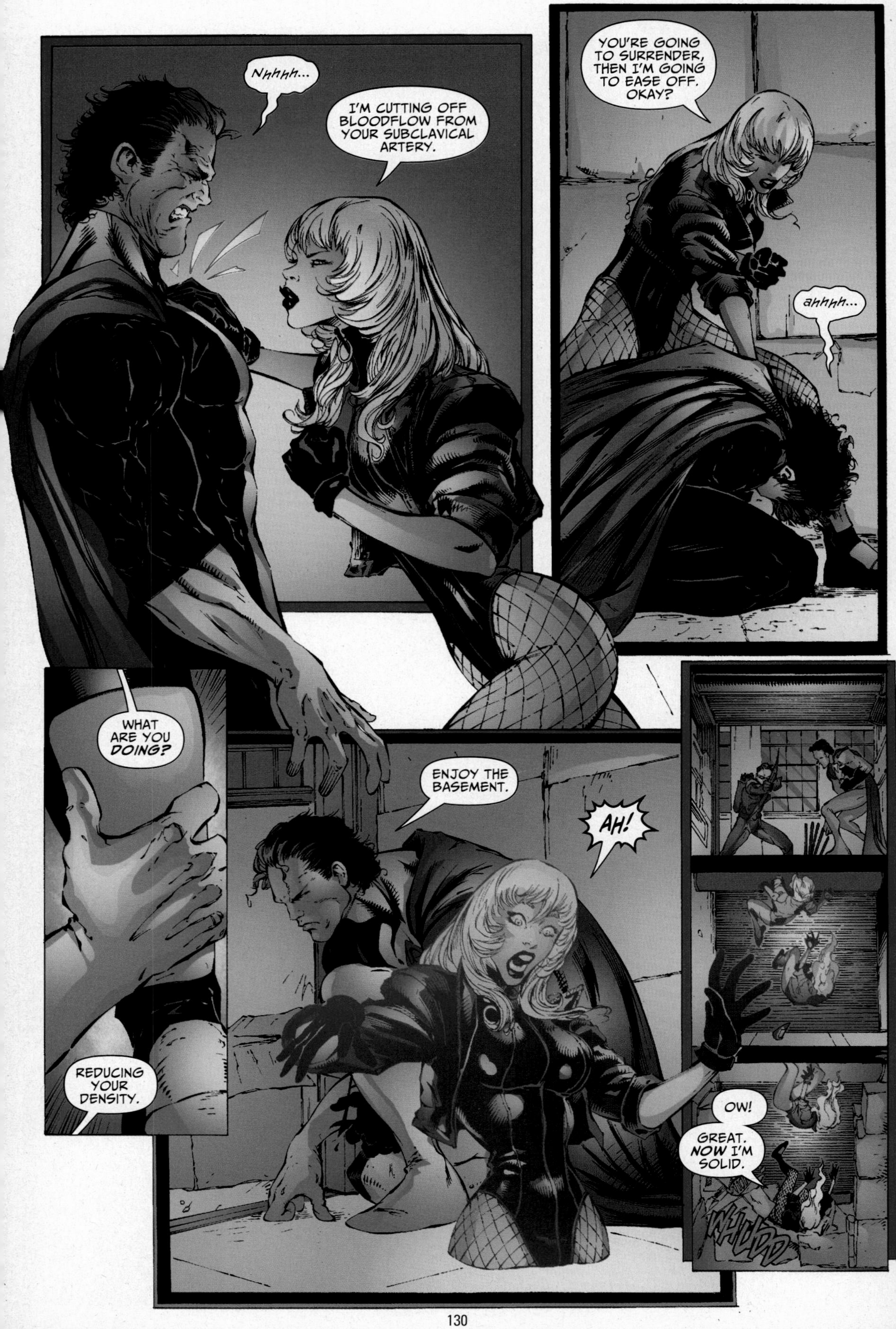
Nhhhh...
I'M CUTTING OFF BLOODFLOW FROM YOUR SUBCLAVICAL ARTERY.
YOU'RE GOING TO SURRENDER, THEN I'M GOING TO EASE OFF. OKAY?
ahhhh...
WHAT ARE YOU DOING?
REDUCING YOUR DENSITY.
ENJOY THE BASEMENT.
AH!
OW!
GREAT. NOW I'M SOLID.
WHUDD

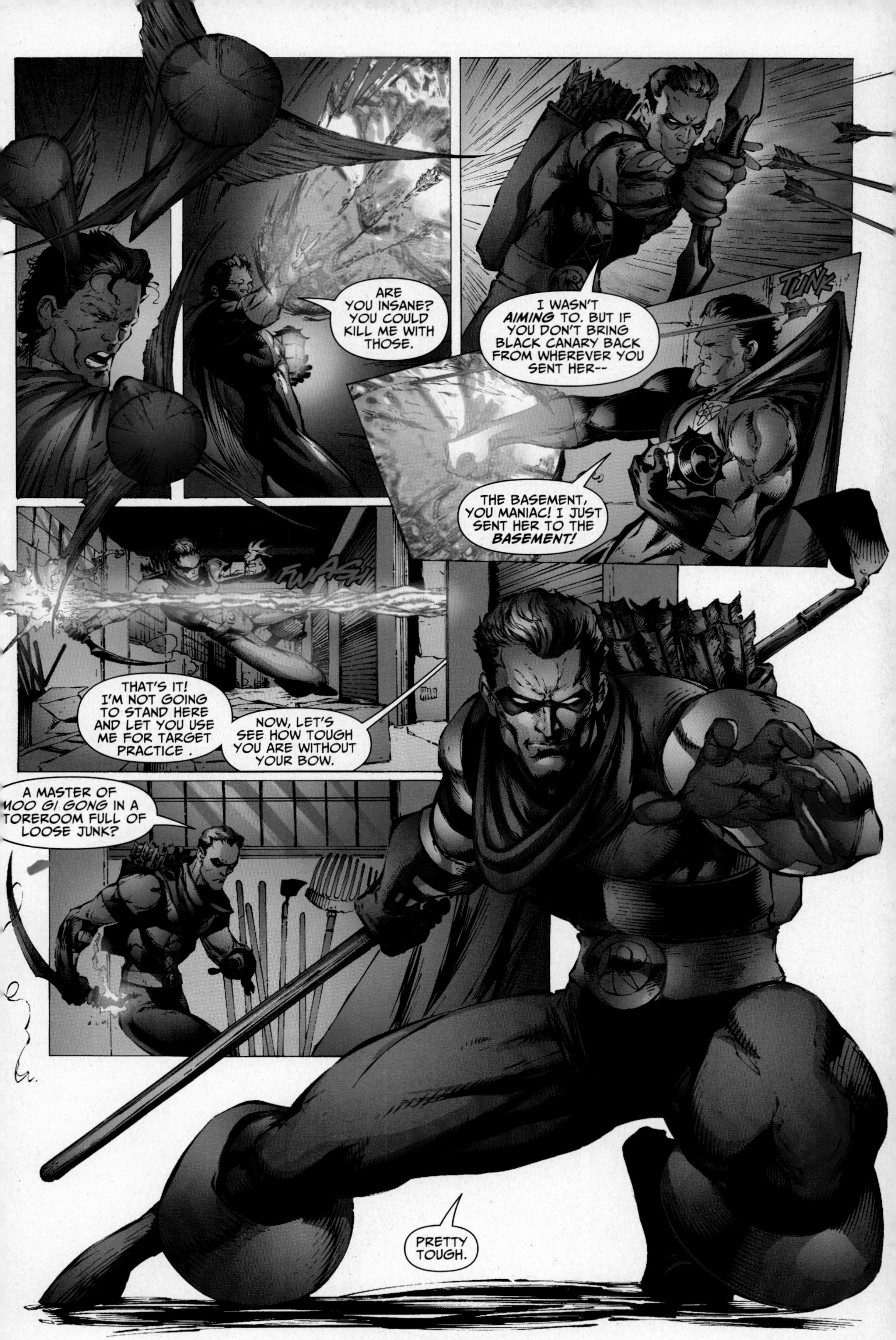
ARE YOU INSANE? YOU COULD KILL ME WITH THOSE.
I WASN'T AIMING TO. BUT IF YOU DON'T BRING BLACK CANARY BACK FROM WHEREVER YOU SENT HER--
TUNK
THE BASEMENT, YOU MANIAC! I JUST SENT HER TO THE BASEMENT!
FWASH
THAT'S IT! I'M NOT GOING TO STAND HERE AND LET YOU USE ME FOR TARGET PRACTICE .
NOW, LET'S SEE HOW TOUGH YOU ARE WITHOUT YOUR BOW.
A MASTER OF MOO GI GONG IN A TOREROOM FULL OF LOOSE JUNK?
PRETTY TOUGH.

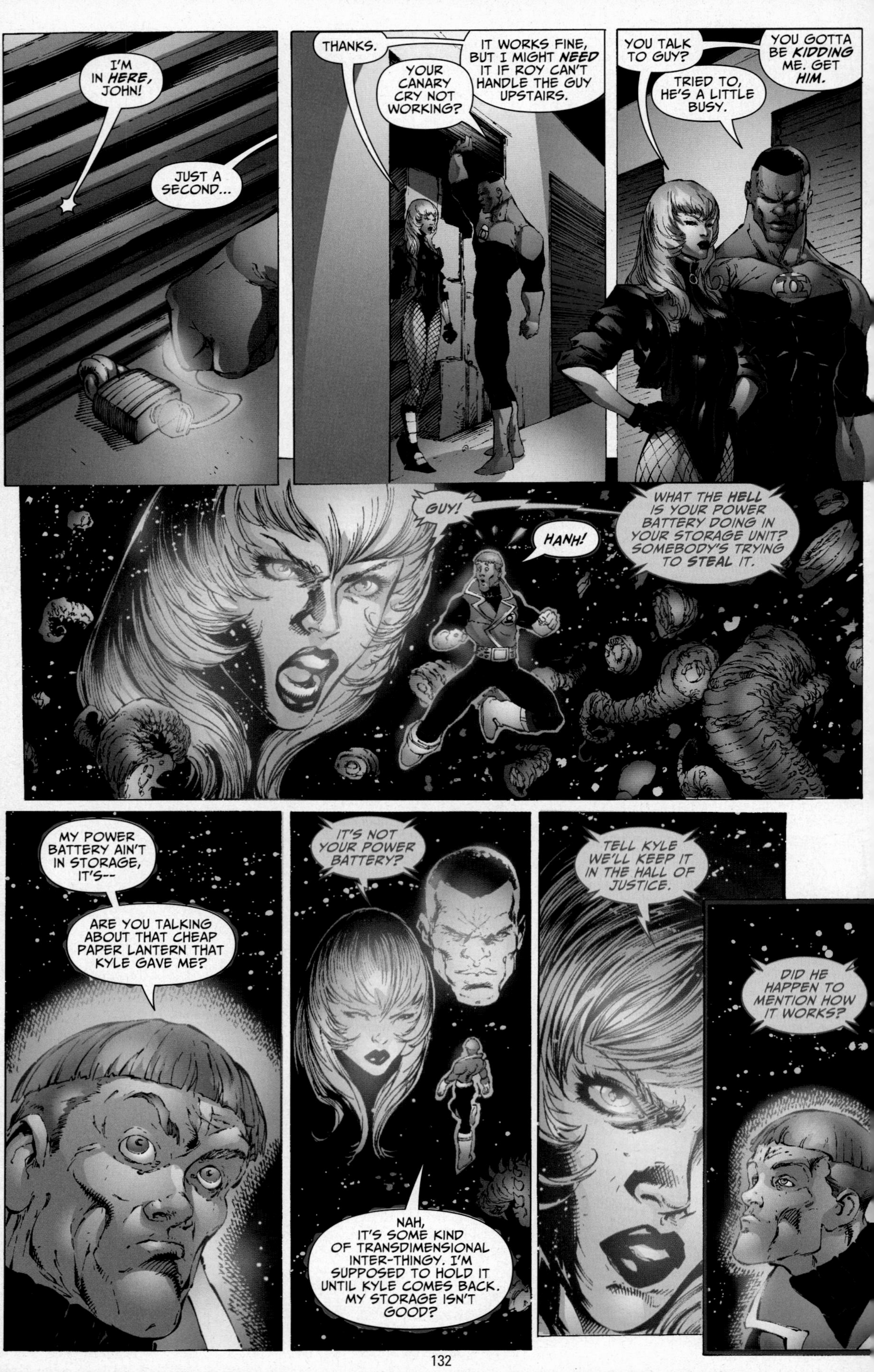
I'M IN HERE, JOHN!
JUST A SECOND...
THANKS.
YOUR CANARY CRY NOT WORKING?
IT WORKS FINE, BUT I MIGHT NEED IT IF ROY CAN'T HANDLE THE GUY UPSTAIRS.
YOU TALK TO GUY?
TRIED TO, HE'S A LITTLE BUSY.
YOU GOTTA BE KIDDING ME. GET HIM.
GUY!
HANH!
WHAT THE HELL IS YOUR POWER BATTERY DOING IN YOUR STORAGE UNIT? SOMEBODY'S TRYING TO STEAL IT.
MY POWER BATTERY AIN'T IN STORAGE, IT'S--
ARE YOU TALKING ABOUT THAT CHEAP PAPER LANTERN THAT KYLE GAVE ME?
IT'S NOT YOUR POWER BATTERY?
NAH, IT'S SOME KIND OF TRANSDIMENSIONAL INTER-THINGY. I'M SUPPOSED TO HOLD IT UNTIL KYLE COMES BACK. MY STORAGE ISN'T GOOD?
TELL KYLE WE'LL KEEP IT IN THE HALL OF JUSTICE.
DID HE HAPPEN TO MENTION HOW IT WORKS?

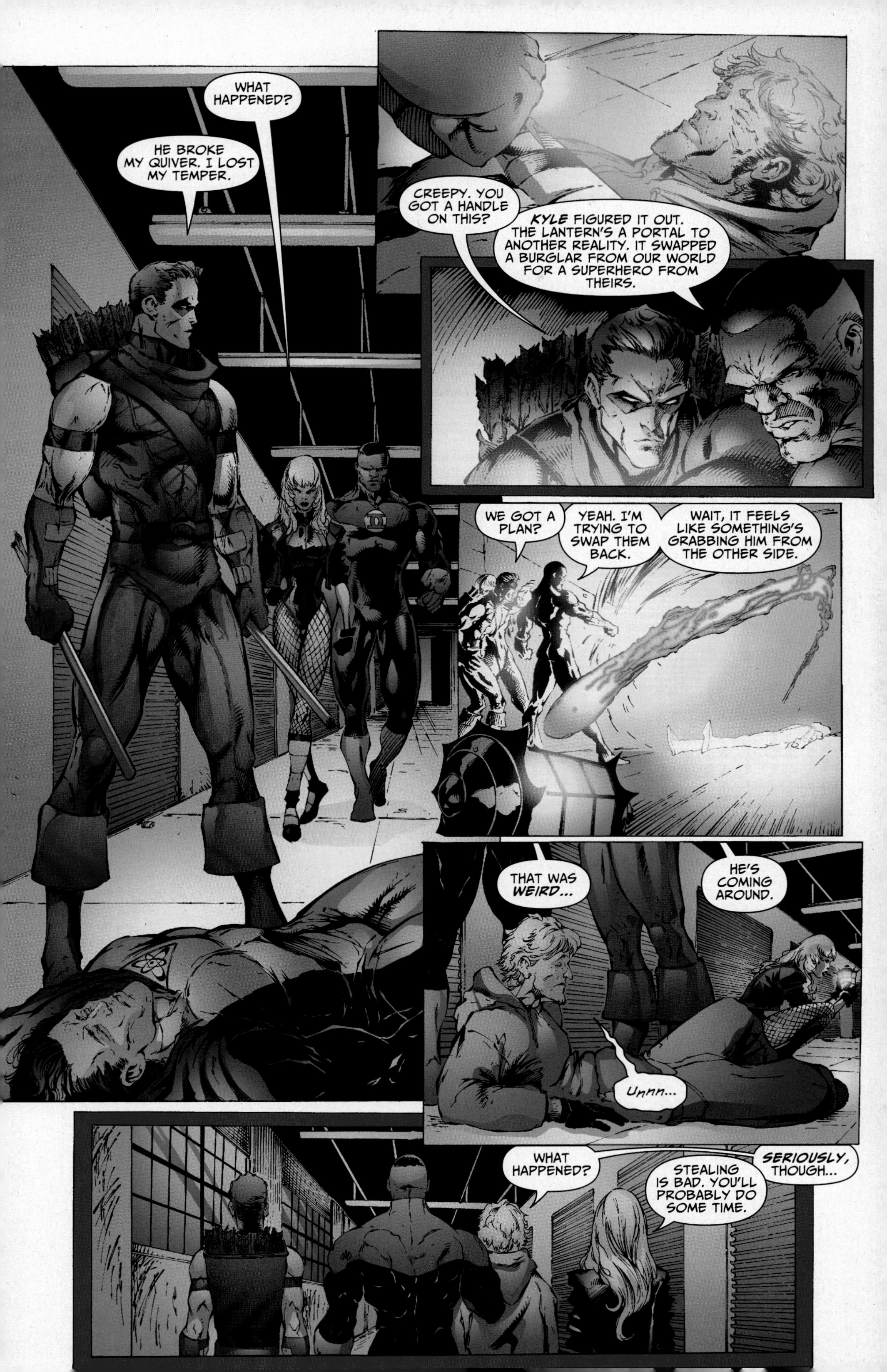
WHAT HAPPENED?
HE BROKE MY QUIVER. I LOST MY TEMPER.
CREEPY. YOU GOT A HANDLE ON THIS?
KYLE FIGURED IT OUT. THE LANTERN'S A PORTAL TO ANOTHER REALITY. IT SWAPPED A BURGLAR FROM OUR WORLD FOR A SUPERHERO FROM THEIRS.
WE GOT A PLAN?
YEAH. I'M TRYING TO SWAP THEM BACK.
WAIT, IT FEELS LIKE SOMETHING'S GRABBING HIM FROM THE OTHER SIDE.
THAT WAS WEIRD...
HE'S COMING AROUND.
Unnn...
WHAT HAPPENED?
SERIOUSLY, THOUGH...
STEALING IS BAD. YOU'LL PROBABLY DO SOME TIME.

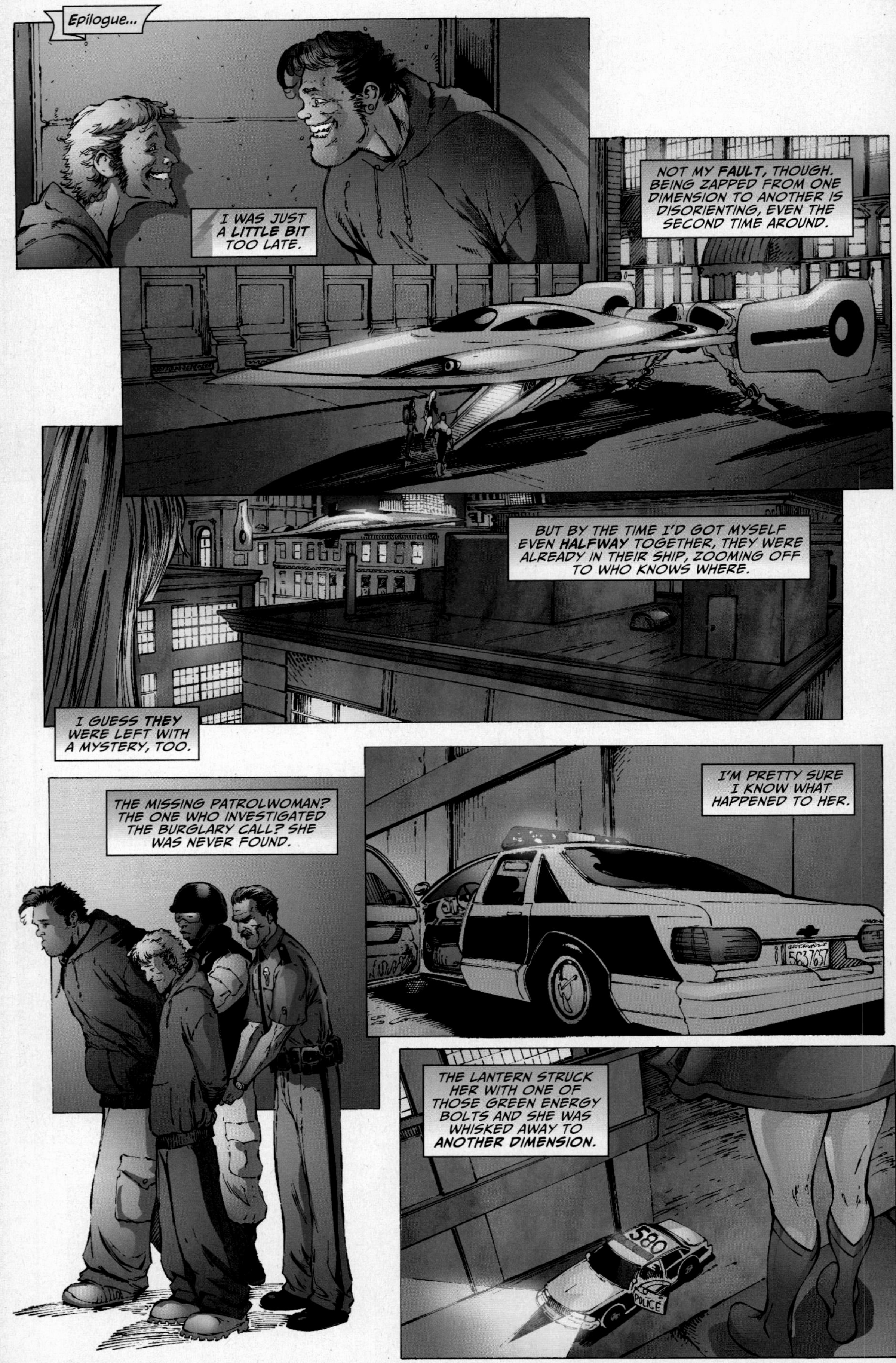

Epilogue...
I WAS JUST A LITTLE BIT TOO LATE.
NOT MY FAULT, THOUGH. BEING ZAPPED FROM ONE DIMENSION TO ANOTHER IS DISORIENTING, EVEN THE SECOND TIME AROUND.
BUT BY THE TIME I'D GOT MYSELF EVEN HALFWAY TOGETHER, THEY WERE ALREADY IN THEIR SHIP, ZOOMING OFF TO WHO KNOWS WHERE.
I GUESS THEY WERE LEFT WITH A MYSTERY, TOO.
THE MISSING PATROLWOMAN? THE ONE WHO INVESTIGATED THE BURGLARY CALL? SHE WAS NEVER FOUND.
I'M PRETTY SURE I KNOW WHAT HAPPENED TO HER.
THE LANTERN STRUCK HER WITH ONE OF THOSE GREEN ENERGY BOLTS AND SHE WAS WHISKED AWAY TO ANOTHER DIMENSION.
580
POLICE

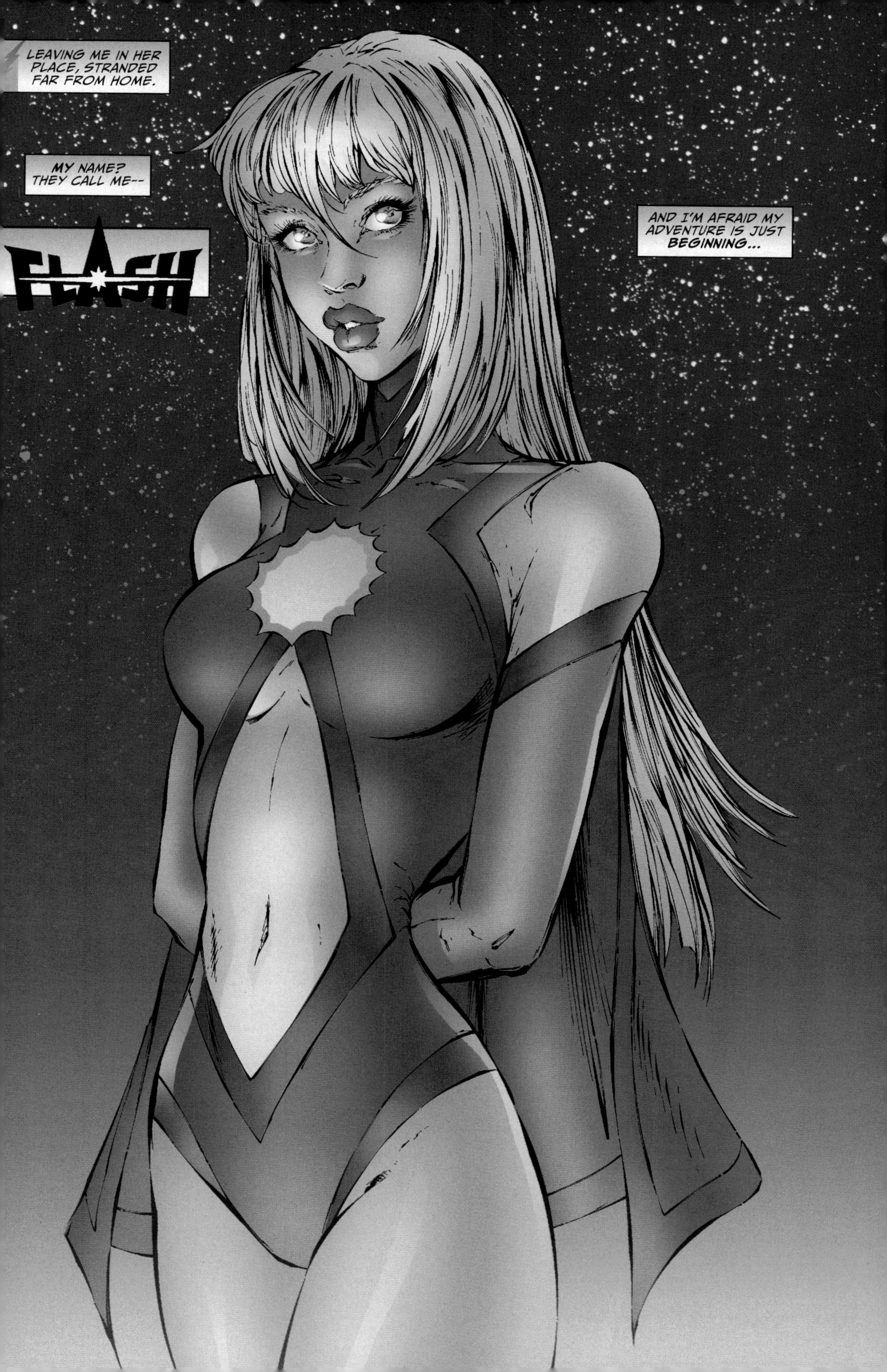
LEAVING ME IN HER PLACE, STRANDED FAR FROM HOME.
MY NAME? THEY CALL ME--
FLASH
AND I'M AFRAID MY ADVENTURE IS JUST BEGINNING...

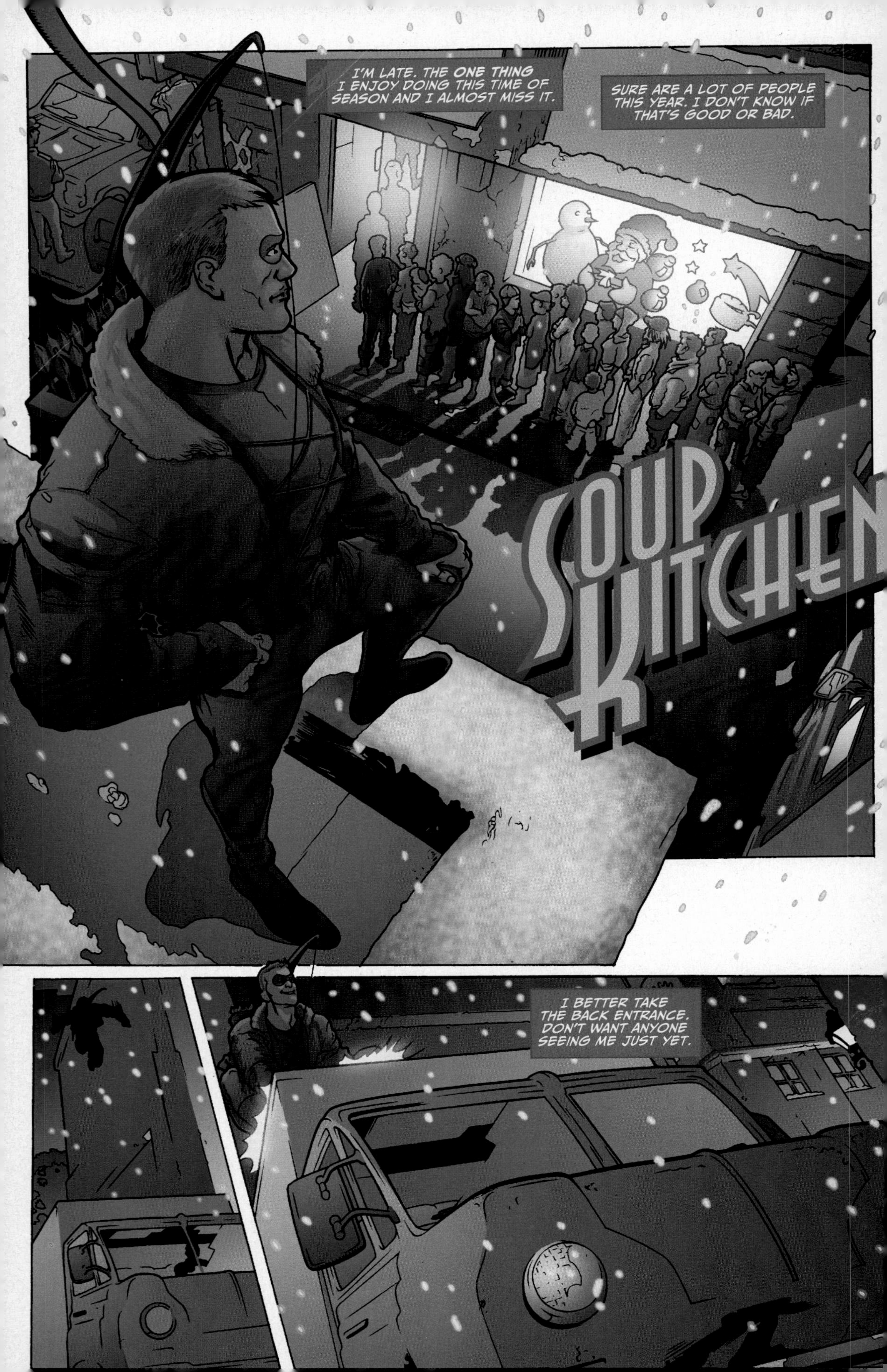
I'M LATE. THE ONE THING I ENJOY DOING THIS TIME OF SEASON AND I ALMOST MISS IT.
SURE ARE A LOT OF PEOPLE THIS YEAR. I DON'T KNOW IF THAT'S GOOD OR BAD.
SOUP KITCHEN
I BETTER TAKE THE BACK ENTRANCE. DON'T WANT ANYONE SEEING ME JUST YET.

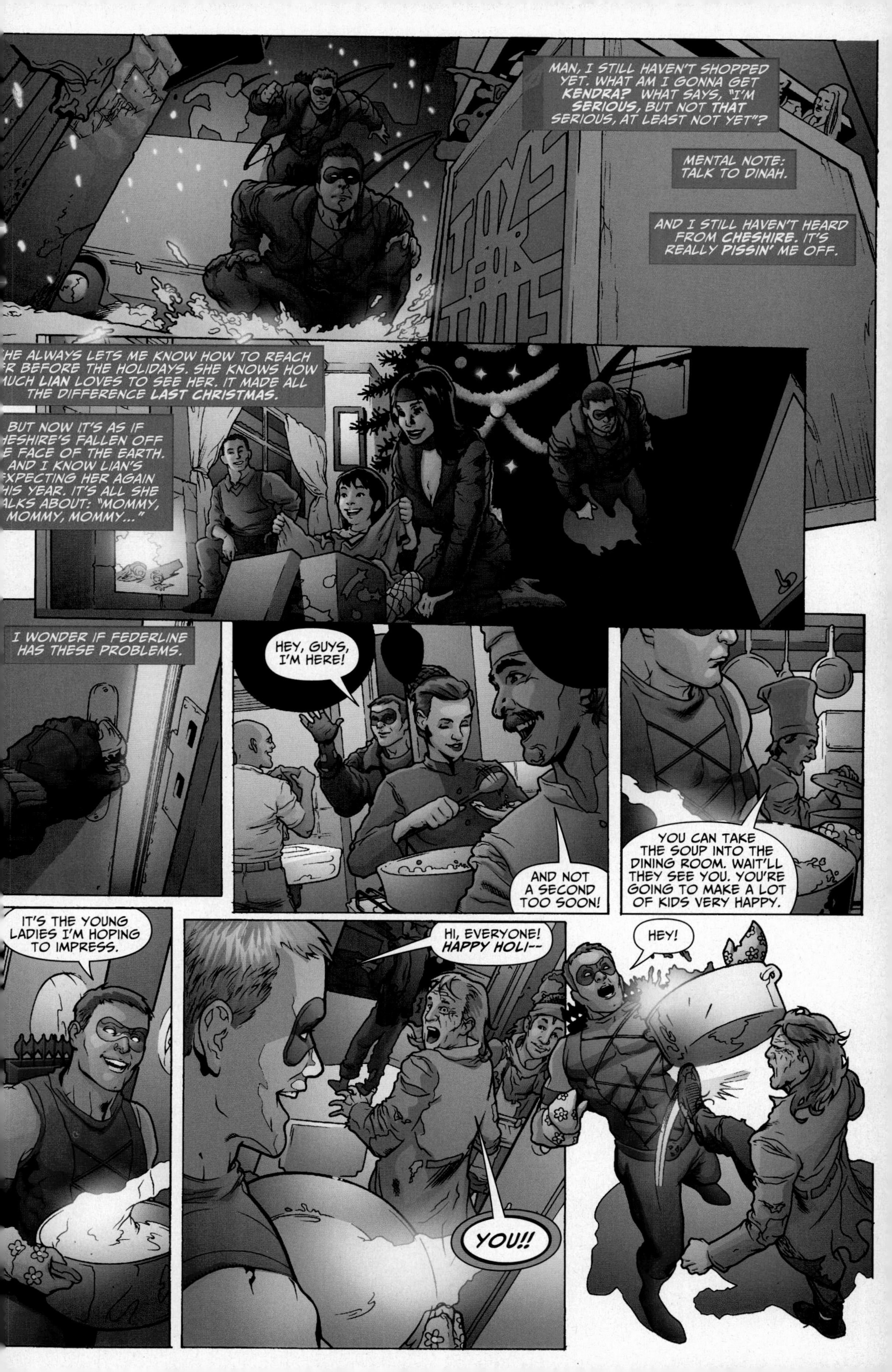

MAN, I STILL HAVEN'T SHOPPED YET. WHAT AM I GONNA GET KENDRA? WHAT SAYS, "I'M SERIOUS, BUT NOT THAT SERIOUS, AT LEAST NOT YET"?
MENTAL NOTE: TALK TO DINAH.
AND I STILL HAVEN'T HEARD FROM CHESHIRE. IT'S REALLY PISSIN' ME OFF.
TOYS FOR TOTS
HE ALWAYS LETS ME KNOW HOW TO REACH R BEFORE THE HOLIDAYS. SHE KNOWS HOW MUCH LIAN LOVES TO SEE HER. IT MADE ALL THE DIFFERENCE LAST CHRISTMAS.
BUT NOW IT'S AS IF HESHIRE'S FALLEN OFF E FACE OF THE EARTH. AND I KNOW LIAN'S XPECTING HER AGAIN HIS YEAR. IT'S ALL SHE ALKS ABOUT: "MOMMY, MOMMY, MOMMY..."
I WONDER IF FEDERLINE HAS THESE PROBLEMS.
HEY, GUYS, I'M HERE!
AND NOT A SECOND TOO SOON!
YOU CAN TAKE THE SOUP INTO THE DINING ROOM. WAIT'LL THEY SEE YOU. YOU'RE GOING TO MAKE A LOT OF KIDS VERY HAPPY.
IT'S THE YOUNG LADIES I'M HOPING TO IMPRESS.
HI, EVERYONE! HAPPY HOLI--
YOU!!
HEY!

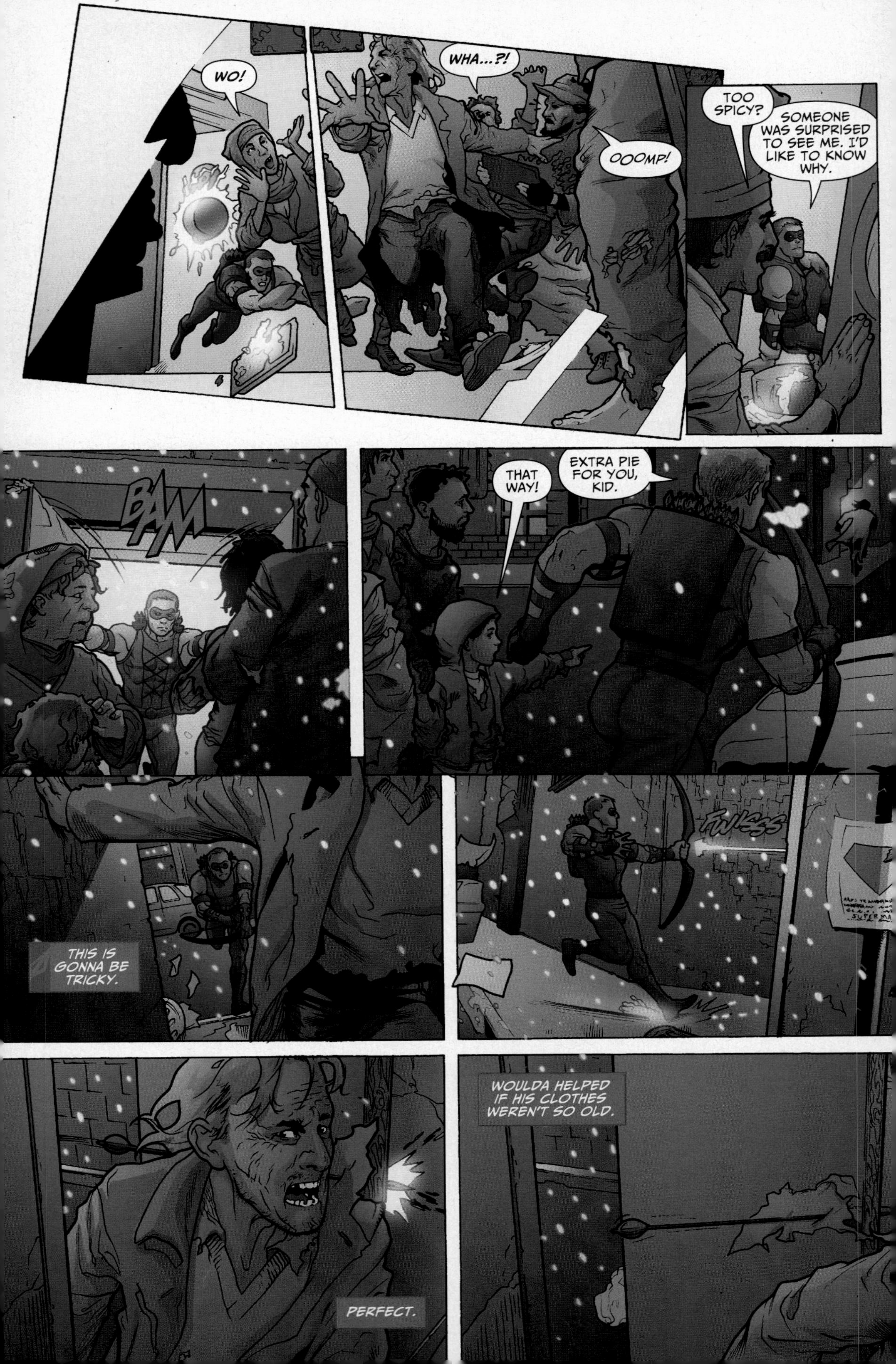
WO!
WHA...?!
OOOMP!
TOO SPICY?
SOMEONE WAS SURPRISED TO SEE ME. I'D LIKE TO KNOW WHY.
BAM
THAT WAY!
EXTRA PIE FOR YOU, KID.
THIS IS GONNA BE TRICKY.
FWISSS
PERFECT.
WOULDA HELPED IF HIS CLOTHES WEREN'T SO OLD.

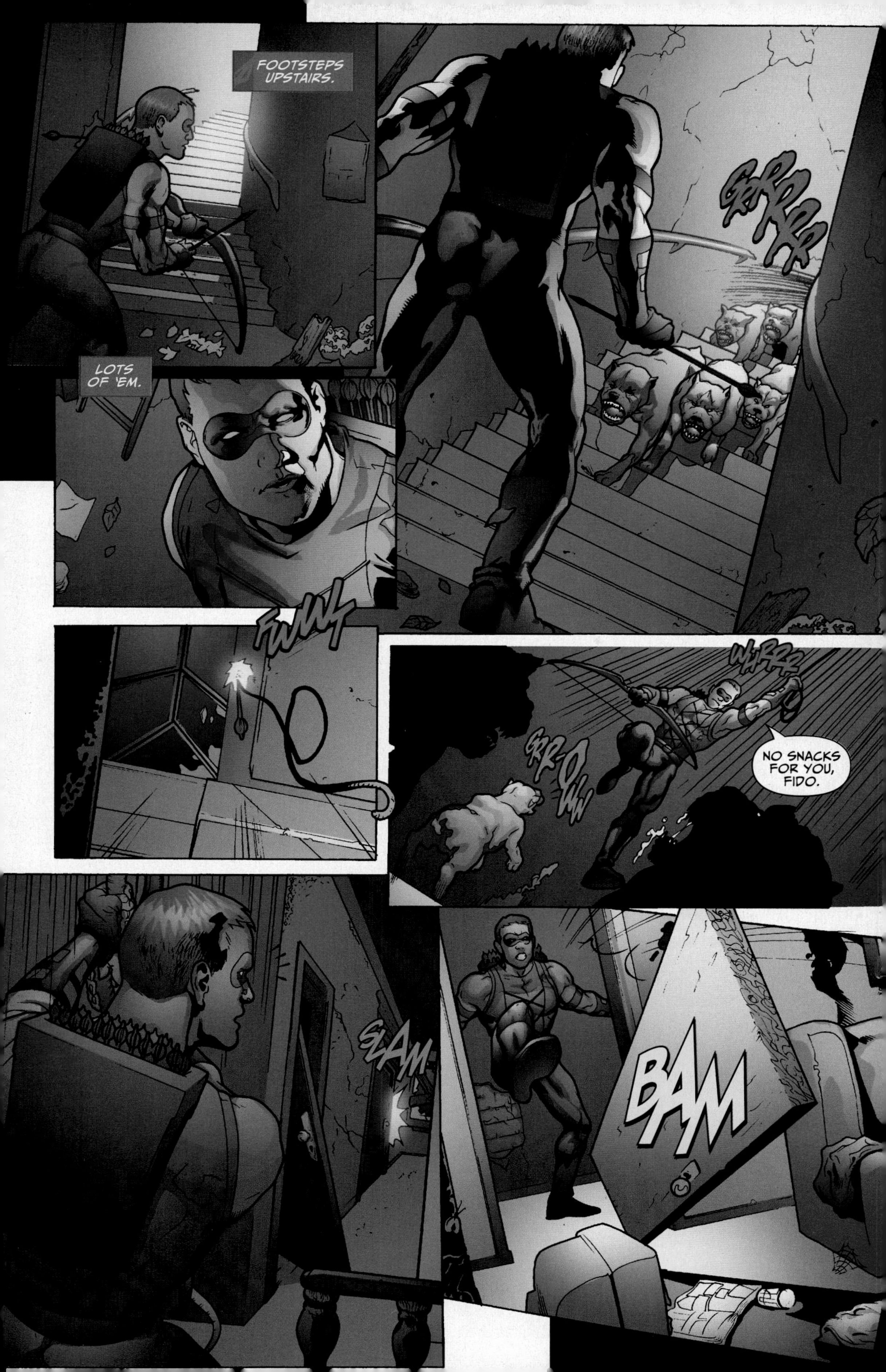

FOOTSTEPS UPSTAIRS.
GRRRRR
LOTS OF 'EM.
FWUNG
WHIRRR
GRR-OWW
NO SNACKS FOR YOU, FIDO.
SLAM
BAM

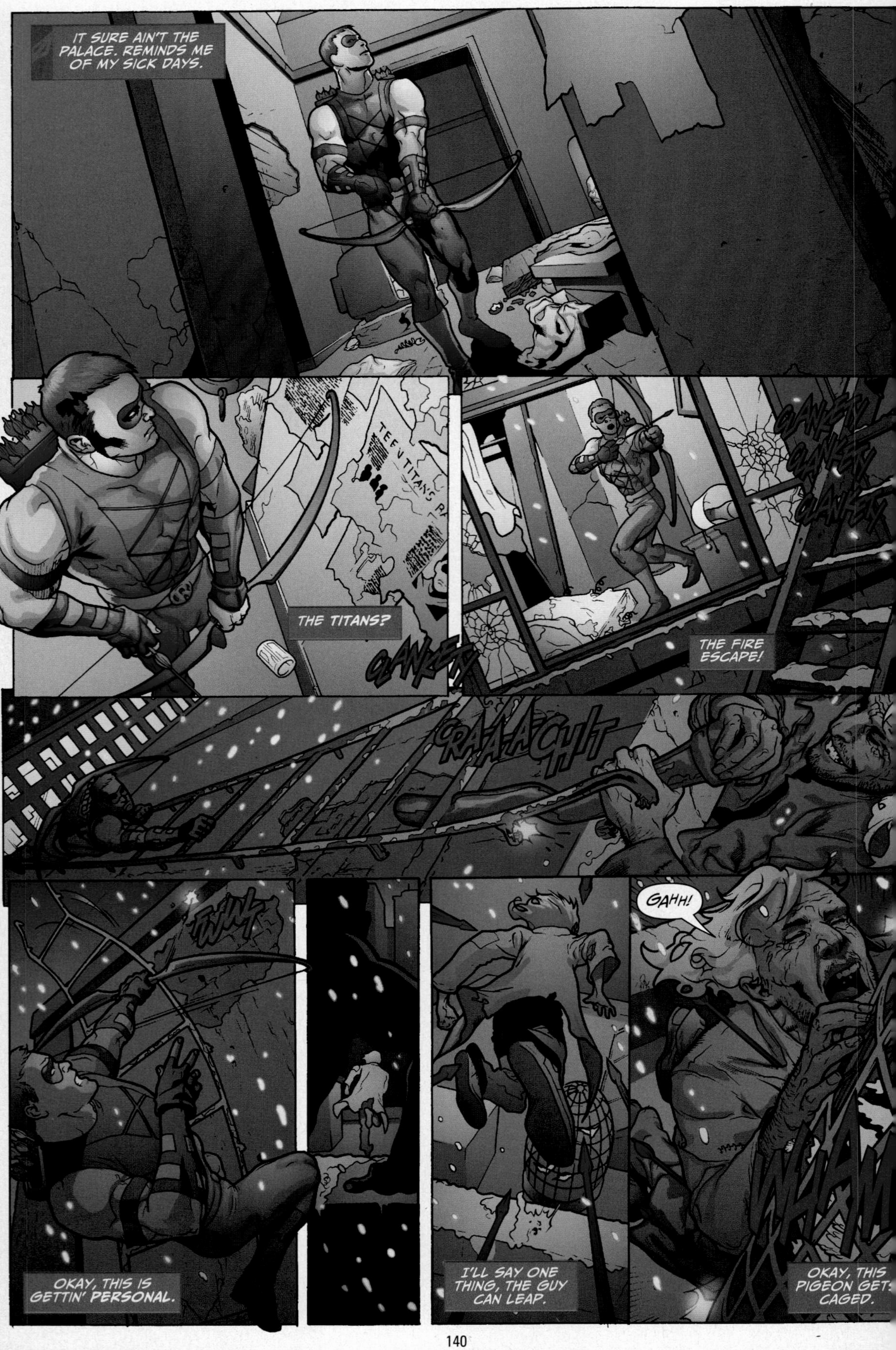

IT SURE AIN'T THE PALACE. REMINDS ME OF MY SICK DAYS.
TEEN TITANS
THE TITANS?
CLANKETY
CLANKETY CLANKETY CLANKETY
THE FIRE ESCAPE!
CRA-A-ACHIT
GAHH!
OKAY, THIS IS GETTIN' PERSONAL.
I'LL SAY ONE THING, THE GUY CAN LEAP.
OKAY, THIS PIGEON GETS CAGED.

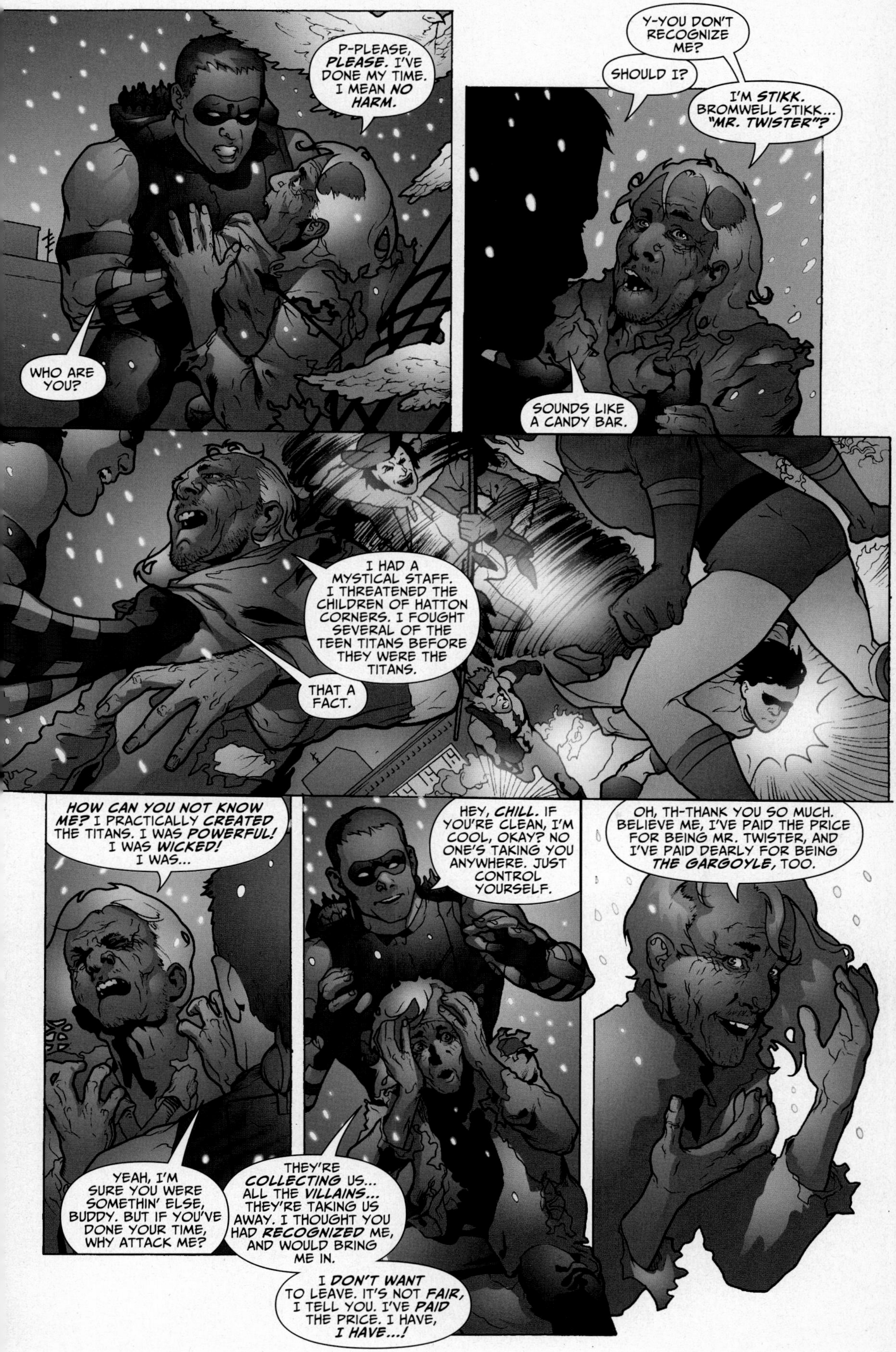
P-PLEASE, PLEASE. I'VE DONE MY TIME. I MEAN NO HARM.
WHO ARE YOU?
Y-YOU DON'T RECOGNIZE ME?
SHOULD I?
I'M STIKK. BROMWELL STIKK... "MR. TWISTER"?
SOUNDS LIKE A CANDY BAR.
I HAD A MYSTICAL STAFF. I THREATENED THE CHILDREN OF HATTON CORNERS. I FOUGHT SEVERAL OF THE TEEN TITANS BEFORE THEY WERE THE TITANS.
THAT A FACT.
HOW CAN YOU NOT KNOW ME? I PRACTICALLY CREATED THE TITANS. I WAS POWERFUL! I WAS WICKED! I WAS...
YEAH, I'M SURE YOU WERE SOMETHIN' ELSE, BUDDY. BUT IF YOU'VE DONE YOUR TIME, WHY ATTACK ME?
THEY'RE COLLECTING US... ALL THE VILLAINS... THEY'RE TAKING US AWAY. I THOUGHT YOU HAD RECOGNIZED ME, AND WOULD BRING ME IN.
I DON'T WANT TO LEAVE. IT'S NOT FAIR, I TELL YOU. I'VE PAID THE PRICE. I HAVE, I HAVE...!
HEY, CHILL. IF YOU'RE CLEAN, I'M COOL, OKAY? NO ONE'S TAKING YOU ANYWHERE. JUST CONTROL YOURSELF.
OH, TH-THANK YOU SO MUCH. BELIEVE ME, I'VE PAID THE PRICE FOR BEING MR. TWISTER, AND I'VE PAID DEARLY FOR BEING THE GARGOYLE, TOO.

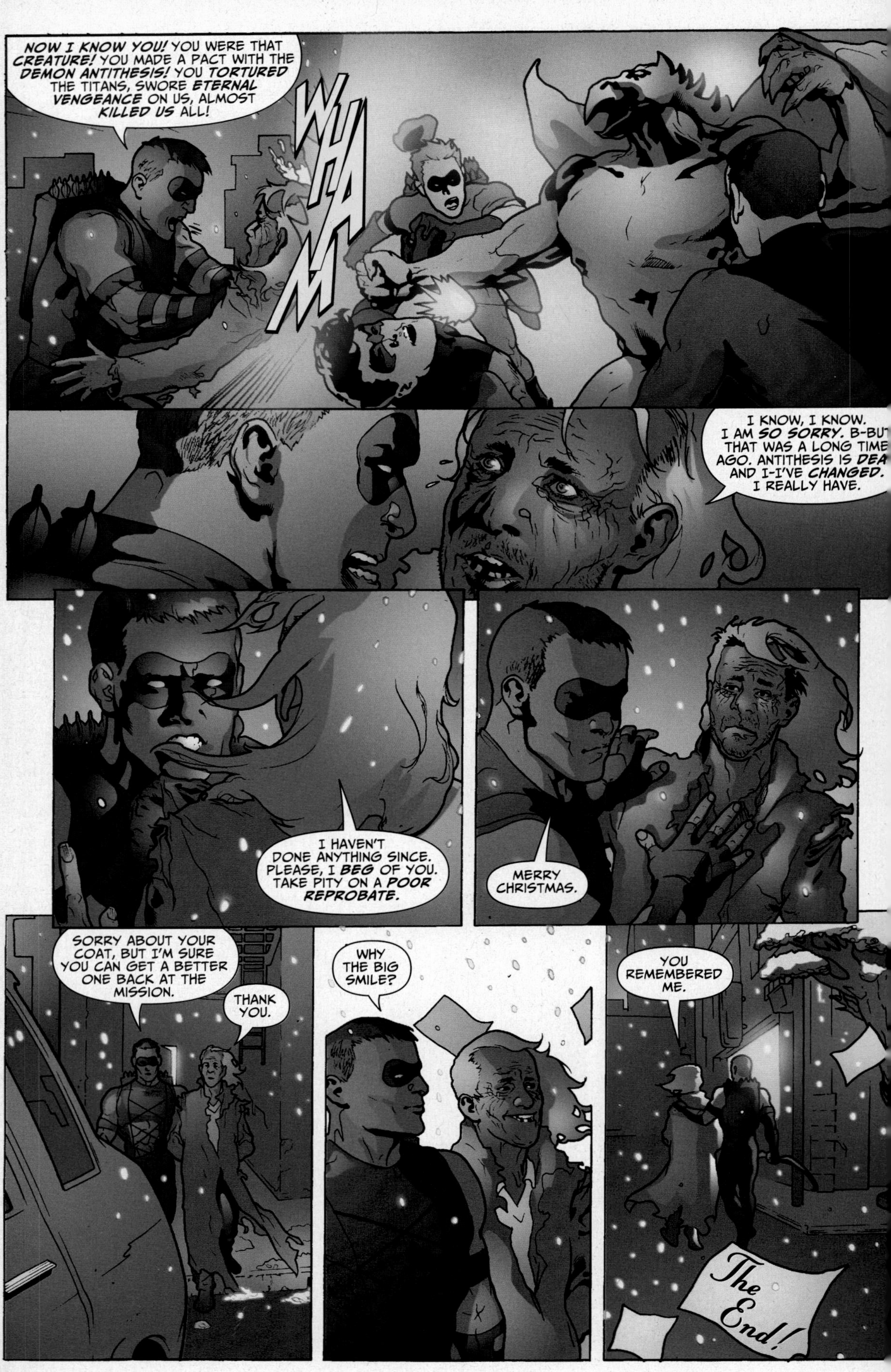
NOW I KNOW YOU! YOU WERE THAT CREATURE! YOU MADE A PACT WITH THE DEMON ANTITHESIS! YOU TORTURED THE TITANS, SWORE ETERNAL VENGEANCE ON US, ALMOST KILLED US ALL!
WHAM
I KNOW, I KNOW. I AM SO SORRY. B-BUT THAT WAS A LONG TIME AGO. ANTITHESIS IS DEAD AND I-I'VE CHANGED. I REALLY HAVE.
I HAVEN'T DONE ANYTHING SINCE. PLEASE, I BEG OF YOU. TAKE PITY ON A POOR REPROBATE.
MERRY CHRISTMAS.
SORRY ABOUT YOUR COAT, BUT I'M SURE YOU CAN GET A BETTER ONE BACK AT THE MISSION.
THANK YOU.
WHY THE BIG SMILE?
YOU REMEMBERED ME.
The End!

JUSTICE LEAGUE of AMERICA

READ MORE ADVENTURES OF YOUR FAVORITE HEROES IN THESE COLLECTIONS FROM DC COMICS:

KINGDOM COME

THE GREATEST SUPER-HERO EPIC OF TOMORROW!
DC
ELSEWORLDS
KINGDOM COME
Mark WAID Alex ROSS

Mark Waid and **Alex Ross** deliver a grim tale of youth versus experience, tradition versus change and what defines a hero. KINGDOM COME is a riveting story pitting the old guard — Superman, Batman, Wonder Woman and their peers — against a new uncompromising generation.

WINNER OF FIVE EISNER AND HARVEY AWARDS, INCLUDING BEST LIMITED SERIES AND BEST ARTIST

IDENTITY CRISIS

NEW YORK TIMES BEST-SELLING AUTHOR OF THE ZERO GAME
BRAD MELTZER
RAGS MORALES MICHAEL BAIR
IDENTITY CRISIS
Introduction by JOSS WHEDON, creator of BUFFY THE VAMPIRE SLAYER and FIREFLY
"The IDENTITY CRISIS mystery involves the biggest DC heroes... and uses all of Mr. Meltzer's skills as a thriller novelist." — The New York Times
DC

BRAD MELTZER
RAGS MORALES
MICHAEL BAIR

CRISIS ON INFINITE EARTHS

CRISIS
ON INFINITE EARTHS
MARV WOLFMAN & GEORGE PÉREZ
DC

MARV WOLFMAN
GEORGE PÉREZ

DC: THE NEW FRONTIER VOLUME 1

DC
DC: The New Frontier
VOLUME ONE
BY DARWYN COOKE WITH DAVE STEWART

DARWYN COOKE
DAVE STEWART

SEARCH THE GRAPHIC NOVELS SECTION OF

www.DCCOMICS.com

FOR ART AND INFORMATION ON ALL OF OUR BOOKS!

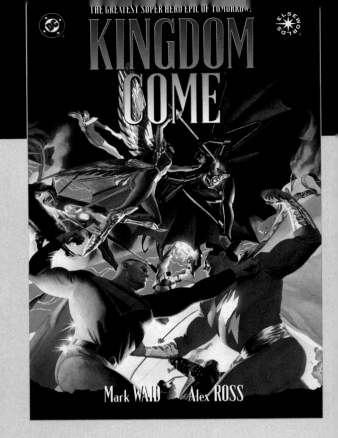

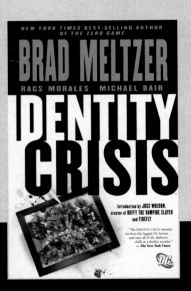